Please Don't Bomb the Suburbs

A Midterm Report on My Generation and the Future of Our Super Movement

BY WILLIAM UPSKI WIMSATT

Published by Akashic Books
©2010 by William Upski Wimsatt

ISBN-13: 978-1-936070-59-6
Library of Congress Control Number: 2010922720
All rights reserved

First printing

Akashic Books
PO Box 1456
New York, NY 10009
info@akashicbooks.com
www.akashicbooks.com

TABLE OF CONTENTS

Introductions

Harlem After Dark

I got off the bus just before midnight on 125th and Lenox—the picture of a white traveler lost in Harlem. Except I wasn't lost. I had lived and worked in Harlem for the past six years. Despite its wide, impersonal avenues, it was starting to feel like home. Struggling to carry four bags from three weeks of travel, I lumbered down Lenox to 121st and made a right onto my block. As soon as I turned the corner I got a bad feeling.

Most of the streetlights were out, and I could see outlines of figures in the shadows. My house was at the far end of the block. On the way, I had to pass a darkened schoolyard and a remote section of pavement shrouded behind a row of trees. I could see a big group of guys walking toward me. They took up the whole sidewalk. I could hear their voices. I could feel their energy. In a moment they would see me cross underneath the faded orange streetlamp. I imagined them seeing me—a white guy dressed in rumpled business clothes, pulling a suitcase on wheels, with a laptop case and two other bags slung over my aching shoulders and back.

Normally I would feel comfortable. I have been living in urban neighborhoods for most of my life. I often walk home at two or three a.m., by the projects, the hot corners, down dark alleys and side streets. I show respect for everyone. I expect respect. And I never think twice about my safety. But for some reason, in this moment, with my bags and my laptop, an animal fight-or-flight instinct took hold of me. I felt utterly vulnerable and defenseless. I considered crossing the street. Pride stopped me. *I will not be afraid in my own neighborhood. I will not be afraid of young men on my own block.*

That's what I told myself. But my imagination was racing. The tension toward white people moving into Harlem was strong enough to taste. Rents were tripling and quadrupling. Black Harlem families who'd been here for generations were being forced out. White babies could be seen in local parks, pushed in strollers by black nannies. Normally the white and black residents of Harlem just stayed out of each other's way, walking past each other on the sidewalks without acknowledgment. But anger boiled beneath the surface. Lines at the local food bank stretched down the block, young and old waiting for hours to get a bag of groceries. Under circumstances like this, could a band of rowdy, possibly drunk, neighborhood guys on a Friday night simply walk past me on an isolated, dark street? Wasn't this the perfect opportunity for revenge?

They were coming closer. We would meet in the middle of the darkest stretch of pavement, underneath the trees. I should have crossed the street when I had the chance. Why did I have to take my laptop with me? What if it got smashed on the sidewalk? Damn, I forgot to back up the files. I have to re-member to back up the damn files! The thoughts I have at times like this. And then they were upon me. Seven or eight of them. Midtwenties. Swaggering, some with their shirts off. Slowly their faces came into focus.

"Up-ski!!!"

It was my roommate Jameel and his friends, calling me by my graffiti name from the old days. "What up, West Rok?"

He introduced me around to his friends, mostly B-boys visiting from Chi-cago. They had just finished a barbecue at our house, and were headed out to a party. Did I want to come with? Naw, I need to get home and get my life to-gether. We gave each other dap, talked for a while, and parted ways. "I left you some barbecued chicken in the fridge," Jameel called as we were walking away.

I shuffled along the sidewalk feeling so many things: relief, humiliation, joy. Barbecued chicken sounded good. I looked up at the sky and started laughing.

How did this happen? I was always the white hip-hop kid. When did I grow up into the tourist-looking white guy fearing his own friends in his own neighborhood?

Adulthood Hits You Like Whoa

At its heart, this book asks a simple question: What does it mean to be a grown-up at this pivotal moment in history? How do you embrace the good aspects of growing up and leave the bad ones alone? And how do each of us as adults find our calling, live up to our potential, and meet the challenges of our time?

This is a coming-of-age story about me and my generation, Generation X (born 1961–79), and the generation after mine, the Millennials (born 1980–2000). We both grew up on hip-hop. My generation grew up on raw political hip-hop. Y'all grew up on guns-and-bubblegum hip-hop. But that's okay. We both got slapped out of our faces by September 11. We were profoundly shaped by the Bush and Obama years, Iraq and Afghanistan, climate crisis, financial crisis, student loans, the BP oil mess, and Hurricane Katrina. We began to flex our political muscle against Bush in 2004. We swept Republicans out of Congress in 2006. And in 2008 we elected a black community organizer from the South Side of Chicago as president of the United States of America.

Overall, the Millennials are light-years more politically and professionally astute than we ever were. They are growing up in the worst economy since the Great Depression. Sixteen-year-olds, without blinking, will send you a resume and a PowerPoint presentation from their phone. And still can't get a job! They are growing up with the existence of a strange new phenomenon: an organized and strategic progressive political movement. In fact, Millennials are statistically the most progressive generation in U.S. history. I am proud of them. And I'm scared they're going to take my job.

(Note: I use "my generation" to refer to both Generation X and the Millennials, together.)

The Most Progressive Generation in History

So yeah. Young people are the most progressive generation in history. Look at the preceding chart of voting patterns from young people over the past twenty-five years.

In the 1960s and '70s, young people were halfway decent politically. In the '80s, we fell for Reagan's charm. In the '90s, we started to be semi-okay again. But then in 2000, we voted at only 41 percent. And we voted in equal numbers for George W. Bush and Al Gore. What were we thinking?

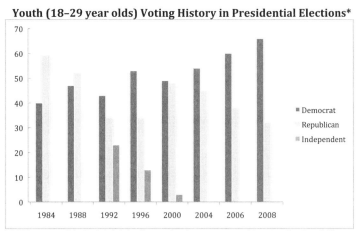

Youth (18–29 year olds) Voting History in Presidential Elections*

*2006 Congressional election is included to illustrate that the progressive trend is not just about Barack Obama.
Sources: CIRCLE (civicyouth.org) and Future Majority (futuremajority.org).

By 2004, things began to change. A lot of us realized we could no longer afford to ignore the whole voting/electoral politics game, or take it for granted. On November 2, 2004, we voted for Kerry over Bush by 9 points. In the 2006 midterm elections, we voted for Democrats over Republicans in Congress by 22 points. In 2008, we voted for Obama over McCain by a whopping 34-point spread (66–32).

Not bad!

What this means in simple terms is that if we keep going like this, a progressive vision will shape the future of our country. Every two years, there is a national election. And every two years, a few million more of us enter the electorate. If progressive folks—by which I mean you and me—play our cards right, we can begin to repair this country over the next ten to twenty years. We are the Clean-up Generation. We have been left with a huge mess by previous generations. It is our responsibility to clean up the mess so we don't pass it on to our kids.

I have no illusions that everyone is going to read this book. I didn't write this book for everyone. I am writing this book with a specific purpose for a very targeted audience. My realistic goal is to reach 50,000–100,000 key cultural and political "influencers" between the ages of fifteen and forty-five. My goal is for these leaders to develop a deeper sense of the history of the past twenty-five years, and a fearless, deliberate vision for how to navigate the challenges and opportunities ahead.

Statistically speaking, there are probably more than a million people between the ages of fifteen and forty-five who have been connected in some way to the political and cultural movements of our time. They have read books, written blogs, gone to rallies, organized voters, joined a campus group, recorded an album, performed a spoken-word piece. I figure if even 5,000 of us read this and become more strategic players, the 5,000 will influence the 50,000. The 50,000 will influence the million. And the million will transform this country. At least a little bit.

Question: Where do you see yourself in these circles?

Please keep in mind, this book is written for two audiences at the same time: the seasoned forty-two-year-old leader in the inner-most circle, and the bright-eyed seventeen-year-old in a Freshman 101 course who grew up in a small town, didn't listen to hip-hop, and has never encountered a progressive movement in his or her life.

If all of this is new to you, then I want to say a warm *welcome to the movement*! A whole new universe is about to open up to you. It might seem like a foreign language at first, but you'll catch on soon enough. As you'll see, you have a place in this conversation. In a very real way, you—the new people, the young people—are the ones who will decide whether or not we succeed. Your role is the decisive one.

Children of the '80s

Looking back, the children of the '80s were in many ways a Lost Generation who grew up in a backward and confusing political time where anything left-of-center was seen as irrelevant, extreme, or a punch line in a political-correctness joke. There were no out gay people in either of my high schools. The Democratic Party was a tired old mule. Hip-hop was the only vibrant and hopeful social movement that we had. I wore an "Upski" belt buckle with no sense of irony, and my friends and I came to school wearing clocks around our necks trying to look like Flavor Flav. The Internet wasn't big yet. Thankfully, there are no pictures.

Eigth grade graduation, Kenwood Academy.
One of the few photos I have from this time.

During this time, politically, young people were the most conservative segment of the population—voting overwhelmingly for Reagan in 1984. It's no accident we were called Generation X—endless articles were written about how conservative, apathetic, and obnoxious we were. Survey after survey showed we had rejected every aspect of the '60s (except the drugs) and were only interested in making money. Crack wars, AIDS, deindustrialization, and the prison boom were unraveling what was left of urban social fabric. *The Wire* and worse was the prevailing reality in most urban communities.

Gentrification hadn't exploded yet (white folks were too scared to even drive through black and brown neighborhoods, let alone live in them). White flight and suburban sprawl were wrecking the urban tax base. The War on Terror hadn't been dreamt up yet. My God, we were still supposed to be fighting Russia! This was before the Columbine and Virginia Tech massacres. The major public violence involved black and brown kids killing each other and white kids like Kurt Cobain killing themselves. Looking back, a lot of the stuff we did back then seems immature and unstrategic. Yet, during those "lost" years, we were laying many of the bricks for the new progressive era. At the time, we were wandering in the wilderness, taking our political cues from Spike Lee movies, and MTV.

Please Don't Bomb the Suburbs is an intimate personal history of America's cultural and political movements from 1984–2010. From the death of Chicago Mayor Harold Washington to the rise of Barack Obama. From the golden era of hip-hop to the dawning of a new progressive age. From "No More Prisons" to the green-collar economy. From the Battle of Seattle to the Coffee Party movement. From getting arrested and booked at the police precinct to using sophisticated data to organize a voter precinct. From juvenile delinquents to JDs. From B-boys and B-girls to MBAs. From anarchists to the PTA. From pissed-off voters to grown-up community organizers who win elections, wear suits, sustain marriages, raise kids, and take on the ultimate responsibility: governing the United States of America in the midst of an all-out war for the soul, control, and the future of our country.

This is a book about how far we've come, about remembering the last twenty-five years, and about preparing ourselves for the next twenty-five.

Which leads to a scary question: how can we step up our game before we find ourselves cast as extras in one of those end-of-the-world sci-fi thrillers we love to watch—*The Day After Tomorrow*, *The Book of Eli*, *Minority Report*, *The Road*, *Avatar*, *2012*, or *Children of Men*? Popular books in recent years have titles like *The World Without Us*, *The Long Emergency*, and *Collapse*. One of the most common cultural themes is the scenario in which human beings in the next hundred years or so annihilate ourselves—in really cool ways with lots of flooding and screaming and explosions, just like the video games we love to play.

Wait . . . what?

Is it just me, or is there an eerie fiddling-while-Rome-burns quality to modern life? At the very least, there is a bizarre disconnect. On the one hand, there is a public conversation now and some actual trends that could plausibly wipe out civilization as we know it (not to mention most of the Earth's other species). On the other hand, we're all supposed to go on acting like everything is normal and okay. Can you please take out the trash? What's up with Miley Cyrus's hair?

I mean, let's take stock for a second: we're running out of oil, water, fish, trees, animals, topsoil, and icebergs. We've got close to seven billion people now (compared to one billion in 1800, two billion in 1930, and 4.5 billion when I was born). We're headed for more than nine billion by 2050. Everyone wants to live like Americans, the pinnacle of civilization, with our fancy cars, houses, and shiny new things ordered on Amazon.com. Meanwhile, we're clear-cutting the Amazon.Rain.Forest.ForRealY'all. And we're playing a game of global warming/nuclear chicken.

Here's what I have to say: will someone please stop this roller coaster? I want to get off. Will someone please grab the steering wheel of this *Titanic?* I want to go back to shore. Mayday! Mayday! All hands on deck! We need to turn this ship around! Hello? Anybody there? Are there any *adults* up there driving this ship?

Um, yeah, that would be us.

It's like when your parents get older and you have to take care of them. They become like children again. You have to tell them what to do. That's the situation we're in as a generation. And that's the situation our kids and grandkids are going to be in with us.

At some point, someone needs to stand up and behave like a real adult.

When I started this book, right after the 2008 election, I had spent more than twenty years helping build a youth movement in the United States—since I was a fourteen-year-old graffiti writer in Chicago calling all-city meetings to hit up the train yards with political messages.

I believed that working to strengthen the youth movement was the most strategic thing I could do to change history. For several reasons: One, young people have time and energy. Two, young people are smart, idealistic, and willing to take risks. Three, young people have played a central role in leading every major historical change movement in history. Four, older people are gonna die.

I'm not saying that to be mean. It's just a cold hard fact. Young people are going to die too, but hopefully not for another sixty years. Political organizing is good training for future leadership. Someone who's in college right now is going to be president in thirty years. Could be that quiet Latina woman sitting next to you. Finally, five, as a field, youth organizing is so neglected and underfunded that a little bit goes a long way. Youth politics is like an undervalued stock. It's a smart investment with a lot of upside. So whip out those pocketbooks!

Every three to five years, I've seen wave after wave of young visionaries, artists, activists, and organizers "graduate" from the youth movement. As I watched each successive group of my homeys disappear into the normal adult world, I made a conscious decision to stick around, serve as institutional memory, and try to help the generations coming up behind me to improve their game.

The longer I stuck around, the more my game evolved—from hip-hop to journalism to social entrepreneurship to prison organizing to philanthropy to electoral politics to the green economy. My story is almost like a *Where's Waldo?* of movement evolution over the past twenty-five years. While some people may see a string of random causes, I see one movement for the survival of life on Earth. We need all the tools in the toolbox to tackle such a multifaceted challenge.

Along the way, I have probably met as many people in as many different sectors of the movement as any living person. Over the past twenty years, I've worked with dozens of groups; published five books in collaboration with hundreds of people; worked as both a funder and a fundraiser to move more than $8,000,000; worked on the Obama campaign in a key swing state; helped create the League of Young Voters and the Generational Alliance (a national alliance of youth organizations). Together, we mobilized thousands of young people, played a role in passing more than a dozen laws and swinging more than a dozen elections, including a House race, a governor's race, and a Senate seat. The Senate seat was the most satisfying. Right after I left the League, our group in Minnesota helped Senator Al Franken win by 312 votes.

I was starting to do pretty well as a youth organizer. I was really starting to get the hang of it. Then a terrible thing happened to my youth organizing career. I turned thirty-six.

This brought about a small midlife crisis. I was no longer a youth in any way, shape, or form. I knew it was time to move into the adult world. But what did that really look like? Getting a job, settling down, buying a house, having kids. It sounded okay. Not bad, actually. But there had to be more! Maybe writing a book would help me put the clues together. Worst-case scenario, I had some good war stories and an oral history to pass on to the next generation.

Please Don't Bomb the Suburbs

When I was twenty-one, I published a book called *Bomb the Suburbs*.

My grandmother told me right away it was a bad idea. But did I listen? No. "Don't name it that," she said. "Why would you name your book such a crazy thing? Why don't you name it something else?" She was grasping for an idea. "How about: *A Comparison of Life in the City and Suburbs* ..."

"Nonny," I patiently tried to explain, "no one will buy a book called *A Comparison of* ... whatever you said."

In Miami Beach with Nonny, age 98 (approximately).

How was my ninety-year-old grandmother supposed to understand? Bombing was another word for graffiti. My book wasn't about bombing. It was about hip-hop, graffiti, race, fear, suburban sprawl, adventure, political organizing. She had grown up in a different era. What did she know about books, let alone hip-hop?

She told me I was being *meshugana*—a Yiddish term for crazy.

Now I realize she was a prophet.

Six months after the book was released, on April 19, 1995, at precisely 9:02 a.m. (just after parents had dropped their toddlers off at day care) at the Federal Building in downtown Oklahoma City, a man named Timothy McVeigh detonated a truck bomb outside, killing 168 men, women, and children; injuring more than eight hundred. His aim was to attack the federal government. His actions echoed the "government is the problem" chorus of right-wing politicians and talk show hosts.

I had nothing to do with the Oklahoma City bombing. It was 180 degrees opposite of my values and worldview. Yet suddenly, the title of my book wasn't so cute anymore. After September 11, it became even less cute.

Fast-forward to 2008. A lot of my friends were involved in the Obama campaign. I had been organizing for social change for twenty years. This was the most exciting and important campaign of my lifetime. I was already volunteering. And one of my friends asked me to be on an advisory committee. Exciting! *Just send me your resume, you'll be vetted and then—*

Screeeech.

Whoa, vetted. Forgot that part.

There's this book I wrote called . . . Well, it's called . . . Bomb the Suburbs. *It wasn't really about bombing anything but . . .*

Now there are right-wing bloggers and Fox News, and the last thing Obama needed was a guy who wrote a book called *Bomb the Suburbs.*

I did not want to do anything to hurt the campaign. I walked around feeling sorry for myself for a couple of weeks. Then I got over it.

This is all part of growing up. A lot of us made less-than-wise decisions when we were younger. A lot of us went to prison for stupid reasons. Or killed people. Or got killed. Or killed ourselves. Or went crazy. And what about those of us who survived? A lot of us became "normal adults" with families and jobs, never to be heard from again. Growing up and becoming an adult is hard under the best of circumstances. It can be heartbreaking and boring, confusing and clarifying, profound and humbling. Sometimes we make mistakes. And thanks to the Internet, everything we have ever done will now be on public display forever. People change their relationship status on Facebook, and suddenly random people start posting: *Are you okay???*

Part of being an adult is owning our mistakes. We have to take responsibility. We have to forgive ourselves and be forgiven. We have to make amends with people we have wronged and those who have wronged us. And sometimes we need to eat humble pie. Sometimes we need to face harsh realities and rethink our strategies in light of new facts. Sometimes we need to admit we were wrong. Nonny, I admit it. You were right about the book title, wherever you are up in heaven.

The issue was highlighted again for me when I went to work for Van Jones in 2009. Here was this incredibly brilliant thinker. One of the best this generation has produced. He wrote a best-selling book called *The Green Collar Economy*. He is a Yale-educated lawyer. He is one of the world's experts on green jobs and finance. I think by now he has won every award someone can win short of the Nobel Peace Prize. He gets appointed by Obama as a special adviser for green jobs. He's doing great. He's working in the halls of government on boring wonkish stuff like weatherization, retrofitting buildings, and partnering with industry to create jobs in Appalachia.

I quote Van a lot throughout this book because I have learned so much from him and because I have gotten to watch his thinking evolve over the years. "My entire social justice career, I was using the wrong metaphor," he reflected a few years ago. "I thought I was on the *Amistad* and the goal was to free the slaves. But actually I was on the *Titanic*. I was in the wrong movie. I was on the wrong boat. We still have to free the people at the bottom of the boat. But we also have to turn the whole ship around or we're going to run into an iceberg and we're all going to drown."

Van is a person who has grown tremendously. But that doesn't matter, because here come the right-wing bloggers and talk show hosts. The Glenn Becks of the world. The good residents of Salem looking to find a witch. The good Senator McCarthy looking to rid the land of communists. Glenn Beck features Van on his Fox News show no less than twenty times, ripping and tearing this man's reputation.

Here Van is, a midlevel staffer, trying to weatherize buildings and put people to work.

But he can't escape the high-tech mob, Twittering for blood, demanding his head, making it hard for him to do his job. And this isn't even about him. This is a power struggle. It's about taking down Obama. Tear down the Democrats. Derail their hard work to fix health care, education, the economy, and global warming. Ultimately, rather than allow the administration to be distracted from its important work, Van Jones took one for the team. He decided to resign. It was the honorable thing to do. But what does it say about us as a country?

Watching Van get ripped to shreds was an especially painful and humbling experience for someone like me who decided to publish a book called *Bomb the Suburbs* at the tender age of twenty-one. So before I go on, I want to send a special shout out to all you right-wing bloggers. You did a good hit job on Van. If I'm at all successful, you'll do a good hit job on me too. Just for the record, here are the facts: I do not like bombs. I do not like bombing. Bombs and I are not friends. We're not cool. Not on speaking terms. We don't hang out or associate with each other. I've never seen a real live bomb, and if I did see one I wouldn't want to be friends with it. And since we're setting the record straight, I am very good friends with the suburbs. I do NOT want to bomb them. When I was a kid growing up, I used to live in the suburbs outside of Columbus, Ohio. I liked it there. I liked the people. I liked to ride my bike on the tree-lined streets and play fun sports and games with my friends at the parks and rec center. I have lots of friends from the suburbs and in the suburbs. I love suburbs, suburbanites, and everyone with a letter S in their name. I do not under any circumstances agree with bombing them.

Everybody got that? Okay, good. Glad we set the record straight.

So, *Please Don't Bomb the Suburbs*. What does it really mean?

Let me count the layers.

Please Don't Bomb the Suburbs is my one-line response to the right-wing bloggers. It is a difficult personal reckoning. It is a message to my twenty-one-year-old self, a movement strategy memo to all you young whippersnappers, political organizers, activists, hip-hop heads, and other hot-blooded pissed-off young artists and troublemakers out there: maybe you can avoid some of the potholes I've fallen in a few too many times. *Please Don't Bomb the Suburbs* is a book about not sabotaging yourself. I still get letters from young folks who read my old books for the first time and get excited and say it changed their lives. Knowing what I know now, this makes me say: *Hold up, player. Pump the brakes. Let me holler at you. The game has changed.* For everyone who liked my old books (in the words of Beyoncé): let me upgrade you.

The world has changed a lot in the sixteen years since *Bomb the Suburbs* came out. The suburbs aren't what they used to be. Neither are the cities. Who would have guessed? For four decades, from the 1950s through the 1980s, there was a mass exodus of people, especially white and affluent people, to the suburbs. White flight was the game. Chicago lost 750,000 people—nearly a quarter of its population. It was a government-subsidized evacuation and disinvestment program.

During the 1990s, that trend started to flip faster than most of us could imagine. Historic black and brown neighborhoods from the South Bronx to Bed-Stuy, Cabrini Green to West Lawndale, Columbia Heights to Anacostia, North Philly to South L.A., Hunter's Point to Roxbury, the east side of Cleveland to the east side of Austin. Neighborhoods that were seen as off-limits to white people for fifty years or more were suddenly becoming "cool, trendy, and livable"—that's right, folks. Time for gentrification!

During the Bush years, from 2000–08, suburban poverty grew a whopping 25 percent. According to the Brookings Institution, suburbs now house one-third of all poor people. In our ninety-five largest metro areas, the poverty rate grew five times as fast in the suburbs as in the cities they surround. The poorest city on record is not even a city. It's a suburb called Ford Heights, Illinois, twenty-five miles south of Chicago. Chicago's inner-ring southern suburbs are some of the poorest places in America, a thick band of fifteen separate municipalities like Robbins, Phoenix, Harvey, Thornwood, Hazelcrest, Chicago Heights, and Dalton—just like the South Side of Chicago, but spread out—with worse services, and limited transit to shopping, schools, and jobs. Meanwhile, large swaths of cities have become like suburbs now, complete with big-box stores.

In short, everything has become more complicated. Our strategies and analyses need to reflect our current reality.

From a moral standpoint, *Please Don't Bomb the Suburbs* is a meditation on the responsibilities of adulthood. In the tradition of Gandhi and Martin Luther King Jr. (and, um, the majority of women on the planet), being an adult includes a principled practice of nonviolence. Without reservation, we must oppose terrorism in all forms. This might seem obvious, but it's important to spell out because progressive folks are sometimes labeled wrongly as "soft" on terrorism. Some on the left have romanticized violence and/or justified violence as self-defense. Self-defense is justifiable, but only as a last resort to protect yourself or another from being hurt or killed. People often associate the idea of being left-of-center or being "radical" with being "militant." People often use the terms "radical" and "militant" interchangeably, when in fact they mean two very different things. "Radical" means "of the root." It means seeking the truth, get-

Top Ten Reasons to Love the Suburbs

1) More Americans live in the suburbs than in cities or rural areas . . . duh.
2) Suburbs are becoming more like cities, diverse and with more character.
3) Cities are becoming more like suburbs, whiter and with more chain stores.
4) Suburbs are becoming more progressive, politically and socially.
5) Most swing districts are in the suburbs and rural areas.
6) Suburbs will decide the future of our country.
7) They need love.
8) If they don't get love, they could turn to fear.
9) If you didn't love them before, it's a prejudice you can overcome.
10) Because I said so, and I'm the one who talked bad about them in the first place.

ting to the root of things. "Militant" means aggressive, violent, employing the use of force. Two very different concepts. Getting to the root is a good thing. Violent use of force, not so much.

Let's be very clear. Al-Qaeda, the Taliban, and Islamic terrorist groups in general are a right-wing phenomenon, not a left-wing phenomenon. They are not demanding women's rights, worker's rights, universal health care, a clean economy, peace, democracy, and respect for all. They are intolerant right-wing fundamentalists and we oppose them for the same reasons we oppose intolerant ring-wing fundamentalists in our own country. We oppose Osama bin Laden for the same reason we oppose Timothy McVeigh. We oppose violent fundamentalism wherever it is found, whether in Iran, Iraq, Afghanistan, Pakistan, India, Israel, Palestine, or in this country. And, by the way, we oppose violent left-wing fundamentalism too (although admittedly it has died down a lot since the collapse of the Soviet empire). Most people in the world want peace. So the issue is never Israel vs. Palestine. Or the U.S. vs. Iran. There are violent, usually right-wing *meshuganas* in every country and we are opposed to all of them. Plus, on a personal note, I ride public transit. The idea of bombs is very scary. Don't do it!

Human civilization is entering a very delicate stage and we don't need anybody to bomb anything right now. We need to just chill for a minute. Everyone needs to take a step back. Take a time out. Take a breather. Go work out at the gym. And then we need to ask some very adult questions about how our children and grandchildren will survive on this planet. What quality of life we want them to have.

Bottom line, we need to grow up.

As individuals. As a movement. As a country. As a species.

On top of all these substantive reasons for giving my book a controversial title, the comedian in me couldn't resist the temptation to have someone who wrote a book called *Bomb the Suburbs* write another book sixteen years later called *Please Don't Bomb the Suburbs*. It was just too funny. Someone needs to laugh at how my generation of hot-blooded anti-everything rabble-rousers has turned into boring normal adults who aspire to own a house, have kids, and buy ecological smoothie makers. There's a lot to laugh at—the crazy things we did when we were younger, and the way we are now. Just look at those old pictures of us, for Christ's sake, with our names on our belt buckles, looking hard as hell in our B-boy stances. We used to look ridiculous. And guess what? We still do!

We were a generation who grew up talking so much shit about how special and different we were and how we were the hip and the hop. How we were going to change the world. Now, as rapper Phonte from Little Brother says: "I hear us talking about SpongeBob SquarePants." Not to mention credit scores, aging parents, 501(c)(3)s, and, if we are lucky, 401(k)s and Roth IRAs. At some point, we deserve to have a good laugh at ourselves—at who we thought we were and who we have become. Our parents deserve to have a good laugh too. They told us so. They told us one day we'd understand. How humbling it is to admit they were right.

This is a difficult pill to swallow for a generation that grew up hating everything mainstream and chanting "Fight the power" with our fists raised in the air.

A Sobering Thought from My Fifteen-Year-Old Cousin

A few years ago, I was at my relatives' house in Los Angeles, sitting in the kitchen, talking to my fifteen-year-old cousin Miro. The last time I saw Miro was at his Bar Mitzvah. He and his friends were into the Beatles and they all had bowl haircuts, bangs falling over their eyes. I think it was some type of trend.

So here we are two years later. Miro is several inches taller—he's towering over me now. I'm asking him what kind of music he likes and he tells me he's into underground hip-hop.

"Underground hip-hop???" I say.

"Yeah . . . you grew up in Chicago, right?"

"Yeah."

"I love Chicago hip-hop." To my amazement, he starts naming artists and hip-hop blogs from Chicago, most of which I'd never heard of, because I haven't lived in Chicago for the past ten years. Then he stops me cold. "I like Pugslee Atomz . . . The Cool Kids . . ."

"Pugslee Atomz?"

"Yeah."

"How do you know about Pugslee Atomz?"

He gets online and starts playing me songs and showing me blogs.

Shit. I couldn't believe it. Pugslee was a kid I used to know in Chicago back in the '90s. He was six or seven years younger than me. He went to my high school. He was friends with my roommate Jameel (a.k.a. West Rok). I used to go to their breakdancing practice at the local community center. I remember buying a tape from him back in '97. Not a CD. A tape. Pugs was super talented, but I didn't know anyone outside Chicago had ever heard of him, let alone my fifteen-year-old Jewish cousin from L.A.

Ah, the Internet.

"What was it like to grow up in hip-hop in the '80s?" Miro wants to know.

"I don't know," I say. "What do the '80s seem like to you?"

"It seems like such a cool era to grow up. The golden era of hip-hop. Back when kids used to breakdance in the streets, deejays spun on vinyl, graffiti was still on the subways."

Whoa. How does he know all this stuff? I start reminiscing and feeling lucky to have grown up with Chicago hip-hop in the '80s. It *was* a golden era. I'm touched that my fifteen-year-old cousin has some concept of how amazing it was.

He says he wished he got to grow up in the '80s too.

I tell him I wish I got to grow up now. This is the golden era of progressive politics. In my youth, there was no organized progressive political movement.

I start to do the math. I was born in 1972. Miro was born in 1992. The 1980s are ancient history to Miro in the same way the 1960s were ancient history to me when I was his age.

Back then, I used to sit in the back room of 57th Street Books in Hyde Park, reading endlessly about the 1960s, the Black Panthers, and Malcolm X; the sit-in movement with the Student Nonviolent Coordinating Committee (SNCC), the antiwar movement, and Students for a Democratic Society (SDS), feeling like I had missed out on the golden era. It had all seemed so long ago. The people who came of age in the 1960s were the baby boomers. The baby boomers were old!

And then I start to have a very sobering thought. I still think of myself as young. But to my cousin Miro, I am old. As old as a baby boomer.

The thought rings in my head.

As old as a baby boomer. As old as a baby boomer. As old as a baby boomer. Whoa.

To Miro I am a baby boomer! Dear God. Me.

And then I have an even more sobering thought.

If my generation is as old as the baby boomers, what great historical accomplishments do we have to show for it? The baby boomers built all these movements in their younger years which—like them or not—dramatically transformed American life. The civil rights movement, the black, brown, yellow, and red power movements, the antiwar movement, the women's movement, the gay liberation movement, the consumer rights and environmental movements. Not to mention the entire field of community organizing.

And what type of love did they get for doing all of this? No love. Not from us. No love at all. We still thought they sucked. We still thought they were self-centered, irresponsible, hypocritical sellouts. Not so hot as leaders. Not so great as parents. So then came my even more sobering thought: what is Miro's generation going to think of us?

We did create hip-hop . . . kind of. But really it was invented in the '70s. We made skateboarding big—twice. We brought the world Spike Lee and Ani DiFranco, YouTube and *South Park*. We built a network of local youth organizing groups. We revived campus activism with United Students Against Sweatshops, and fights over higher education access. Our global justice movement put a dent in the WTO, third world debt, and international trade policy. We pioneered online organizing, blogs, and sophisticated data management. We launched the climate justice and green jobs movements and held the biggest climate lobby day in history—three times. We held the biggest antiwar rallies in history. We held the biggest immigrant rights rallies in history. We built an antiprison movement. We built AmeriCorps programs like City Year, Public Allies, and Teach for America. We made it okay to be lesbian, gay, bisexual, transgendered, intersex, queer, questioning, and even metrosexual. We made mixed babies in record numbers. We even elected a mixed baby as our president. We turned Congress and a bunch of state governments blue . . . When you start to add up all our accomplishments, we haven't done half bad.

The 1960s generation created all these movements. It was our generation's job to unite them into an integrated progressive movement capable of governing. We were halfway there.

Historically, the lost generation of the '80s and '90s was parallel to the silent generation of the 1950s (which, for the record, actually started the civil rights movement and community organizing). Our lost generation helped pave the way for the Millennials to become the most progressive generation in history. We laid the foundation for a new progressive era, not just in the streets but in the halls of government. So take that, baby boomers!

And *thank you*, baby boomers. Thank you for all the foundations you laid for us. You weren't perfect. Neither are we.

But when you add it all together, we have a lot to be proud of.

At the same time, we have a long way to go.

Why Good People Need Power

I do a lot of college speaking and everywhere I go, many cool, progressive, hip-hop, social-change type people show up at my events. I sometimes ask: "How many of you are artists or writers?" A bunch of hands go up. "How many of you plan to become teachers or work in nonprofits or do some kind of social change work?" Most of the rest of the hands go up. "How many of you are planning to go to law school or business school or get a corporate job?"

From a crowd of two to three hundred people, usually only a few hands go up. Those are the smart ones.

We have a serious problem, people. It's called power. We don't have it. We don't want it. We think it's dirty and bad. The people who read my books and show up at my talks are the *good* people—people who are motivated by wanting to do good, fighting against bad things, and creating beauty in the world, people who at a deep level aren't primarily motivated by money and power. I tell them they need to go to business school or law school. I say this metaphorically, since obviously there is more than one path to power. I don't care how you get there. An MBA, a JD, a legit hustler mentality. Whatever works for you. I'm just saying: it is a *moral imperative* for good people to get power.

That's when they all start giving me blank looks. Isn't power what we're fighting against? Doesn't power corrupt and absolute power corrupt absolutely? Isn't that what we good non–power hungry people have been taught all our lives?

To an extent, yes. Now that Democrats are in power, they will begin to be more and more susceptible to corruption and co-optation. This is why Democratic machines in cities tend to become crooked and self-dealing. This comes as no surprise.

The more surprising point, as my man Bernard Dory, a community organizer in L.A., says, "Powerlessness corrupts too. Absolute powerlessness corrupts absolutely." When you have no power, you are forced to play by the rules of the people who control your life. When you have to spend fourteen hours a day working in a sweatshop with no union, just to make ends meet, and you're only allowed to go to the bathroom for five minutes twice a day, and if you try to organize a union you get fired or beaten or killed, then your actions are severely constrained. And your thinking tends to become constrained as well. It is harder to have empowered thoughts. We are corrupted—mind, body, and spirit—by powerlessness as much as by power.

It's also possible—and this is my pet theory—that the types of people who are attracted to power tend to be the worst kind. That's why I'm talking to you. You're the ones who *don't* want power. You are uncomfortable with power. You think power is bad and evil. And that's exactly why you're the people who I trust the most to get power and use it for good.

I want good people to have actual power, not pretend power. I want you to own your home when you get old, not be in debt. I want you to be able to take time off, blow the whistle on a corporate scandal, and not worry how you're going to pay your bills or legal fees next month. The more you make smart career and political moves now, and avoid doing unstrategic things like naming your book *Bomb the Suburbs* when you're young, the more leverage you will have to do good when you're fifty-five years old and at the apex of your career.

Don't get me wrong, it's also easy to go off the rails in the other direction, to get corrupted by power, to get too comfortable, isolate yourself from pain and suffering and reality, and lose your purpose, your vision, your fire in the belly for change. Only you know where you are on this spectrum. Only you know, at any given point in your life, whether you need more power or whether you need to take a long slow bus ride through Latin America. Only you know whether you need to apply for a corporate internship, or volunteer with homeless veterans.

It is a lifelong balancing act. But honestly, people who read my books are less in danger of getting corrupted by power. I know my audience pretty well. With few exceptions, you're more in danger of not being very effective because you don't have enough power.

To my twenty-one-year-old self, and to everyone out there thinking you're too smart and too down for all that boring reformist mainstream grown-up stuff, take it from me and Nonny: please don't bomb the suburbs!

Please Don't Bomb the Suburbs is nothing less than a call to my generation, the one after mine, and everyone else I care about, to do three things:

1) Be good.
2) Get power.
3) Don't do stupid things to mess up your life.

These are what you might call Billy's Three Rules. They sound simple, but very few people manage to follow them. If you follow them, you are likely to have at least a halfway decent life.

Let's take examples of four men who did not follow Billy's Three Rules: Bill Clinton, John Edwards, Eliot Spitzer, and Jesse Jackson. They all tried to do good. Okay, some tried harder than others. They all got power. And they all ruined their lives (at least temporarily) and undercut their moral credibility because they couldn't keep their pants zipped up.

I don't want this to happen to you. So follow Billy's Three Rules, okay?

My friend Rha Goddess came up with her own three rules. Rha is a rap artist, actor, spiritual teacher, and all around one of the best people I know. Her system is similar to mine. Rha's Three Rules:

1) Stay true.
2) Get paid.
3) Do good.

It probably doesn't matter if you use Rha's rules or mine. Rha's are focused on money, mine are focused on power. Mine starts with being good, hers ends with doing good. Hers starts with being true to yourself, mine doesn't talk about that. Use whatever system works for you. I have to admit, hers is a little bit catchier. So go ahead and use her system. Just please, whatever you do, don't do anything stupid to mess up your life.

Eli Ceballos

Welcome to the Movement

I love social movements.

When most people think of social movements, they still think of news clips from the 1960s. Black people marching in the South. Sitting in at lunch counters. Getting sprayed by fire hoses. College-aged hippies in the streets, protesting the Vietnam War.

I want to demystify and deromanticize the idea of movements. Movements are very important and useful—utterly necessary to creating real change. We need to understand what they are, how they work, how they succeed. And the common roadblocks that hamper their success.

The word "movement" gets thrown around a lot. But what is a social movement exactly?

Here is my definition: a social movement is a group of people, connected by a common vision, acting to achieve shared goals, who think of themselves as a community.

Some complain that the term "movement" is used too casually. Some argue it is a sacred word that should be reserved only for the biggest, most transformative, most history-changing movements.

I too think movements are sacred, but in an everyday sort of way, like washing your hands or chewing your dinner, not like a magical unicorn that you place on a pedestal. To me, the romanticized way we use the word "movement" contributes to a fuzzy-headed way of thinking about how to actually build one. And because our idea of movements tends to be not very well thought out, we often don't set ourselves up to succeed. Romantic notions, images, and expectations of what a movement looks and feels like are demoralizing to the real-life everyday practice of movement-building.

The main question isn't whether something is a movement. Anything in motion is a movement. It's *what kind of movement*? How big? How good? How powerful? How lasting? How transformative?

When you take away the mystique and analyze movements functionally, they can be found everywhere. Big-box stores spreading to every corner of the globe is a movement. Cars and highways are a movement. Bottled water is a movement. So is the movement to stop these things—a much smaller, less powerful movement, to be sure. Two people falling in love is a movement. So is one person dancing. So is a small group hatching a plan. Evolution is the world's greatest biological movement. Capitalism, religion, ethnic solidarity, and nationalism are probably the world's four strongest social movements. What we think of as the progressive social change movement is probably #5 on the list, globally.

We are always in movement. There are always millions of movements going on at any given time. Some are big, most are small. Some are good, some bad, some social, some cultural, some technological, some a combination. Some movements are growing, some are dying off.

I love feeling like I am part of a great social movement, or even an innovative little one. Good social movements at their best feel like the beloved community Martin Luther King Jr. talked about. They have the very real power to transform everything. Movements are a core thread in my life. And vastly underappreciated. I love to understand the history and circumstances that give rise to movements. I love to understand the leaders, pioneers, behind-the-scenes players, and unsung heroes. I love to watch how they spread and grow, the bumps and bruises. And to understand how they stagnate, adapt, die, and suddenly rise from the ashes.

I have questions about how we build them better.

My biggest question: how do we create an unprecedented new movement that truly includes everyone—not just college kids, union members, activists, and people who recently got screwed by a particular issue?

How do we bridge that disconnect? How do we build a movement that everyone wants to be part of? With the Obamas, we took a big baby step in the right direction. What do the next ten steps look like?

We are at a historical turning point in the nature of movements. Naomi Klein writes about the development of a "movement of movements," as millions of local and issue-specific minimovements slowly converge. Paul Hawken writes about it simply as "the largest social movement in history." Yet the vast majority of people in our movement are not even aware of themselves as part of this movement.

At the end of the day, movements, like nations, are imaginary. They exist in our minds. Which means that to some extent they can become a self-fulfilling prophecy. The more that we think of ourselves as part of a movement, the more our movement becomes real. Let the greatest movement in the history of the world become aware of itself! What if we decided to create a Super Movement?

Twenty-five Years of Movement History: 1985–2010

It's also good to have a sense of history and perspective. The chart on page 28 is a very basic snapshot of movement history over the past twenty-five years. It is a living document. Howard Zinn, God rest his soul, created a much more extensive version of this for the past five hundred years. But I think it's important to tell the story of the past twenty-five years—the period when most people reading this book have been alive.

Five things to notice about the following timeline and the nature of movements:

1) There are a lot of minimovements that don't often recognize themselves as part of a whole.

2) At least a few big crises happen every year. These often provide the biggest opportunities for change, yet we're usually unprepared to respond.

3) Usually, at least a few big breakthroughs happen every year. To the public, they appear to happen overnight. In reality, they're often decades in the making, courtesy of millions of unsung organizers.

4) There are major evolutions in every sector of the movement every five to ten years. What are the next set of trends in your sector? Let's try to anticipate them.

5) Successful movements go in phases, they ebb and flow over the years.

Movement Timeline: 1985–2010

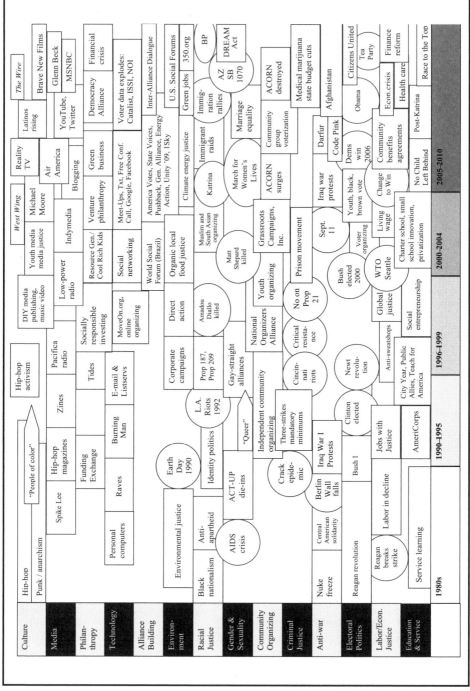

Most people get impatient and demoralized during the ebb stages. Successful movement-builders are like sailors: they study the current, patiently ride the waves. Successful movement-builders stick around, adapt to changing conditions, and are always prepared to go all hands on deck when the right wave comes in.

The Future of Organizing

It's not at all clear what our movement will look like in fifty years. Will non-profit organizations even exist in anything like their current form, or will all political, philanthropic, and community action be self-organized much more efficiently via GoogleTwitterFacebook 8.0?

It's not even clear what the movement will look like in ten to twenty years. The pace of evolution has been so rapid that our current movement would be almost unrecognizable to someone from the 1990s. They would need to put on 3-D glasses to even understand how amazing it is.

Ten or twenty years ago, few movement people thought voting was cool. The idea of labor, environment, and community groups collaborating sounded like an exciting new idea. Community organizing was mostly small and invisible. Almost no one had cell phones—people still kept their contacts in address books, like . . . on paper. Blogs were just starting to exist. Social networks did not exist. Solar panels sounded like weirdo space devices. Data management was done in Excel. There was virtually no relationship between social justice groups and the Democratic Party. And the movement was even more racially segregated, white-male dominated, and insider-y than it is today.

When you think of the progress we've made over the past ten to twenty years, it's incredible. We have gone from the wilderness to having a quasi-decent, quasi-progressive, quasi-governing coalition.

What can we do in the next ten to twenty years?

Which brings us to The Future. Or more precisely: Two Futures.

In ten to twenty years, if we play our cards right, we could have a much better country. We could be on the road to greatness. The human race might even survive.

Upward Spirals, Downward Spirals

Life operates in upward spirals and downward spirals.

If you exercise every day and eat right for a week, you put yourself on an upward spiral. Your confidence goes up. Your self-discipline goes up. Your concentration goes up. You feel better. You look better. You have more energy to make friends, to hustle at work and save the world at the same time. You feel so good that next week you set the bar higher. You're ready for more.

If you eat junk food, watch junk TV, and sit on the couch every day for a week, you fall into a downward spiral. You feel like shit. You look like shit. You feel anxious, undisciplined, and insecure. You start to doubt your self-worth. You have trouble sleeping and you're groggy during the day. You definitely don't feel like exercising. So what do you do? Reach for the cookies. Reach for the potato chips. Start drinking. Pretty soon you're depressed and feeling un-motivated at work, withdrawing from your friends and loved ones, consumed with self-defeating thoughts. Your life goes downhill fast. All because you had a bad week.

Civilizations are like people. The Bush years were a bad week. We went from budget surplus to staggering debt and financial collapse. We painted ourselves into corners in the Middle East. We lost our national wealth and mental health with PTSD. In three years, we went from most-favored-nation status to most-hated-nation status. We felt worse about ourselves, our country, our future. Our major institutions were starting to collapse. We were spiraling down. We landed in intensive care.

Under Obama's leadership, we're slowly beginning to turn things around. We had emergency heart and brain surgery. We were in the hospital for a long time recovering. We're still in physical therapy, learning how to walk again. We're beginning to have a good exercise week. We're cutting back on beer, donuts, and credit card debt. At least a little bit. We're investing in education, health care, and renewable energy. At least a little bit. We're planting local gar-dens. At least a little bit. We're stopping the prison-building madness. At least a little bit. We're investing in infrastructure. We're talking about service and responsibility. We're mending our drama in the Middle East. Or at least we're trying. At least a little bit.

But America, how can I say this? We're not spring chickens anymore. We went pretty far down that spiral. We've been making dumb decisions for a long time now. When you're eighteen, you can eat half a pizza, wash it down with malt liquor, walk it off the next day, and still be on top of the world. When you eat half a pizza and chug malt liquor and you're forty, you wake up in the morn-ing and you can barely get out of bed. The lump of cheesy dough sits there in your stomach like a brick. The alcohol is a fuzzy spot on your forehead.

Two Futures

Let's play out two scenarios for the next ten to twenty years.

In one scenario, Obama's presidency falls apart. Republicans take over again. Or we have a stalemate where Democrats stay in power but don't have the strength and numbers to pass bold progressive change. Education, prisons, war, health care, energy, the economy, and the environment all continue to stagnate and drain our national resources and national spirit.

Then things get worse. Without noticing, we eat one too many fish out of the sea. We cut down one too many trees. We burn one too many tanks of gas. We sell one too many weapons to one too many madmen. We hit an unlucky patch and the dominoes start cascading, triggering crises of gas, food, and the global economy. Demagogues rise to power in countries with nuclear weapons. Men get their dicks involved and mushroom clouds explode over cities.

That's one scenario.

In the other scenario, we dodge a bullet—just barely.

The way I think about Barack Obama is that he's the probably the best president we could have possibly gotten at this moment in history, given the current political reality. He understands what we need. He understands the forces we are up against. He understands politically how to get us there, and how to bring the haters along, one big baby step at a time. I wouldn't be surprised if he is yet remembered as one of the greatest presidents in history. He and Michelle together get a plus 100. The problem is that America and the world right now are at minus 3,000. Shit is really bad. The Obamas being a plus 100 brings us up to a grand total of minus 2,900. Which is a beautiful thing. But the Obamas can only do so much by themselves. We still have another 2,900 to go.

Think about where we could be in ten years if we play our cards right. What if we replace thousands of Republican elected officials at every level with Democrats, and thousands of mediocre Democrats with true progressives? In doing so, we could shift the entire political landscape into something resembling sanity. What if we organize a new generation of progressive funders to take leadership in supporting bold and collaborative new organizing initiatives? What if we update progressive organizing for the twenty-first century—with effective organizations in every county and eventually every precinct in the United States? What if we build wind and solar farms and a new smart grid to carry the power?

We could cut greenhouse gas emissions by 20 or 30 percent in the U.S. and worldwide. We could replace hundreds of prisons with community colleges and drug treatment facilities. We could create an incredible upward spiral and launch a new progressive renaissance.

If we play our cards right, the next U.S. president could be even better than Obama. Our kids might even put us in eco-friendly hip-hop retirement homes.

Upward spiral or downward spiral.

Ten to twenty years.

We get to choose.

Road Map of What's Ahead

The next three sections are my fun personal history of movements from hip-hop through Obama. The last four sections are shorter reflections on lessons learned and strategy memos for "Where do we go from here?"—as a generation, as a movement, as a country, as individuals, and as a species. At the very end is a workbook for you to reflect on *your* story and the next chapter in *your* book. My hope is that you will use it as an opportunity to reflect on and strategize the next moves in your chess game. Also, if you haven't already, think about starting a little book club. The best thing about movement-building: we don't have to do it alone.

Part I

The Hip-hop Generation Comes of Age

(1984–1996)

*"Next time y'all underestimate me. Recognize I just turned eighteen.
That means I got seven years to catch up. So what's up?"*
—R&B singer Mario

A Brief History of the '80s and '90s

For my cousin Miro and the generation after mine, I want to give a little background on how we got here—my little version of Movement History 101. This isn't remotely comprehensive. So maybe it's better to think of this as my *personal* movement story.

It's difficult to imagine how exciting hip-hop was when it burst into our lives in the mid-1980s like sweet salvation.

During most of the late 1970s and early '80s, there wasn't a lot going on in the world of cultural movements that captured the imagination of young people. There were video games. There were the Harlem Globetrotters. House music was just being born. So was punk. And skateboarding. Spiked bracelets and mohawk haircuts were starting to pop up. Those were cool. Sort of. But I couldn't fully relate to them.

Hip-hop, born out of—and as a creative response to—gang culture in the early 1970s, was revolutionizing New York City. The trains were covered top to bottom. Breaking, rapping, and deejaying were everywhere. But no one outside of New York knew about it.

More than a decade after the birth of hip-hop, it had barely arrived in Chicago. A few early pioneers like my mentor Dr. Groove were starting to rap in clubs, and a few kids like Akbar and P-Lee Fresh, who had moved from New York in high school, began to tag in the early '80s. But no one knew what the hell they were doing. I was completely unaware.

Then in sixth grade, something happened that changed my life. Henry Ofori-Atta came to school with a Sony Walkman—an early predecessor to the iPod. Henry put the earphones in my ears and pressed play.

I said a wikki wikki wikki wikki—shut up!

I was spellbound. What on Earth was I listening to? Was it a song? I didn't know. All I knew was that it was the coolest, funniest, most creative and addictive sound ever invented. It seemed to have been invented just for me—a sixth-grade boy—designed precisely for my sensibilities. It painted a fantasy world complete with ghetto superheroes, cartoon battles, funny voices, mesmerizing beats. I had entered a vibrant new world, a magical mystery tour—a self-contained black planet with hyperintelligent life-forms. It was my first rap song, "Jam on It" by Newcleus. I had no idea what I was listening to. All I knew was that I was hooked.

There was virtually no hip-hop on TV or radio, so my sixth grade friends and I had to search for clues, like the little detectives in Encyclopedia Brown stories. My friend Seth saw a clip on TV of someone doing the centipede. Someone else saw the moonwalk, the wave, pop-locking, the turbo walk, the backspin, the helicopter. We would bring our discoveries to school and compare notes in the hallways between classes, endlessly practicing the moves, trying to figure them out. By the summer of 1984, breakdancing was everywhere. Anytime you would leave the house, you would encounter a group of boys. Someone would be carrying a boom box. And they would battle right there on the sidewalk. Or someone would run into a store to get a piece of cardboard. For a summer or two, it melted away the barriers of race and class for urban boys. For a summer or two, we were all just boys (and a few girls) trying to breakdance.

Breaking was cool, but what really got me was graffiti. Pieces started appearing under the 47th Street viaduct. Tags materialized on phone booths downtown and in the back windows of the 55th Street bus. They were messages in secret code from a culture that I yearned to be part of. Soon I was. My parents had sent me to the local private school—the University of Chicago Laboratory Schools (where the Obamas would send their kids twenty years later). It was a racially integrated institution, but still very sheltered. In seventh grade, I convinced my parents to let me transfer to Kenwood, the neighborhood public school.

First Day of Seventh Grade

"I ain't play the hand I was dealt. I changed my cards." —Kanye West

Transferring to Kenwood was like hip-hop utopia to me. The first day of seventh grade, kids were breakdancing in the cafeteria. Kenwood was a magnet high school with a seventh- and eighth-grade program. It was 90 percent black but attracted kids from all over the city. There were Puerto Rican kids from the Northwest Side. Mexican kids from the Southwest Side. Street-smart white kids from Uptown. And black kids from the poorer neighborhoods surrounding Hyde Park all the way south to the wild hundreds. Our major rival was Whitney Young on the West Side (where Michelle Obama went to school).

Kenwood was not a gang school. We did have some Black P. Stones, who were the original black Chicago street gang founded by a Hyde Park high school dropout in 1958, but they were a tiny presence. Mainly, Kenwood was known on the South Side for having the finest girls and a great music teacher, Ms. McLin. Chaka Khan, R. Kelly, Da Brat, Twilight Tone (Common's producer), and, yes, Pugslee Atomz and the Cool Kids all came through Kenwood.

My new classmates were more cosmopolitan than I was. I had never taken a public bus before, except for the 6 Jeffrey Express to go shopping downtown with my mom. Hyde Park was an embattled upscale island in the middle of Chicago's black South Side. If you were white, or even if you were black and from Hyde Park, you were told never to cross 47th or 61st Street. A bombed-out ghetto landscape surrounded us on all sides. My new friends took me on the bus and train lines all over the city, showed me how to navigate gang turfs, run the el tracks and subway tunnels, rack markers, paint, climb rooftops, and holler at girls (back before they called it hollering). Walking back and forth to school, I would "bomb" the outsides of five to ten buses a day. Then I'd go out again after soccer practice and paint ten or fifteen more. I set numerical goals for myself. My buses were transferred all over the city and everyone began seeing me up.

My friends and I called ourselves The Union Crew. Our leader was a charismatic Puerto Rican kid named Joe Iglesias. Joey told us he made up the name Union Crew. We later found out he got it from the movie *Wild Style*. Most other crews were from one particular neighborhood, train line, and race. We were a multiracial crew of magnet school kids from all sides of the city. In addition to buses and trains, we targeted mail and newspaper boxes downtown that no one else was hitting. Before I knew it, *Upski* and *The Union Crew* were known all over the city. My goal in life was to be All-City King, and I thought I was invincible in the way only a thirteen-year-old can be.

The summer I was thirteen, I was a camp counselor at the Hyde Park Jewish Community Center. I would get off work, wearing Hawaiian shorts and T-shirt with a Pilot marker tucked in my drawers. I would ride the train to 95th Street, the end of the line, then ride back downtown against rush hour traffic. I would start at the back of the train and walk through the cars, bombing. By 63rd Street, people would be on the train, so I would move in between cars, kneel down, and write on the outside doors. Later, when the train cars decoupled, *Upski Union* would appear on the front or back of the train.

One bright summer afternoon, I was doing my routine, in between the cars, bending down to write, when the door swung open and a train conductor tried to grab me. In a split second, I dodged him, bolted through the opposite door, and ran through the train, with passengers cheering me on. I ran car to car, without looking back, until I got to the front of the train. In the front car was a crew of quasi-official-looking workmen. Shit. They looked at me suspiciously, but it didn't appear that they had been radioed yet. I tried to catch my breath and appear normal. Meanwhile, the train was approaching Cermack 22nd Street/Chinatown, an elevated station close to the headquarters of the Chicago Police Department. I had to plan my escape. Fast. The station only had one exit at the rear of the platform. If I waited until the train stopped, I'd be stuck at the front of the platform and would have to get past the conductor and the police, who were probably already on the way. I was trapped. What would Houdini do?

As the front of the train approached the station, I pulled the cherry (red emergency-door release), which opened my door. No one else was standing near me but people started gasping. I jumped out onto the platform. I tried to leap in a running motion to cushion my fall, but we were still going full speed. As soon as my foot touched the platform, I flew face-first and hit the platform floor like a pancake. In a daze I got up, hopped the turnstile, and began running down the stairs. I sprinted into Chinatown, weaving through narrow egg-filled alleys past bizarre housing projects, which looked like regular housing projects but were filled with Chinese people and decked out in red and green pagoda trim.

Winded, I dashed under a train viaduct and emerged on Halsted Street, where a southbound 8 Halsted bus was miraculously stopped at a red light. I boarded the bus, paid my fare, walked to the back. Home free! Still panting, I lifted up my shirt to inspect my stinging midsection. It was covered in blood. "You got shot," the dude next to me blurted, eyes wide.

"Nah, just a little scrape." I got home okay, snuck past my parents into the bathroom, and sat in the shower. My stomach burning, I felt like James Bond.

The 1980s were a depressing time politically. The movements of the '60s had either been destroyed by government repression, imploded, or run out of steam. Reagan's defeat of Carter in 1980 was a giant cowboy smackdown of all things remotely liberal. Reagan set the pattern for Bush twenty years later. He cut school budgets and community programs, and created stiff sentences for nonviolent drug offenses. He broke the backs of working people and he deregulated financial markets, which led to scandals, recession, massive debt, and the virtual collapse of the savings-and-loan industry.

Wall Street was riding high on the dubious financial inventions of the day: junk bonds and leveraged buyouts. In the 1984 election, Reagan demolished Mondale, winning every state except Minnesota. Young people were the most conservative part of the electorate—voting for Reagan by a three-to-one margin. *Time* profiled college students as the most apathetic and selfish generation in American history.

The movements of the '60s hadn't actually gone away. But they had become less visible, more localized, less wide-eyed, more practical. A network of Ralph Nader–style consumer groups like the PIRGs; statewide middle-class groups like Citizen Action; environmental groups like Greenpeace; and low-income community-based organizations like ACORN, were quietly spreading. An alphabet soup of nonprofit advocacy organizations was mushrooming in Washington, D.C., and around the country to speak up for the public good. Underneath the layer of official groups in D.C., an entire ecosystem of innovative grassroots organizations was quietly sprouting through cracks in the sidewalk. Movements, for better and worse, had become institutionalized. Members of SNCC and the Black Panthers were running for office and entering the business world.

The antiwar movement of the 1960s had evolved into an antinuclear movement by 1981 in response to Reagan's game of chicken with Russia. A 1982 protest gathered nearly one million people in Central Park. A famous postcard from the rally showed a sea of bodies and a sign: *Hell No, We Won't Glow.* In 1981, a TV special aired called *The Day After*, a dramatization of what would happen following a nuclear war. There were huge controversies across the country about whether kids should be allowed to watch it. My fourth grade teacher told us that the U.S. and Russia had tens of thousands of nuclear weapons pointed at each other and if someone pushed the wrong button we could all be destroyed.

What do you mean we could all be destroyed?

Are you kidding me?

My fourth grade brain tried to comprehend this. It all seemed so stupid. I remember seeing maps with concentric circles showing how most of Chicago would be vaporized instantly. The entire metro area would be burnt up in a firestorm. I had nightmares of my family fleeing for Indiana before the mushroom cloud disabled our car's engine and enveloped us in radioactive ash. Obviously the adults of the world didn't have their shit together. What were they thinking? The world was in danger of being destroyed and everyone was just going to carry on like normal? Everything will be fine as long as you practice baseball and turn in your math homework. Really?

I convinced my friends that we needed to do something. We had all seen *Star Wars*. It seemed simple enough. All we had to do was use the Force to fight the Death Star. We decided to hold a march through the neighborhood against nuclear war. We made fliers that said *Peace or Destruction?* with a hand-drawn illustration of Chicago getting blown up. We marched around the neighborhood handing them out on the street, shouting "Peace or Destruction!" trying to get people to come to our march. This was my first lesson in event turnout: fliers by themselves don't work very well. You need word of mouth and buy-in. The only people who showed up were my three friends, our parents, and our teacher Ms. Kalk.

The focus of U.S. military intervention had shifted from Vietnam to south of the border. Reagan was authorizing paramilitary actions to destabilize left-leaning governments throughout the Americas. The Iran-Contra scandal broke in 1986 when it came out that Reagan had been covertly selling weapons to Iran to finance right-wing militias to overthrow the elected government of Nicaragua.

Hip-hop vs. House vs. Gangs vs. Crack

There was a growing movement on campuses against apartheid in South Africa. Rap groups like Stetsasonic were making songs like "A.F.R.I.C.A." A divestment and sit-in movement began on campuses that pressured international companies to withdraw investments from South Africa and eventually forced the apartheid regime to allow universal elections in 1994. Meanwhile, a little disease that didn't have a name yet was killing thousands. ACT UP (AIDS Coalition to Unleash Power) was born in 1987 and began staging "die-ins" on Wall Street and at the Centers for Disease Control. Jesse Jackson ran for President in 1988 and won eleven primary states—sparking both a movement and a backlash within the Democratic Party.

I was barely aware of this. The only movement that existed for me was hip-hop. My friends and I grew up on hip-hop and hip-hop grew along with us. Every year from 1984 to 1988, hip-hop became more sophisticated, more creative, more intellectual, and more politically charged. KRS-One was our teacher. Album by album, he educated us about the streets and the larger world. *"Cocaine business controls America. Ganja business controls America."* He made a song about the meat industry. About black history. He even made a song explaining stories in the Bible.

You couldn't believe he was writing lyrics about this stuff. There was a whole cohort of artists doing the same thing. MC Lyte made songs like "I Cram to Understand U" and "Cappucino," about drug addiction. Slick Rick made songs like "Children's Story," discouraging kids from crime. De La Soul made the song "Millie Pulled a Pistol on Santa" about child abuse. Run-DMC made "Proud to Be Black." Public Enemy wrote countless songs about racism, including "By the Time I Get to Arizona" about that state's refusal to recognize Martin Luther King Jr.'s birthday. Ice Cube, by some measures the biggest-selling gangster rapper, was also the most political.

In the late '80s, there was tremendous excitement about building a hip-hop political movement. It was popular to wear leather African medallions around your neck with the shape of the continent in red, black, and green. Chuck D from Public Enemy teamed up with the Nation of Islam and pledged to train five thousand young black leaders in five years.

Spike Lee came out with *Do the Right Thing*, a movie about a race riot in the Bed-Stuy neighborhood of Brooklyn. He opened a store in nearby Fort Greene and made the area a mecca for young black artists and professionals.

Students at Harvard started a magazine called the *Source*, which began featuring groundbreaking political essays and commentary from James Bernard, a law student in the same class as Barack Obama. Bernard's "Doin' the Knowledge" column took KRS-One's scholarship a step further. He wrote a series of stirring essays that articulated an ethos for a generation: *"In the course of human events, it becomes necessary for a generation to declare its own values and vision,"* he wrote. *"We need to harness the very same anger that drove the American colonies into a war against the British. This is not only a political war. It is also a cultural war and a spiritual war . . . The hip-hop Nation needs its own Declaration of Independence."*

Bernard and others at the *Source* created the field of hip-hop journalism, which spawned a slew of magazines: *Vibe, Rap Pages, XXL,* and eventually an entire cottage industry of ghetto reality books.

There was a lot to write about.

By the late '80s, crack, AIDS, drug wars, and the prison epidemic were in full wrecking-ball mode, demolishing the fabric of urban communities. Basically, all hell broke loose.

Chicago was known for having the most organized and sophisticated gang structure. L.A. gangs got famous from movies like *Colors* and spread across the country like wildfire, partly as a copycat phenomenon. But Chicago gangs had rules, and for most of the 1980s they actually kept crack out of the city.

It was well documented that Irish and other white ethnic street gangs had served as the social foundation for the Chicago political machine. Mayor Richard Daley the elder had come out of the Hamburg Athletic Club, an Irish street gang on the Southwest Side, as Mike Royko documented in *Boss*, his classic book on the Daley machine.

The white ethnic neighborhood gangs fed into the ward and precinct political organizations, which operated on a patronage system. They cut deals in black and Latino wards to include so-called leaders who were effective in turning out and securing votes for the machine. It was a vertically integrated patronage model which had roles and perks for everyone from ward bosses to business and church leaders to the thug leaders on the street.

Beginning in the 1950s, an independent progressive political movement formed to challenge the Daley machine—it later went on to nurture the career of a young state senator, Barack Obama. The movement was a joining of three forces: Lakefront liberals, led by legendary Hyde Park Alderman Leon Despres; black independents who built an organization called the League of Negro Voters, which used the slogan *Protest at the Polls*; and a growing Latino cohort that challenged the white ethnic machine in majority Latino wards.

These three forces came together to elect the city's first black mayor, Harold Washington, in 1983—the only nonmachine mayor in recent Chicago history. Harold Washington's election set the stage for Obama. Many of Obama's early supporters, including David Axelrod, cut their teeth on Washington's campaign. After Washington's death from a heart attack in 1987, the Daley machine returned to power. Independent political forces were vanquished. I remember the day Harold Washington died. I was in math class when we got the news, and I immediately made plans with my friends to paint a Harold Washington piece in the subway downtown after school. Unfortunately, the police arrested us before we could even pull it off. But my graffiti friends and I soon created numerous Harold Washington pieces and memorial messages around the city.

Throughout the '80s and '90s, gang, house, and hip-hop cultures in Chicago competed for the hearts and minds of urban youth, and sometimes cross-pollinated. The El Rukns were one of the most infamous and sophisticated black gangs on the South Side. Influenced by the Black Panthers and the Nation of Islam, they incorporated quasi-Islamic teachings. At one point they created a community organization which managed to secure government funding for community nonviolence programming. Their leader was a guy named Jeff Fort who went to prison in the 1980s for attempting to purchase weapons from Libya.

At first the authorities couldn't tell the difference between hip-hop and gang culture. They both did graffiti. And they were both driven by angry young men, fueled on testosterone. As graffiti writers, we did our best to steer clear of the gangs. Once, on the North Side, I got chased by the Puerto Rican Stones. They caught me on a side street when my shoe fell off in the snow.

"What you ride? What you be about?" they yelled as they held me down in the snow.

"I'm a graffiti writer. I don't ride with no gangs."

They went through my pockets and found my black Griffin shoe dye, which they used to write a PR Stones symbol across my bare stomach. I got off easy. Another time, my friends and I were painting a rooftop off of Sheridan Road, and we heard an eagle cry in the alley. "Shit, it's the Latin Eagles, they saw us. Get down." The Latin Eagles were sometime rivals of the PR Stones and they probably assumed we were from another gang.

We scaled down the roof into a gangway on the front side of the building and ran out onto Sheridan Road. Undercover cops had also been monitoring us and thought we were burglars. The police chased us. I got away, but they caught my friend David and beat the hell out of him with phone books that didn't leave marks. As hip-hop kids, we operated as best as we could in the narrow space between gangs and the police.

A lot of the early hip-hop kids in Chicago saw hip-hop as a way of getting away from gangs. Meanwhile, house started out as a gay-oriented dance culture, but it became so popular by the time it reached teenagers in the mid-'80s that we had no idea of its roots. Hip-hop and house were in competition for space on Chicago's airwaves and clubs. But the house promoters and deejays were five to ten years older. They already had the infrastructure of clubs set up, so they shut hip-hop out of the venues and radio until the 1990s.

On a winter night in 1986, the South Side graffiti writers had gathered at Caution's house to paint the nearby B train yards on 63rd and King Drive. On the radio at midnight, legendary house deejay Farley Jackmaster Funk held a call-in contest over whether people wanted to hear house or hip-hop. House won. Hip-hop lost. We all thought it was rigged.

While the house scene had an openly gay undertone, a lot of the early hip-hop kids also had secret lives. They were the creative kids in the ghetto, looking for an outlet to be different, to escape from their neighborhoods and still be accepted. One of my best friends, K-Lite, a hip-hop genius from the Bronx, was seen at clubs around Boys Town on the North Side. Another Chicago legend, Kool Rock Steady, died of AIDS. No one was expecting that. A bunch of original hip-hop legends were gay or bisexual. I'm not gonna name names but it's a part of our history that deserves to be told—a secret ingredient in hip-hop's creative genius.

Nationally, during the '80s, radio formatting became much more racially segregated. This wasn't simply a holdover from the past. It was largely the work of one man, Lee Abrams, a radio-formatting consultant whose firm went around the country to stations in the late '70s and told them that white people didn't want to listen to black music anymore. Music industry historian Dan Charnas wrote his college thesis on this. Before that, radio was more racially fluid; disco and R&B music had wide crossover appeal. This division in the music separated youth culture on racial lines. It wasn't until the mid-'90s that hip-hop's pervasive power broke through this formatting barrier. Today, most popular music has its foundation in hip-hop production and aesthetics. Races and genres are mixed together now. Youth music and culture became integrated.

In the 1990s, black gang leaders on the South Side tried explicitly to copy Daley's Irish Hamburg model to build a political machine. Quick background: There are two major groupings of gangs in Chicago. Like Crips and Bloods in L.A., Chicago-based gangs are divided into two denominations: Folks and People (People are also known as Brothers). You have to watch how you talk in Chicago. I remember when I first went out to California, everybody calls each other "Folks, folks, 'sup, folks." I was like: *Whoa whoa whoa, calm down.*

Folks was an alliance created in the late 1970s in the Illinois prison system. Folks-affiliated gangs typically wore black and blue, and used the six-point star, pitchforks, and banged their hats to the right. The major gangs that rode under Folks were Gangster Disciples, Black Gangster Disciples, Black Disciples, anything with Disciples in the name, and then a bunch of Latin gangs like the Spanish Cobras. The official leader was Larry Hoover, who had been in prison since 1973. Folks also sometimes loosely allied with Crips—who also wore blue.

In response, the People alliance was formed by the leaders of the Vice Lords, the Latin Kings, and the El Rukns, a.k.a. the Black P. Stone Nation. People-affiliated gangs used the symbol of the five-point star. The Latin Kings wore black and gold, and the black gangs generally wore black and red. In the prison systems, nationally, they were loosely allied with the Bloods. It is notable that both major gang alliances included both black and brown gangs, and even some white ethnic gangs. The Simon City Royals and the Popes, a historically white gang from the Northside, rolled with Folks. Another historically white Northside gang, Gaylords, aligned themselves with People.

At various moments, older, more mature gang leaders would become politicized, develop a conscience, and try to steer their gangs away from illegal activities into more positive and political endeavors. In the late '60s, the Black P. Stones marched with Martin Luther King Jr. to protest segregation and worked with the Woodlawn Organization (the original group that community organizing guru Saul Alinsky helped to form). Many gangs marched with Jesse Jackson in the 1970s and '80s, and were involved in a national gang peace summit process in the 1990s. They also stopped calling themselves "gangs" and began referring to themselves as "nations."

In 1993, Larry Hoover officially changed the name of the GDs to Growth and Development, and put out an official word that the members should cease all negative behavior, including drug selling, cutting school, and even littering. Some of the leaders started a nonprofit organization called Save the Children, and later a political group called 21st Century Vote. They organized a protest at City Hall with thousands of young people, and a national gang peace summit in Cabrini Green (the infamous housing projects featured on the original '70s TV series *Good Times*).

In 1995, one of the GDs' top leaders, Wallace "Gator" Bradley, ran for city council in Chicago's 3rd Ward, which included the Robert Taylor Homes—the same ward where Harold Washington began his political career. The election drew national attention and Gator won 31 percent of the vote.

Chicago politics post–Harold Washington was a sad affair. Daley Jr. came back with a new, improved version of the machine. He first drove a wedge in Washington's coalition by gathering key whites and Latinos, left blacks politically isolated, and gradually co-opted almost everyone. Even David Axelrod, who had strategized Harold Washington's campaign, eventually came to work for him.

It is fascinating to read Barack Obama's account of organizing on the South Side and hear him deal with the same dynamics from a more professional standpoint.

As a young person growing up and searching for my political home, I didn't find anything. The closest models I encountered were black nationalism, white leftism, and hip-hop. None of these seemed up to the task at hand. The independent progressive political space was narrow and tenuous.

By the late '80s, grassroots hip-hop was in decline. Graffiti had been buffed from the train lines. Breakdancing was considered dead. I mean completely dead. Like, if you were caught breakdancing, you would be laughed at. The Union Crew had scattered. Joe Iglesias had gotten deeper into gangbanging and became a Spanish Disciple. In ninth grade he transferred to Sullivan High School which was run by Latin Kings, so he had to drop out of school. In 1988, when I was fifteen, I interviewed my mentor K-Lite, an original hip-hop hard rock from the Bronx. "I feel like a unicorn," he said. "I feel like I might be the last one doing hip-hop when everyone else fades away." K-Lite was mad. He felt like his culture was dying. He felt desperate. And he felt alone. Looking back, his sentiment seems absurd. The year 1988 is remembered by rap fans as the greatest period for conscious hip-hop. There was Public Enemy, KRS-One, Brand Nubian, De La Soul, Queen Latifah, A Tribe Called Quest, X-Clan, MC Lyte, Large Professor. But for grassroots hip-hop culture, 1988 looked like a dry spell.

The political narrative of the '80s and '90s was dominated by high-profile racial incidents. Michael Stewart, a black graffiti artist, was strangled to death by white cops. Then Yusef Hawkins was beaten with baseball bats and shot in outer Brooklyn by a gang of white youths who wrongly suspected him of dating a neighborhood girl. Michael Griffith got chased by a white gang in Howard Beach—he ran out onto a highway and got killed. Hasidic Jews in Crown Heights killed a young black boy in a car accident and touched off a riot. Al Sharpton was always involved. Louis Farrakhan would give a speech. A black leader or professor would make a controversial statement about Jews. Jewish groups would denounce that person, and try to get other black leaders to do the same. Activist and author Mumia Abu-Jamal was imprisoned and put on death row as a cop killer—he became a major focal point of organizing and counterorganizing by police groups. The black mayor of Philadelphia dropped a bomb out of a helicopter on a black activist house in West Philly, killing eleven men, women, and children. There were open threats of violence on both sides. Controversy, controversy, controversy.

Video cameras captured the beating of Rodney King, an unarmed black man, by four white cops along the side of a highway. The police were acquitted by an all-white jury in suburban Simi Valley. This led in 1992 to riots which lasted three days, killing fifty-three people and burning a huge section of Los Angeles to a smoky char. Significantly, the majority of the rioters were not black but Latino. Still, the dominant image was helicopter footage of black rioters beating a white truck driver, Reginald Denny, apparently in retribution for Rodney King. Some Korean stores were burned down (there had also been an incident of a Korean woman shooting a black girl for shoplifting in a grocery store) and there was massive civic dialogue about black-Korean relations. Federal funding went to support gang truces and community development in L.A. America's cities were on fire with racial tension, and the dialogue was reflected in rap music and Spike Lee movies. Ice Cube, who predicted the 1992 L.A. riots, chronicled them and concluded: "Riots ain't nothing but diets for the system."

To take a step back, the generation who came of age in the '90s was exposed to a radically different political story than the generation who came of age after 2000.

Two of the most iconic public incidents to shape the public consciousness in the '90s were the L.A. riots and the Battle of Seattle. Both were about angry people rising up to fight the system and battling with police. In contrast, two of the biggest public incidents of the 2000s had a completely different theme: 9/11 and Hurricane Katrina. Both of these were stories about larger outside forces wrecking U.S. cities, the U.S. government failing to protect us, and, at least in the case of 9/11, *working together with police.*

The '90s incidents were stories of a marginalized urban poor and an angry left-wing movement, which had to shut down cities and resort to direct action in the streets to be heard. We grew up on Reaganism, then eight years of Clinton centrism, capped off by the officially sanctioned disenfranchisement of black voters in Florida and a blatantly stolen election in 2000. The overall message: Race is the defining issue. You need to fight the system to get change. And at the end of the day, you're still going to get screwed.

By contrast, the Millennial generation grew up with a completely different narrative: Americans face real external threats from climate change and terrorism. The right-wing is sometimes the real bad guy (not necessarily the system as a whole). You actually can change the system through community organizing, voting, and policy. Race doesn't always have to be the defining issue. And at the end of the day, we can win, make government good, and create real change—at least a little bit. It's a much more hopeful, nuanced, and solution-oriented political story line to grow up with.

Violent racial incidents and controversies didn't go away. They continued unabated as before, but they were no longer the main story. They had been eclipsed by a bigger one.

The Best Teachers I Ever Had

In tenth grade I got sent back to private school. My parents threatened to send me to military school. I threatened to run away from home. Private school was our compromise.

In three short years, from 1985–87, I had been arrested eight times, and was caught four times for shoplifting. I was putting my parents through hell, sneaking out every other night. In one case, I got off with a year's probation and narrowly escaped being sent to the Audy Home (Chicago's juvenile hall), in part because of an unofficial policy not to send white kids there, except in extreme circumstances.

Bored by private school, I got a job in the school library and started reading everything I could get my hands on about race and politics. I also found the best teacher of my life, Mr. Brasler. He is one of the funniest people I have ever met. Sometimes I couldn't believe he was actually a journalism teacher. He used to get up on the desks and sing the Supremes. The phone would ring for a student and he'd answer: "Emily, someone named Tom Cruise is on the phone for you. Emily can't talk right now, Tom. Yes, this is Emily's secretary. She is very busy, Tom. She is on deadline writing an article about the food in our high school cafeteria!" He would mercilessly make fun of students in the most ingenious way—it was part of his teaching method. The first day of class, we were supposed to go around and say our names. I literally couldn't even say my name the whole forty-five minutes because I was laughing so hard.

Mr. Brasler was also dead serious. Our school paper, under his leadership, was one of the most award-winning newspapers in the history of high school journalism. One day he gave us a lesson on interviewing. "Okay, I'm going to be a person, and you're all going to interview me. Ask me anything you want." We asked him questions. What was his name? "Jim Andrews." Where did he live? "Chicago." What did he do for work? Um . . . fifteen minutes later, we were out of questions.

"Are you all done?" he asked.

"I guess so." We looked around the room at each other, unsure.

"Okay, you didn't find out *anything* about me. You didn't find out about the murder. The maid. The affair." He continued: "Why didn't you find out anything about me? Because you were too afraid to ask! And you weren't curious enough. In normal conversations and normal life, people don't ask a lot of questions. In a normal conversation, you say: *I saw this movie. Oh, I saw this movie too. Didn't you like this part? Oh, I liked the part where this happened.*

"When someone is telling you their story, it reminds you of *your* story. You start seeing your own movie in your head, so you fill in the blanks with your own story. In interviews, the goal is to see the other person's movie. Make them show you every scene. How did we get there? What happened next? Why did they do that? What were you thinking when this was happening? You have to make sure you are seeing the other person's movie. Okay? Movies have a beginning, a middle, and an end. They have a narrative structure. They have characters, scenery, dialogue, feelings. Make them show you their movie, frame by frame. And a lot of the best material happens outside of the actual interview. It happens before the interview or after the interview. It could be the message the person leaves on your answering machine."

I took Mr. Brasler's advice. My first interview lasted more than fourteen hours. I interviewed a substitute teacher named Hanah Jon Taylor who was also a semifamous jazz musician. I got him to tell me his life story. He told me about the time he got out of being drafted into the Vietnam War by putting peanut butter in his butt crack. During his interview with the draft board, he stuck his hand down his pants and started smearing it all over his face. He told me about the time his band was playing a club on 53rd Street and the owner refused to pay his band. He called the police and reported a "robbery-in-progress." He said: "Damn, son, I told you stories I've never even told my wife."

I was hooked on interviewing.

I loved Mr. Brasler's class because it was the only one that seemed relevant outside of school. He would encourage us to think of ourselves as professional journalists, to call up random people and interview them. "Networking, networking, networking," he would say. I used to stay at the journalism office until ten p.m. hanging out, asking him questions. He joked that I was trying to make a flowchart of his life. I was.

Around this time, I also started learning about the environmental crisis.

News reports detailed how the ozone layer was being depleted and there was increasing talk about a theory called the "greenhouse effect" which might lead to global warming. But it was still a strange new idea. Even my high school biology teacher didn't believe it.

Earth Day 1990 was the most high-profile environmental event since the original Earth Day in 1970. It coincided with the first major international climate treaty, the Montreal Protocol, which set limits on ozone-destroying chemicals. In 1990, the newly formed Student Environmental Action Coalition (SEAC) held a rally with close to 10,000 people at the University of Illinois.

I tried to convince the graffiti writers of Chicago that we needed to stop using spray paint and start using brush paint because we were destroying the ozone layer. I didn't get very far. One of the kids in my crew, Little Frank, did change his graffiti name to "Earth Baby." That was one step in the right direction. Then he went to jail for shooting someone.

Recycling was only happening in a few places at this time. I started an environmental club at my high school. It was called the Young Conservatives.

I thought it was hilarious to call ourselves the Young Conservatives. We were the real conservatives, damnit! I was all about reclaiming the language. Why should people who support policies that are destroying life on Earth get to call themselves conservative and pro-life? We were the real conservatives. We were the real pro-life. Other members of the Young Conservatives were not so thrilled with this idea. After I graduated, they changed the name to Eco Club.

The Moral Imperative for Good People to Get Power

My plan after high school was to move to New York to paint trains and become a journalist. My parents said no. I ended up at Oberlin College in the middle of Ohio.

Well, it was halfway to New York.

At Oberlin, I had a professor named Paul Dawson who taught American politics. He used to do crazy antics in class. In his Introduction to American Politics course, he had a rule that anyone who was late for class had to pay a dollar. He announced this on the first day. It was a huge class. On the second day of class, he publicly humiliated students who walked in late, calling them out in front of class and making them pay a dollar.

On the third day of class, he walked in ten minutes late and refused to pay his dollar. He essentially invited an open rebellion. The point of the exercise was to get students to question authority. To get us to understand the responsibility of ordinary people to stand up against abuse of power. I was obsessed with Professor Dawson. I sat in on many of his classes in college just to watch him teach.

In another exercise, he got the room to break up into teams to write legislation to make a peanut butter and jelly sandwich. This was an exercise to illustrate how government bureaucracies work, and how difficult it is for government to interpret and implement laws.

To illustrate this, he stood at the front of the room with a loaf of bread, a jar of peanut butter, a jar of jelly, and a knife. One by one, he read aloud each team's instructions on how to make a peanut butter and jelly sandwich.

"Open the jar of peanut butter . . . Take the knife. Put it on the bread."

But the instructions never said to take the twist-tie off the bread bag . . .

None of the instructions actually succeeded in making a peanut butter and jelly sandwich. We were rolling on the floor.

My favorite part was case studies. We would study in-depth cases from government and corporate America. We basically studied how different people and institutions messed up. Why did the New Coke flop? Why did the Centers for Disease Control fail to respond to the AIDS epidemic?

I used to go to Professor Dawson's office hours with a list of questions. I would get up at six a.m. to go jogging with him and get him to talk to me.

Oberlin was full of creative, well-intentioned, naïve kids, many of whom became teachers, artists, and nonprofit workers. Professor Dawson told us: "You're all good people. You just need to get power." When I first heard this piece of advice, it clobbered me over the head. And it still does. Like a good liberal arts student, I was sitting there constantly questioning myself on whether I was being good enough. I always seemed to find myself coming up short. But it made me realize that there was this whole other set of kids who were going to business school and law school and who were not constantly questioning whether they were good. They just assumed they should have money and power. As I mentioned earlier, many of us movement people are oriented to think all the time about how to do good. What Professor Dawson taught, and what I now believe, is that it is a moral imperative for good people to get power. Otherwise, we leave all the power in the hands of the people who are not oriented to constantly think about how to do good.

Professor Dawson told us: The problem with Oberlin students is that you're good people and you're not going to have any power. I like your values, but you have a stupid strategy. You all want to go into nice professions like social work and become teachers. But you're afraid to get power because you think it's bad. So the people who end up getting all the power are the people who want the power. This is one of the most difficult lessons I've ever had to learn.

He told me he was working on a book entitled, *How Not to Shoot Yourself in the Foot When It's in Your Mouth.* I was like, "Please hurry up and write this book because I need to read it." Paul Dawson and Wayne Brasler were the best teachers I ever had.

I once asked Mr. Dawson how he got to be so good at teaching. Did he start out like this?

"Oh no, before I learned to teach there were the awful years."

"How long did the awful years last?"

"My first five years of teaching. Then I finally started figuring it out."

Five years! What a relief. It can take a long time to really figure out what the hell you're doing.

My Experience at an Aryan Nation Meeting

For some bizarre and unknown reason, the Aryan Nation decided to try to recruit at Oberlin. Stacks of fliers advertising a recruitment meeting were found in various public places. Predictably, there was an outcry. My progressive friends on campus dutifully collected the fliers and wrote bland statements about racism. I had been to protests against the Klan before. I remember taking a bus down to Springfield, Illinois, to yell at ten white guys in hoods surrounded by police and thousands of protesters. I was more concerned about the covert institutional racism than a couple of hateful goofballs in costume.

I decided to go to the Aryan Nation meeting. I was a little bit scared. Have I mentioned I'm Jewish? The meeting was going to be held at a very remote location, way off in the country. It could be a trap.

My friend Jennifer dropped me off. She was the most Aryan-looking person I could find. But she refused to come in with me. Light was fading as her car pulled away from the parking lot. It was just me, a country lodge, and a muscular dude in his forties wearing a black security outfit standing at the door. I walked up and said hello. He acknowledged me and waved a metal-detector wand around me. Strange, I thought. What exactly are they looking for?

I walked into the main hall, where sixty to seventy people, white people to be sure, most looking to be in their forties and fifties, sat quietly around tables. The mood was tense—it was mostly men and a sprinkling of women, who seemed generally rural and not very well off. I went right over to the table in the corner with a bunch of big biker guys. I nodded my head. "How's it going?" I said under my breath. They acknowledged me in return. Will they suspect I'm a Jew? I wondered. I had visions of them seizing on me, making a sacrifice of the Jew in their midst.

The program was about to begin. An intense-looking man with dark hair and black fatigues who appeared to be in his late thirties paced at the front of the room.

"We are at war!" he yelled, and then took a dramatic pause. "I said that to get your attention," he continued somewhat awkwardly. "But also because we really are at war." He introduced himself as some kind of preacher and went on for about thirty minutes. I forget most of the rest of what he said, except for one chilling line: "When you're at the shooting range, don't be talking. Don't be talking. Just do whatever you're going to do. Don't talk about it." The whole time I was waiting for him to call me out as a Jew and for the room to descend upon me. It never happened.

He delivered a garden variety demagogue rant. There were no jokes. There was no question-and-answer period. No audience participation. No food or drink. No one asked us our names or asked us to write down our contact information. No one even smiled. And no one offered me a ride home. Not a very good recruiting technique. The preacher guy mentioned pamphlets that could be bought at the front of the room. And that was that. The program was over. I did not judge the preacher nor the attendees. They seemed sad to me. I wondered about their lives and what brought them here. Other than the fact that they were at an Aryan Nation recruitment meeting in a lodge in the woods, they seemed like normal folks who were generally frustrated with life and looking for a way to feel better. More than anything, it reminded me of some of the black nationalist events I'd been to in Chicago: mostly hot air and angry rhetoric, masking real lived feelings of pain and humiliation.

There was one big difference. Black nationalists in Chicago weren't talking about shooting people.

Identity Politics and the Culture Wars

Even more so than today, activism in most of America was by and large a racially segregated affair—even at Oberlin College.

Oberlin, like many liberal campuses in the early '90s, was ground zero in the Culture Wars. The term "political correctness" had just made an early appearance in a comic strip called *Thatch* in the Brown University *Daily Herald*, in which a character named "Politically Correct Person" was constantly making absurdly oversensitive corrections, insisting that girls should be called "prewomen."

On campuses, and in school curricula, the battles raged. All drama aside, what the progressive forces wanted was simple. First and foremost, we wanted to be able to afford to go to school. In 1995, more than ten thousand Hunter College and other CUNY students marched on New York's City Hall to protest tuition increases.

In addition, we wanted to create access and respect for students who were not born with penises and beige skin. Most of the fights were to improve student services, and recruitment and retention for low-income students and students of color, as well as inclusion of people of color, women, and LGBT folks in the curriculum. Was that too much to ask?

Right-wing students and pundits attacked and lampooned our efforts as the "PC Police."

Identity politics was dissed, made fun of, and generally scorned and lampooned by the general public. Even a lot of leftists, especially older white males, critiqued it as counterproductive. They believed that we should stay focused on class and economic issues—which would unite us instead of dividing us. They had a good argument. Up to a point.

What they missed is that identity-based politics served several important purposes which were absolutely critical to the progressive movement that later emerged. First, they created a shared understanding of interlocking oppressions. We didn't necessarily learn a lot about how to concretely organize for change. But we did get a basic grasp of how racism, sexism, homophobia, and class were intertwined and mutually reinforcing. More importantly, it taught us to be aware of our real differences and to be more sensitive to each other. Ignorance and insensitivity to differences in race, class, gender, and sexuality are a big part of what had imploded many social change movements in the past.

And identity politics opened up new avenues of organizing. Gay rights took hold on campuses and trained a generation that created gay-straight alliances at high schools. The term "queer" came into popular usage at this time, defining an inclusive and unifying identity for people whose gender and sexuality was outside the traditionally defined norms. When I got to Oberlin in 1990, people on campus were wearing pink ribbons on their backpacks in solidarity with queer folks.

Similarly, the term "people of color" came into popular usage around this time. It was key to building a sense of common identity between black, brown, and Asian students—a critical foundation for everything that came after. It also lit a fire in the generation of student activists who graduated in the '90s and decided to take their organizing beyond campus walls into the community.

The best and brightest Stanford activists of color started community organizations in East Palo Alto. Berkeley grads in Oakland. UCLA and USC grads went to South Central L.A. Columbia grads set up shop in Harlem and Washington Heights. NYU grads in Bed-Stuy and Bushwick. Harvard grads in Roxbury and Dorchester. U Penn grads in West Philly. Duke grads in Durham. Vassar grads in Poughkeepsie. Pitt grads in East Liberty and Homewood. And likewise from coast to coast. By 1997, a miniature social entrepreneur revolution was being born.

Too Cool for School

One of my biggest regrets looking back is that I thought I was too cool for everything. I was too cool for college. I was too cool for campus organizing. I was too cool for mainstream politics. So I did everything in my own special way and didn't get the mentoring and actual work experience I needed to succeed. I made up everything from scratch, and I learned every lesson the hard way over and over again.

I treated Oberlin as an intellectual activist summer camp.

I wish I could go back to college again. First of all, I probably would have stayed in school and gotten my degree. Second, I would have done what I tell all college students to do—a trick I didn't discover until junior year, right before I dropped out: don't sign up for classes based on departments or courses; ask around and sign up for the best teachers, no matters what subjects they teach.

The challenge with campus activism: by the time you figure out how to work the system, you're on your way out. Toward the end, I began to apply some of Mr. Brasler's networking techniques. I decided to raise money to bring my Chicago hip-hop friends to campus. I didn't know how to raise money. So I asked twenty people who to talk to. Then I talked to twenty more people until I had mapped all the money sources on campus.

One of the big money sources was Concert Board, which paid for bands. Concert Board was run by people who were not big hip-hop fans. They told me they had never heard of my hip-hop friends from Chicago. When I complained that they weren't bringing any hip-hop acts, they said Concert Board was open to anyone to suggest groups and vote on them. That was all I needed to know. The next meeting I brought a hundred people and a boom box with my friends' music. We turned the music on. Everyone started dancing, and then we took a vote. I went around to every student group, every dorm, and raised more than $5,000. This paid for twelve of my friends from Chicago and 150 cans of spray paint, which we used to paint twenty graffiti murals around the school.

I learned a few other things in college too. I learned that a lot of kids who grow up in rural areas are more cosmopolitan than kids from the city. A lot of the East Coast kids at Oberlin especially annoyed me. They thought they were all that because they were from New York. Meanwhile, most of them were from the tony parts of Brooklyn or Manhattan, Jersey, Long Island, Connecticut, and Massachusetts. Most of them were more sheltered than the Ohio kids. A lot of the rural and small-town kids from the Midwest had gone to high school with a wider spectrum of humanity than the kids from New York. Rural kids went to school with the children of farmers and doctors, newspaper editors and families on public aid living in trailer parks. Rural kids tended to be more humble, more sincere, hungrier, and I liked them better. Oberlin High School, for example, is half black—and a lot more diverse than where most of the supposedly cosmopolitan New York City kids went to high school.

By my sophomore year, I was done with college. I felt like I was wasting time. I wanted to get out there in the world and become a full-time change agent. What made it worse was that I got chosen as an "*Utne* Visionary" by *Utne Reader*. At that time, I was the youngest person chosen, so I thought it was my responsibility to personally try to save the world. So I moved to D.C., but I didn't know anybody and I didn't apply for any jobs. The idea of working for the government or in Congress didn't even occur to me. I was so dumb! I just started freelance writing and trying to come up with a master plan.

I found a room on 10th and Kenyon for $150 a month. I lived off canned soup and fruit that I would freeze and eat like popsicles in the summer. I soon found out that my housemate Michael had AIDS. Every morning he coughed up blood in the sink.

I would sit in bookstores all day, read books and magazines, and draw up huge plans for an organization I wanted to form called the Coordinators Circle. I had no idea how organizations worked and I knew I needed to learn. Some days, I would wander into different office buildings on K Street, look at all the interesting organizations in the building directory, knock on their office doors, ask to read their literature and speak to someone about their organization. I never visited the White House or Congress or even the Smithsonian. For some reason I assumed that everything having to do with the actual government was stupid, uninteresting, and definitely off-limits to me. Unlike ambitious twenty-three-year-olds today, it did not even occur to me that government was a place one could go to make change. Or maybe I was just intimidated and had no idea where to begin.

I think about Kanye's *College Dropout* album, which I listened to obsessively when it came out. And I think about my own books and writings about self-education and dropping out of school. Kanye and I both made fun of school. We both dropped out of school. And we both seemed to get the last laugh. Or did we? Looking back on my own experience as a dropout, I'm not so sure anymore. You really do have to work twice as hard. Four times, if you're a person of color. You really do need to create you own career and mentorship structures. Unfortunately for me, I thought I was too cool for most of those as well.

Where Is Everyone Now?
The Chicago Hip-hop Alumni Association

Old-school Chicago FEDS Crew Reunion.

What happened to my old friends from Chicago? I recently went back and reread my old books, to look through the "thank you" sections. Pages and pages of names of people I have completely lost touch with. It made me deeply upset.

I thought about ten of my best male hip-hop friends from the '80s. Where are they now? I wondered. How did we grow so far apart?

Four of the ten are dead:

REGINALD, A.K.A. K-LITE. Although a close friend of mine, I never knew his last name. One of my major mentors—originally from the Bronx, he could breakdance, deejay, rap, *and* write graffiti. One of the smartest, most charismatic and talented people I knew, he led a mysterious life and died of AIDS.

NAZON "KEP" SIMMONS. A true friend who stuck with me when I was going through hard times in high school. Later got caught up in gangbanging and went to prison. He died of pneumonia. It is assumed he was HIV-positive.

The way I usually tell the story is that my white friends who did drugs got sent to college and my black and Latino friends who did drugs mostly ended up dead or in jail. But that isn't true anymore.

Two of my closest white friends are also dead:

HUNTER "TOAST" BRUMFIELD and WYATT "ATTICA" MITCHELL. These were the two people who were in some ways the most similar to me in high school. We read *The Autobiography of Malcolm X*, James Baldwin, Maya Angelou, Kurt Vonnegut, and the Beatniks together. We listened to Miles Davis, memorized every interesting rap song that came out, and a lot of not-so-interesting ones. We all wrote graffiti and they both rapped and went to majority black schools and we disobeyed our parents and talked philosophy and got arrested. We were cut from the same cloth: creative as hell and thought we were badass white kids—the next generation of precocious, creative political artists who would soon be discovered . . . after we got out of high school.

A few months before Hunter died, I ran into him on the subway in New York. He was living in St. Louis at the time, rapping and playing music under the name Toast. For some random reason he happened to be in New York on the subway at three a.m., on the same car I was on. Out of the corner of my eye, I notice this guy halfway down the train car talking to strangers about music, making jokes.

"Hunter!!!" I yell.

"Billy!!!" he yells.

And we're jumping around the train hugging each other like old best friends who haven't seen each other in ten years. He comes to meet me the next day at my office up in Harlem. We walk all over Harlem together for hours talking about life. He seems happier than ever and crazier than ever too. He has been diagnosed as crazy and he's on meds and getting SSI from the government. "I used to not accept myself. I was always fighting against it and feeling guilty for being an alcoholic and being on medication. But now I can just be who I am. I'm at peace with myself," he said.

A few months later, he went off meds and ended his life like he had been talking about and unsuccessfully trying to do since high school.

I feel sad about Wyatt, Hunter, Kep, and K-Lite not being here anymore. I'm mad at them too.

You guys are supposed to be here with me right now.

Instead, you left me alone. When I hear other grown men talk about hanging out with their "boys" or their "guys," I get sad. Where my guys at?

I know it's kind of low to be angry at your friends after they are dead. Angry at them *because* they are dead. Angry at them for the way they died. Angry at them for leaving me. Angry at them for abandoning me for drugs, alcohol, gangs, and unsafe sex. Angry at them for not staying in the fight. Angry, above all, at larger forces that took them away from me. Maybe if you were still alive, you could be mad at me too.

Two of my friends are doing okay but disappeared from the hip-hop scene:

KEVIN "BET" LUKLAN was one of my best friends in eighth and ninth grades. He had a political conscience, got involved with the Nation of Islam for a while, and changed his graffiti name to We Still Miss You Harold (for Mayor Harold Washington). Though he was intensely bright, he dropped out of high school, had kids at a young age, and went to prison for gangbanging. Later, he turned his life around, began doing construction work, moved to Arizona, and started over. He escaped!

MARIO "AGENT" DEJUAN, also one of my best friends in eighth and ninth grades, had an international graffiti career, spent a lot of time in Africa and Latin America, learned to play drums and other traditional instruments, and is now a documenter and producer of indigenous music from around the world.

One of my friends is in prison:

DERRICK "WARP" MCINTOSH. In some ways, this is the most heart-breaking. Warp grew up in Cabrini Green but he was the moral and spiritual leader of the Chicago graffiti movement. He organized the first-ever all-city graffiti meeting and he was a huge mentor of mine. I practically lived on his couch one summer when I was fourteen. Last time I saw him, he was getting by as an artist, airbrushing and creating woodcut graffiti sculptures. He always had a positive attitude and had stopped doing illegal things a long time ago. Then he got caught robbing banks. No one saw that coming.

To Kevin, Mario, and Derrick—I'm sending you love and looking forward to the next time we see each other.

Two friends I can't find:

ARNOLD "SALAHDIN" BULLOCK. The first person who brought me on the train lines on the South Side and took me to rack spray paint. Last seen living illegally in the projects on 44th and Cottage Grove in a wheelchair (paralyzed after falling off a building). When I was in Chicago recently, I went back to see him. His building had been torn down.

JOEY "IGGY" IGLESIAS. The first person who took me on the train lines on the North Side and to Humboldt Park. Last I heard, Joey went to prison for working at a crack house and shooting people. I hope things got better for him. He was super smart. I keep looking for him to show up on Facebook one day.

To Joey and Arnold, I'm praying you're okay and hope we find each other again in this lifetime.

One of the ten became a teacher and a hip-hop activist:

LAVIE "SUPER LP" RAVEN is still deeply involved in hip-hop. It's ironic: back when we went to Kenwood, he got in trouble for painting the school. Fifteen years later, he came back with a graduate degree, and got a job at Kenwood as an African American history teacher. He started a break-dancing club, and got permission to paint graffiti murals with the kids in the hallways throughout the school. He even got the Board of Education to buy the spray paint. He now teaches at the Multicultural Arts School in Little Village. He also founded a program called the University of Hip-hop and he's on the Board of the Southwest Youth Collaborative. He's getting a PhD at Teachers College at Columbia University.

Out of all my close hip-hop friends from the '80s, only Lavie survived and made the transition from hip-hop and juvenile delinquency to the movement for social change. I'm so grateful we're on this journey together.

I fantasize how much better the world would be if all ten of my friends were alive today and working for change. What if they had all survived and made the evolution with Lavie and me? Imagine what a force we would be right now! All ten of us, working together as team—we would be unstoppable.

Mostly, I just miss y'all. Sending you love wherever you are.

When Graffiti Writers Own Garages

A few years ago, I did an event in Chicago that a bunch of old-school writers came to. Slang was still Slang, but growing white hair. Severe, Casper, and K-So had bellies. Deface has a sixteen-year-old son now and had moved out to Evanston for the good schools. K-So has more kids than I can count, and he has a new CD and book that he just published. We talked about the old days, and about our lives now. We all have a strong identity as old-school writers, but it's an identity that feels for the most part frozen in time, like a long-ago war that seems to us like yesterday but that no one else understands.

Casper, Slang, Erik DeBat (Risk), and Chris Silva are badass professional artists. Erik now owns a building with a garage: "Yeah, these young taggers come and bomb up my garage. I've had to paint over it," he says laughing with a bemused look. "I guess everything comes full circle, what goes around comes around!"

I moved back to Chicago several times during my long slow process of dropping out of college. Ultimately, I had to get out because Chicago was dragging me down. So many people with so many issues. Issues with me. Issues with themselves. Issues, issues, issues, like only a hometown can have. I loved Chicago with everything I had. But I had to get out. I was drowning.

One of the few old-school Chicago cats who made the transition from hip-hop to activism was a guy I barely knew back in the day, a graffiti writer from the deep West Side named Jumaani Bates (Dred One). After a stint in prison, he got out and enrolled in a green-jobs training program at Wilbur Wright Community College and used his smarts to prepare more people from the hood for careers in weatherization, urban agriculture, and the like. He works with many of the green jobs groups in Chicago and is also starting his own organization, New Faces of Urban America. As Jumaani sees it: "Green is the new hip-hop."

How do we get more people to make that transition?

Part II

Building the Movement
(1997–September 11, 2001)

The Blind Spots of a Yale Education

Up until 1997, I thought I was building the movement essentially by myself. Pretty much, I thought I was the movement. Not that I was quite that arrogant. I just didn't see a whole lot else going on. I would go on these book tours all over the country. I would meet interesting young people who wanted to get involved in something. But there was not really a lot out there for them to get involved with.

I did this one talk at Yale Law School. It was titled "The Blind Spots of a Yale Education: What's Missing from Our Conversation about Sex, Race, Crime, and Money."

This was Yale. These kids were going to run the world one day. I felt a personal responsibility to give them a life-changing experience they would never forget. My theory was that well-intentioned people usually stay in their comfort zone and don't do anything unless they are forcibly shaken out of it. My goal was to rub uncomfortable truths in their face in such an upsetting way that the pain of inaction would become greater than the pain of action. So I put all my heart into it, in the most vulnerable way possible, to reach them. What tools did I have in my toolbox to puncture their ivory comfort zone?

I told them that they were the sort of people who got As and that they were therefore in danger of never doing anything important with their lives. That the very thing that got them to into Yale—getting As and high test scores and impressing their teachers and jumping through all the right hoops—was exactly what was going to make it hard for them to do anything interesting with their lives. Because to do something interesting involves risk. And taking risks . . . you might get a B. Or even . . . a C.

I gave all two hundred of them a sealed envelope with a letter and a dollar bill inside—a major portion of my speaking fee.

My strategy worked. They were provoked all right and they ate it up. Several of them cried, and wrote me long handwritten letters. I got invited to speak at two secret societies. Clearly this was filling a niche. There was no space to talk openly about the real things people were thinking about on campus. One kid told me: "I've never seen anyone say any of these things. It's like you and . . . I don't know . . . Jesse Jackson! There's no one out there in our generation who goes around saying stuff like this."

The best letter I got was from Jay Readey. Jay was a white dude who had recently graduated and started a youth program in New Haven called Urban Solutions. It was basically green jobs before it was called green jobs. He trained kids from the hood to do environmental landscaping work, get paid, and learn marketable skills. Jay had just as much swagger and fire in the belly as I did and he told me I wasn't actually doing shit, just going around to colleges talking mess. If I wanted to get down with the real work going on in the hood, I needed to come see his organization in action. Jay and I stayed up late talking and became great friends.

The New Hood Social Entrepreneurs

Jay called me up a few weeks after my Yale talk. My imaginary little world was about to be turned upside down. I was about to learn that I was not in fact the center of the youth movement in America.

"You need to go to this conference."

"What is it?"

"It's called the Vassar Gathering. At Vassar College in Poughkeepsie, New York."

What is it?

"It's hard to explain. See, there was this group called the Black Student Leadership Network. It broke up. But there's a group of really smart young leaders and organizers of color. It was started by a woman named Lisa Sullivan. She was invited to the White House by Bill Clinton. She said, 'No thanks. You're not going to co-opt this movement. We're not going to be a part of your photo op.'"

Say what? I was intrigued.

Lisa Sullivan was a visionary young African American woman from D.C. She had gone to Clark University in Atlanta and then received a scholarship to study political science at Yale. While at Yale, she got involved with the New Haven chapter of the NAACP and became the head of its youth and college division. She built relationships with informal leaders in the community—deejays, party promoters, gang leaders, Five Percenters, barbers, local shop owners and entrepreneurs. Over the course of a few years, she organized them into a formidable political force.

New Haven had been controlled by a mobbed-up Italian machine. In 1988, Lisa ran an innovative voter drive and Get Out the Vote effort which registered and turned out five thousand unlikely black and Latino voters. John Daniels won by four thousand votes—New Haven's first black mayor. At twenty-eight years old, Lisa became one of his closest advisors. She worked with him to re-think government agencies, starting with the police department. He appointed a maverick police lieutenant, Nick Pastore, who would hang out on the corners with gang members and retrained his department to focus on building positive relationships and crime prevention instead of arresting and locking people up.

Over the period from 1990 to 1997, crime in New Haven dropped 22 percent.

Marian Wright Edelman, head of the Children's Defense Fund, heard about Lisa. She was passing through New Haven and asked Lisa to break-fast. Edelman had been a SNCC organizer in the '60s (Student Nonviolent Coordinating Committee, famous for launching the sit-in movement). She had been tight with the Clintons and was considered one of the most power-ful black women in America at the time. She took Lisa under her wing as an apprentice, and recruited her to come to D.C. and start the Black Student Leadership Network (BSLN) as a program of the Children's Defense Fund. BSLN ran Freedom Schools all over the country, and convened young leaders of color—laying the groundwork for an updated version of SNCC.

At a certain point, something went wrong. Marian Wright Edelman pulled the plug. She and Lisa had disagreements of vision and power struggles. I'm not sure exactly what happened. Lisa resigned and was not allowed to use the name or access the funding. A big part of the narrative in the 1990s was that the civil rights and baby boom generation of the 1960s had neglected to pass the torch to our generation.

The Black Student Leadership Network had staged a gathering at Shaw University in Raleigh, North Carolina, the site of the original SNCC found-ing convention in 1960. SNCC had been pulled together by an energetic older field organizer from the NAACP named Ella Jo Baker. Martin Luther King Jr.'s organization, the Southern Christian Leadership Conference (SCLC), had tried to co-opt SNCC into becoming part of SCLC. But Ella Baker had stood up to them and insisted that the students who were more radical needed to have their own independent organization.

Lisa patterned herself after Ella Baker. Her style was to find talented grass-roots leaders and support them to find their own voices. She saw herself as creating space for a new generation of young leaders. After Edelman pulled the plug on BSLN, the Vassar Gathering had been organized to bring together former BSLN people to recreate the network and move forward.

I arrived at the opening session of the Vassar Gathering and was blown away. I thought I was in hip-hop activist heaven. There was Rha Goddess; Donna Frisby, who would become the first black executive director of Rock the Vote. There was a huge crew from El Puente Academy for Peace and Justice (the so-called "hip-hop high school" in Brooklyn), including Héctor Calderón, who would become its principal, and JLove Calderón, who would become a famous hip-hop writer and activist. Also present were: Taj James, who would create the Movement Strategy Center in Oakland; Marta Urquilla, a community-based education organizer in D.C., who would later serve on Obama's civic engagement advisory committee; Van Jones, who had recently founded the Ella Baker Center for Human Rights; and Jay Imani, who would later become its director. On and on and on. I had stumbled into a growing national community of brilliant young organizers who were connecting education, community development, youth organizing, hip-hop, and all the things I cared about.

Jay Readey pulled me aside. "Hey, a couple of things. In case you didn't notice, we're the only two white people here besides a few of the panelists and students who wandered in, so make sure you are respectful—this isn't the space for white people to do a lot of talking. Also, I wanted to point out—don't look now, but that's Lisa Sullivan in the back row behind us. She's probably not going to say anything the whole conference. She doesn't put herself out front as a leader. She believes in staying behind the scenes. But she's the one behind this whole thing."

I looked in the back row to see a large, calm, professional-looking woman in her midthirties with her hair cut low and one of the most beautiful, magnetic faces I have ever seen. She had glowing brown skin and large round features that flashed with vision, curiosity, dignity, purpose, and a deep inner-knowing. I decided I wanted to be friends with her, and it didn't take long. I went to a fundraising workshop which was led by one of Lisa's mentors who had worked in the fundraising office at Stanford. So of course Lisa had to be there. Only four other people showed up. The session was kind of slow so I asked a lot of questions. I remember saying: "How do you raise money from rich people without kissing their asses?" Lisa's mentor told me very gently that when he asks for money, he puts on a three-piece suit. Lisa pulled me aside afterward and said she wanted to talk to me. I had officially been talent scouted.

She told me she was starting a new organization and she needed someone to do a lot of the things I did: writing, organizing, and working with grassroots youth groups, connecting ideas. I was more than thrilled. I sent her my proposal for the Coordinators Circle. Then she called me up and said: "I want you to come do this for me."

She tested me first. She didn't have the money to hire anyone yet so she fed me a string of related projects with allied organizations. First she asked me to write a cover story on hip-hop activism for *Who Cares* magazine, an upstart nonprofit publication for the emerging social entrepreneur sector. She hooked me up with Donna Frisby to do a project for Rock the Vote.

Lisa's organization was called LISTEN, Inc. I was the second employee. It was my first nonprofit job, and I had no idea how to work as part of an organization. I remember my supervisor Ditra Edwards showing me how to fill out a weekly review/preview sheet. The idea that I would need to be *accountable* for doing movement work was a foreign concept. (Now I make other people do it.)

My job title was Information Coordinator. Most information was not online yet. My first job was to go through the past five years of Lisa's boxes of paper files, databases, and business cards, and organize them into a usable system. The project took an entire month. I entered her data, organized her files, and read the notes she had scribbled in the margins. By the end of the month, I had a deep understanding of Lisa's many worlds, and the way her ingenious mind was connecting them all—across race and class, disciplines and institutions, from the ivory tower to the streets.

She was taking ideas from the business world, from the cutting edges of social psychology and nonprofit management, and applying them to young people from the inner city. She understood hip-hop as a form of social capital that could help black and brown youth get jobs and skills. Above all she was a teacher, a connector, and a movement intellectual. She loved interesting ideas, talented people, and cross-pollinating them. She understood how to recognize opportunities and she had a vision to build a twenty-first century organization supporting urban youth.

I loved Lisa intellectually. She was a voracious reader with a huge vision who was always dreaming up new projects and leaving clippings on my desk with notes in the margins: *For our radio station?* She saw her role as a project incubator, matchmaker, and translator between worlds. She got invited to dozens of events and she was oftentimes the youngest person—and the only person of color—in the rooms she occupied. One time, she brought me along to a leadership retreat at Harvard convened by Robert Putnam, author of *Bowling Alone*. I was there to get the group excited about the emerging social movement among urban youth. And there, sitting in the corner, was my old state senator from Chicago, Barack Obama, who listened intently throughout the entire session, barely saying a word.

Lisa had friends everywhere. She was the first real movement mentor I had. She taught me how to fundraise, and she invented the organizational vision and pattern that I operated out of for the next several years: creating space for young leaders, and connecting people, ideas, projects, and money to change the world.

Lisa was the convener of a growing national network of young strategic organizers, activists, youth workers, community development professionals, and a new category: social entrepreneurs starting innovative ventures to empower a generation of kids who had been left to die in America's ghettos.

Lisa did not survive to see her dreams realized. She died at the age of forty from heart and respiratory conditions. With intense pressure on her as a young black woman, she simply worked herself to death.

Lisa influenced a lot of us who are still trying to walk in the path she laid for us. I often think to myself: *Hey, Lisa, I hope we're making you proud.*

Lisa Sullivan, Rest in Peace (1961–2001)

Does the Progressive Movement Have a Brain?

During the late '90s, I became a conference junkie. As I traveled from conference to conference, I began to wonder: does the progressive movement have a brain? It didn't seem to have one, because there were very few people who I saw at more than one conference. The right hand didn't seem to know what the left hand was doing.

In 1998, I was hired by Rock the Vote as their national talent scout to find the best young activist groups in America. I spent eight months traveling the country and I went through a zillion different networks to make a list. By the end I had more than five hundred people and organizations. My friends and I turned it into a book called *The Future 500*. The question was: Why hadn't anyone created this list before? Didn't somebody, somewhere, care to have a list of all the youth activist groups in America? Weren't they the future of the progressive movement?

Wasn't some progressive political strategist in Washington thinking about this?

Around this time, I hooked-up with Resource Generation, a group that was trying to organize the next generation of progressive philanthropists. It was an important step. (I nicknamed it the Cool Rich Kids Movement.) Philanthropy was the biggest bottleneck in progressive movement-building. We needed visionary new philanthropic leadership to take the movement to the next level. You would think this organization would have all the resources it needed. There were plenty of progressive rich people involved. Yet it almost went under due to lack of funds. Despite the excellent work of the organization, very few cool rich kids were actually far enough along in their process to begin moving serious amounts of money, and few who were moving big money saw the need to fund the cool rich kids' organization. Why would an organization for people with money need money?

You would think there would be someone paying attention to situations like this. Paying attention to the progressive movement as a whole and monitoring the pieces to make sure they were functioning properly. Someone to connect the dots and announce over the intercom: "Need more bathroom tissue in aisle four!"

But the progressive movement was organized like the Wild West. Anyone did anything they damn well pleased and there were virtually no standards, coordination, or accountability to a larger movement that entered into the equation.

The Battle of Seattle

The labor movement had suffered a long, slow decline, along with America's industrial base. From a third of American workers in 1960 to only 12 percent today, the labor movement—and with it, America's middle class—has been beaten within an inch of its life.

The American social contract that had created shared prosperity and the rise of the middle class in the 1950s had been decimated by right-wing laws and corporations. The tax rate for corporations had been reduced from more than 90 percent during the 1950s to 35 percent in 1986 and sliced full of loopholes. Wealthy individuals' tax rates were cut from over 90 percent to as low as 15 percent. American workers found themselves assaulted on all sides by aggressive antiunion campaigns, unfriendly laws, global competition, and the loss of manufacturing.

By the 1990s, its back to the wall, the labor movement began getting creative, looking for allies to halt its decline. In 1997, an innovative summer intern program was started at UNITE, a clothing and textile workers union. They sent college students overseas to do in-person inspections and reports on sweatshops in Mexico and Indonesia. The students came back horrified, wrote reports, and immediately started a new organization: United Students Against Sweatshops (USAS).

USAS spread like wildfire to hundreds of campuses. They targeted the multibillion-dollar campus apparel business, and succeeded in winning a series of concessions to source campus clothing from sweat-free factories. The rise of USAS was part of a revitalized economic justice movement. Global capitalism was tearing through national laws and ridding countries of pesky labor and environmental standards.

Passing through Eugene, Oregon, in 1998, I came across a flier in a coffee shop that said something about fighting against MIA, GATT, and WTO.

Huh?

I had to look it up. MIA and GATT were global trade agreements most people had never heard of that could trump any country's environmental and labor laws. The WTO (World Trade Organization) was the body that would enforce these new trade agreements. Capitalism had descended into full crackhead mode.

Suddenly the world began to think of a new acronym: WTF?

No one had ever paid attention to the WTO before. They were planning a meeting in downtown Seattle on November 30, 1999.

On that day, fifty thousand protesters showed up in what would become the most iconic protest action in decades. While labor and church groups marched in a government-approved rally, hundreds of small groups, using handheld technology, organized in real time to disrupt the WTO meetings. The protests outside emboldened representatives of developing countries inside the meetings to defeat the WTO's worst provisions.

Most dramatically, a small group of "Black Bloc" anarchists wearing bandannas smashed the windows of banks and other corporate storefronts. Police arrested more than six hundred protesters and blanketed downtown Seattle in tear gas, which led to a class-action lawsuit, the resignation of the police chief, and the defeat of the mayor in the next election. Images of mayhem were broadcast across the globe and energized the emerging global justice movement, which held similar protests in Washington, D.C., Montreal, Prague, and Italy. The Independent Media Center (Indymedia.org) was launched in a Seattle storefront to cover the protests and soon spawned chapters in 150 cities worldwide.

To the general public, the protests had come from nowhere. All of a sudden, anarchist philosophy was a topic of conversation. In reality, the networks that shut down Seattle had been a decade in the making. Punk anarchist-inspired collectives had quietly built a virtual ant farm of decentralized under-the-radar institutions. From Food Not Bombs to Critical Mass bike rides to Riot Grrrl to Anti-Racist Action chapters; from community garden networks to Radical Cheerleaders; from zines to info shops to pirate radio stations. The grassroots radical networks had literally hundreds of outposts nationwide, a presence in most states, and many small towns—from Auburn, Alabama, to Minot, North Dakota.

Inspired by the Zapatista rebels in Mexico, spread by touring punk bands, intellectually fueled by Noam Chomsky and Oakland-based book publisher AK Press, the radical punk scene by the mid-'90s could loosely claim at any one time tens of thousands of participants nationwide. Seattle was its crowning public achievement. In the following years, the anarchist movement lost momentum, but this loose network deserves a lot of credit for politicizing probably upward of 100,000 youth during the 1990s, and setting a pattern of local organizing that would prepare many for years of community action. They did it with no grants from foundations or formal philanthropic support.

The Battle of Seattle was historically important for several reasons: It drew public attention to the largely invisible global justice movement. It was partially successful in checking the excesses of the WTO. The use of new technology, media, and decentralized network-based organizing was extraordinarily successful. Seattle was the first quintessentially twenty-first century protest movement—one month before the official start of the twenty-first century. It set the stage for the rise of political blogging, and the more mainstream wave of decentralized online-to-offline organizing that followed.

My *New York Times* Fiasco

In the fall of 1999 my second book, *No More Prisons,* was published. I had stumbled onto a formula: Write about serious topics I cared about (prisons, philanthropy, self-education) in an accessible, mavericky way. Connect the topics to hip-hop, urban youth culture, and movement-building. Weave it all together into a punchy, adventurous narrative. Then figure out what the book was "about." Create a theme and a frame and a title for it. Fill in the holes by interviewing friends who had good stories to tell. Sing the unsung heroes. Slap a cover, table of contents, barcode, and ISBN number on it, and call it a book.

The final aspect of the formula was to take the project beyond the medium of being just a book. *No More Prisons* was the chosen title for one reason: it was the name of an underground rap album that my friends from Raptivism Records were putting out, and it was also the website of the Prison Moratorium Project. Individually, each of our projects was too puny to be noticed on the scale of mainstream American culture. But if we used the same name for all three projects and cross-promoted them together, maybe we could be slightly less puny. Being a graffiti writer, my job was to have the words *No More Prisons* written in white letters on the sidewalks of twenty-five cities. Sidewalks were ideal because the words would wear off by themselves. No one had to clean them. It was probably the most successful political graffiti campaign ever. We estimate that several million people noticed the message. Among urban youth for a couple of years, it was almost a household phrase. My talks at colleges became cultural events. We would invite organizers to make cameos and recruit students to get involved on and off campus. Students would get excited after events and we would have strategy sessions that would go on past midnight and continue the next day. It felt like we were really helping build a movement. It was one of the most exciting experiences of my life.

And then it all came crashing down. Because of something stupid I did.

A few months after *No More Prisons* came out, I was contacted by a reporter from the *New York Times* who said he wanted to interview me for an in-depth series on race. The topic was white kids in hip-hop.

The reporter, N.R. Kleinfield, was a nerdy guy who reminded me a little bit of Woody Allen. He said I should call him by his nickname, Sunny. I'd generally had good experiences with the press up until this point, and I was flattered that he wanted to do such a big story on me. He came on tour with me and we spent a lot of time together over a period of months. I was totally transparent with him and made my life an open book.

I ranted earnestly and endlessly about white racism and how we needed to transform society from head to toe. I saw this as my chance to inject a scathing critique of what I saw as the hypocrisy and subtle racism of white liberals into the pages of America's paper of record. I thought I was winning him over. Boy was I wrong.

All this time I thought he was taking me seriously, possibly even learning something, and we spent so much time together that I began to consider him a bit of a friend. He told me I must be the most committed antiracist white person he could possibly imagine. I fell right into his trap.

"Oh no," I told him. "I'm just as racist as any other white person."

"What do you mean, give me an example," he said, seeming not to understand.

I stretched to come up with examples. I worked hard to make myself sound bad. He spun it another 180 degrees and turned my self-critique into a virtual exposé. The half hour or so of me talking about how racist I was got flipped around and became a centerpiece of his article. By the time he was through with me, he had painted a thoroughly convincing portrait of a confused David Duke–type cartoon character who mocked and exploited black people and black culture. Whoa!

It was bad.

The article came out on July 6, 2000. It was a huge story with a picture of my face blasted across the front page of the paper, above the fold. At six a.m., I started getting phone calls: "Oh my God, your face is on the front page of the *New York Times*." At eight a.m., I started getting a different type of call: "What did you tell that reporter?" "Billy, we need to talk. Call me immediately." "I'm questioning: who are you?"

I was shell-shocked. I didn't know what to say. How do you explain that you were trying to get white people to look at their own racism by talking in the most dramatic way about your own? How do you explain that you were intentionally trying to make yourself look bad to a reporter from the *New York*

Times? People don't do that. No one does that. Why would anyone do that? It doesn't make any sense.

It was a traumatic experience. Two of my colleagues publicly disowned me. One wrote an essay about it. Even some of my best friends were questioning whether they wanted to be associated with me. A lot of people got my back too and reassured me. It's times like this when you learn who your real friends are. I needed to get away and clear my head. I needed to go to the beach. I had never been to a beach in New York before. I looked at a subway map and saw that if you took the A train to the end of the line, you would end up in Far Rockaway, where it looked like there might be a beach. I bought a notebook and I spent the week at the beach writing.

One thing I wrote was a fifteen-page public response, correcting and refuting the article in excruciating detail. And I decided to take a step back from public life. I decided not to talk to the media or do any public writing or public speaking. For a long time. Maybe forever. I felt like my career might be over. The organizations I worked with weren't sure they wanted to be associated with me. So I focused on helping out behind the scenes. I also felt depressed. My creativity, risk-taking, and honesty is what had gotten me in trouble. My creative juices ran cold. I couldn't even write in my diary most of the time.

For the past decade, I had been giving birth to a new book every five years via C-section. *Bomb the Suburbs* collected my writings from ages seventeen to twenty-one. It came out in 1994. *No More Prisons* collected my writings from ages twenty-two to twenty-six. It came out in 1999. I had to write the books and go on tour with them in order to move on from that period of my life. Get over them psychologically. Make space in my head to learn new things.

The *New York Times* fiasco interrupted my formula.

September 11

Meanwhile, the whole country was about to have its formula interrupted.

I was staying at my friend Gita's house in Fort Greene, Brooklyn. Every time my life fell apart, I ended up crashing on Gita's futon.

"Oh my God," she said, running into my room. "Look out the window."

Black smoke over Manhattan . . . What was going on? Gita had heard something on the radio about planes hitting the World Trade Center. We had no TV. Who had a TV? Adam Mansbach lived down the street. Hey Adam, we're coming over. We walked over to his house and watched the TV in disbelief. When we came back outside, thousands of people were streaming across the Brooklyn Bridge, mostly black people covered in white dust.

We walked to David Jacobs's house in Park Slope. He had a direct view of

Manhattan and a TV. We spent four hours watching images of planes crashing into buildings, people jumping out of windows, buildings collapsing, people running for their lives. Then we watched George W. Bush and New York
Mayor Rudolph Giuliani on TV pretending to be tough guys. Afterward, I felt
sick. I went outside and smelled burning plastic and dead bodies—the stench
lingered over the city for an entire week. I started calling my friends. We heard
rumors that Arab and Muslim stores were being attacked. My friend Ibrahim
and I went to Atlantic Avenue and Sunset Park to make sure everything was
okay.

The next day, we heard that people were holding a vigil in Union Square in
Manhattan, so we went over there and found an incredible scene. A nineteen-
year-old college kid named Jordan Schuster had accidentally organized it.

"We were trying to figure out what to do," he recounts. "It was strange. Everyone in the city was just walking around aimlessly. I'm an event organizer. So
my friends and I went to Union Square and rolled out two big pieces of butcher
paper. We put markers out. Within ten minutes there were fifty people writing on it. Within an hour there were five hundred. There'd be twenty people
writing at a time. People were looking and they were crying and people would
say: 'Do you need a hug?' By the end of the day Tuesday, we had acquired
about twenty volunteers and thirty-five sheets of butcher paper had been filled.
People brought candles and flowers. People were handing out free food, free
water. And then someone would walk by and yell: 'How can you people just sit
there? We need to bomb Arabs!' And someone else would say: 'That's not going
to solve things.' And it would start a political discussion.

"The political discussions were popping up all over the place. My friend
James would go in between the circles and create order. He'd institute a talking-
stick system—delegate responsibility to people and then move on to the next
circle. By noon the second day there were two thousand people. We had at
least a thousand people there all week, usually until three a.m. People were saying: 'Thank you, I needed somewhere to go.' All the media came: ABC, NBC,
CBS, Fox. At least 90 percent of the messages people were expressing were
pro-peace. But the media kept looking for that other 10 percent that wanted
vengeance."

This was true across the board. In the weeks and months that ensued, we realized we needed to get out the stories and voices for peace—to break through
the drumbeat for war. I didn't know what to do. So I did what I always do:
pulled my friends together and published a book: *Another World Is Possible:
Conversations in a Time of Terror*. We collected stories and photos and got the
book out by December 11, 2001. We worked hard to make sure it was the first

book published about September 11 so the media would have to pay attention to it. They ignored it anyway.

September 11 was a profound turning point for our country in so many ways. And it was a profound turning point for the movement.

The energy from Seattle and the economic justice movement shifted into a new peace movement. Suddenly, wearing black bandannas over your face, staging street confrontations with police, and smashing corporate storefronts wasn't cool anymore. A climate of fear set in with new security restrictions and reports of Arab Americans being racially profiled and attacked. People on all levels hungered for a more peaceful approach.

For Arab American, Muslim, and South Asian communities who were often apolitical or had leaned Republican, this was a political wake-up call. Students organized more than four hundred vigils on campuses in the week following September 11. A huge new coalition, United for Peace and Justice, was formed—including over a thousand groups—and later organized rallies with 200,000–500,000 people against the war in Iraq.

A twenty-one-year-old named Eli Pariser created an online petition calling for a measured, multilateral response to September 11. He sent it to fifteen friends. It was forwarded and forwarded and ended up reaching more than 500,000 people. Eli's website 9-11peace.org merged with a semidormant group called MoveOn.org, and a new era of online organizing was born.

Artist vs. Organizer

During the 1990s and well past 2000, my role model was novelist and social critic James Baldwin because he would say *anything*. He said the job of the artist was to be honest. The more provocative, the better. The more cans of worms opened, the better. The more people felt uncomfortable, the better.

This is part of how I saw my calling in the world as well: to learn my lessons the hard way and to share them with excruciating vulnerability, like a car wreck on the side of the highway. You're afraid to see it but you can't look away.

I was caught between two paradigms as a writer: my old paradigm said tell all—flesh and blood. My new paradigm said protect myself and everyone around me. The way Barack Obama in his first book admits to doing blow as a youngster. How much was self-revelation, and how much self-protection?

I have spent a lot of my writing and organizing career as a political bomb thrower. Calling shit out. Challenging people. Dissing people publicly. Creating tension. Testing boundaries. Being angry. Being self-righteous. Being immature. Pushing, pushing, pushing. Some of this has been positive, skillful, and with pure intention. But some of it hasn't been positive, skillful, or pure. I have needlessly hurt people's feelings in the process.

One of the main people I have hurt is myself. It's a very common dynamic for people with a lot of fire and passion. Our flame is hot. We have the power to generate heat, to ignite people. To thaw ice and burn away lies. If we're not careful, the flame will burn us and everyone around us too. My anger at the political system seems married to an anger just as deep at myself. As hard as I have worked to change the political system, I have probably worked nearly as hard to sabotage myself and my career.

Like so many of us, some deep part of me feels unworthy, less than, insecure, not okay. Over and over again, I have undermined myself, my reputation, and my career for a supposed greater cause: to tell an uncomfortable truth, to provoke a reaction, to make a point. I have paid a price personally and professionally for speaking out, breaking the rules, and going against the grain as much as I have. I have shut myself out of a lot of opportunities. I have pushed myself outside the mainstream. Quite selfishly, for my own aspirations in life, and not-so-selfishly, to fulfill my larger purpose, I want another chance.

Bottom line, artist and organizer are two very different hats. For people who can do both, it's a powerful combination. And it's a tricky balance that can get you in a world of trouble.

This is part of what derailed Van Jones's mainstream political career. Someone asked him why when Republicans are in power, it seems like they can pass anything they want, but when Democrats are in power, they can't do the same.

He thought about it for a while and came up with a comedic response. You can watch it on YouTube.

"Well the answer to that," he said, "is they're assholes."

He said this to huge laughter and applause. "That's a technical political science term," he continued. "And Barack Obama is not an asshole. Now, I will say this. I can be an asshole. And some of us who are not Barack Hussein Obama are going to need to get a little bit uppity."

Now obviously, from a political standpoint, it's a no-no to call Republican members of Congress assholes. But was he actually calling Republicans assholes in a real sense? No. Right after he called Republicans assholes, he called himself an asshole. He was using humor to make a point. The point was that Democrats and progressive-minded people need to learn how to play hardball. A fair point. Politically, that's exactly what he should have said. Substantively, that is exactly what he did say.

But if that was all he said, it would have been boring. No one would have remembered it. And it wouldn't have made anyone laugh. So the comedian in him probably said: *Go for it—it's funny.* And the political organizer in him paid the price. Which may be why most politicians and political organizers are so deadly boring and no one wants to listen to what they have to say.

The Artist Trap

Many creative, talented young people fall into what I call the Artist Trap. In high school, if you're creative, there is a box for you. It's called the arts: music, visual arts, dance, theater, writing, new media, etc. That's where creative people find our identities and thrive. And that's fine. Millions of people find their callings, their identities, and even gainful employment working in the arts. But what they don't tell you is that creativity is needed in all sectors of society. So what we have is a glut of creative people trying to be "artists" who can't find work, who don't have much social or economic power, who feel discouraged beating their heads against a wall in the arts game. And then we let every other sector of the economy and society (business, politics, real estate, religion, science, etc.) be dominated by not-so-creative people who are focused on making money, amassing power, covering their asses, and doing things the wrong way.

Meanwhile, millions of the most creative, risk-taking, imaginative, truth-seeking, and God-loving people who we need to take leadership, get power, and transform our society have locked themselves up in a ghetto called *the arts*, which is mostly very safe and has a limited impact on the status quo. Not that the arts have no impact. But they operate within certain boundaries.

The same is true for teaching, social work, and the nonprofit sector in general. It is filled with people whose heart and politics are in the right place, but who aren't maximizing their impact and more often than not are getting their spirits crushed by the systems in which they operate (especially under the No Child Left Behind ideology of one-size-fits-all testing and metrics-based evaluation).

The silver lining is that new media and technology are blurring the lines between arts careers and other sectors of the economy. Now that everyone needs new technology, there are openings for creatives with new media and tech skills to lead in business, politics, and mainstream media. The rise of social media and communications technology is one of the most promising developments of the past few decades. It was key to the rise of Obama and it is core to the new progressive era we need to build. Over the next ten to twenty years, we have the opportunity to take a quantum leap forward.

Turning Thirty

When I was about to turn thirty, I went on a little retreat to reflect on my life and how I wanted it to be.

Our *Future 500* book had just come out. We had the release party in Oakland on my thirtieth birthday. My life was at a crossroads. The three organizations I had helped to create were falling apart.

I needed some time and space to think about my life. My friend and mentor Ellen Furnari had a house in San Diego and she said I could come stay with her for a few months while I figured it out. Her house rested along a canyon. Every day, I would head out to the backyard, hop the fence, and go running in the canyon.

I reflected on every year of my life, starting when I was four. I asked myself: Who was I when I was four? What grade was I in? What year was it? What are all my memories? What was I interested in? Who were my teachers? Who were my friends? What did I learn that year? How did I grow? Who was I when I was five? I went through and thought about my whole life, year by year. It took me a couple of days.

I learned a lot about myself. In hindsight, most of my friends who I invested time and energy into turned out to be temporary. Looking back, we didn't end up having that much in common after all. Most of the projects I tried to do didn't pan out. I spread my energy around and I did a lot of cool projects. Books and organizations. But nothing that would substantially change the course of history.

I looked back on my twenties, and I realized I had spread myself thin. I had tried to do a lot of different things. My thinking in my twenties was: *How many organizations can I help start? How many books can I create? How many boards can I sit on at once?*

I had to face facts: quantity over quality wasn't working for me.

I always lived my life as though I was about to die. I'd had friends die. And I always felt like: *Let me finish this book before I die.* I felt like if I can only finish this one thing, then I can die happy and I'll have done what I was put on Earth to do. By my late twenties, I started realizing that I wasn't dead yet. And that I might in fact live to be seventy or eighty. Then what? What if I really had another forty or fifty years to play with? Forty or fifty years . . . I could do a lot with that!

I decided that in my thirties, instead of doing a whole bunch of things, I would do one thing well. One thing that would last. One thing that would make an impact hundreds of times beyond anything I had done before. And for that one thing I would say no to everything else. It's called maturity, I guess. Getting over the fantasy that you can do everything right now and have it all work out great. Everything takes longer than you think. Everything is more complicated than you think. And after a certain point, every additional thing you try to take on reduces the quality of everything else you are doing. As someone who had always tried to do more and more and more, this was a revolutionary thought.

Part III

Dawn of a New Progressive Era
(2002–2008)

How MoveOn.org F#*ked My Head Up

I had been doing some form of organizing and activism for fifteen years at this point. Over the next seven years, my model was about to be blown apart. And then blown apart again. And again.

I had met Eli Pariser when he was a student at Simon's Rock College and I was going around speaking about *No More Prisons*. When he graduated in the summer of 2000, he and his friends created something called the American Story Project. They went around the country in a converted bus and interviewed regular Americans about their experience with politics. I agreed to be an adviser on the project and they came to visit me where I was living in Raleigh, North Carolina, right before election day.

After MoveOn had really started to take off, I went to visit Eli at his apartment in Manhattan. We were talking in his tiny room, which was barely big enough to fit a bed, a desk, and a small bookcase. "Where's your office?" I asked.

"This is my office." He pointed to his laptop on a desk.

I looked around. There were no filing cabinets. There was no bulletin board. There wasn't even one piece of paper.

"Do you have a printer?"

"Nope."

"What if you have to print something?"

"I don't," he said. "Maybe once in a blue moon. Then I'll just use my roommate's printer."

This was so weird. I was trying to wrap my mind around it.

MoveOn, for anyone who doesn't know, is arguably the most powerful, effective, and dynamic progressive organization of the twenty-first century. Eli, at this time barely twenty-three years old, was its driving force.

"Let me show you something," he said. "Right now we're organizing a lobby day in 535 congressional offices . . . So let's type in one in Alaska. Okay, there are twenty-one people signed up to lobby Representative Murkowski at noon. Up to twenty-five people can sign up for each group. We don't want them to get too big."

"But how did you schedule all the appointments?"

"We don't. We just say: twenty-five of your constituents are going to show up at your office at noon on this date. We suggest you be there."

"But who organizes these lobby visits? Do people just show up or how does that work? It seems like it would be disorganized."

"No, we have about a thousand coordinators who organize the lobby meetings."

"Where do you get the thousand people?"

"They're coordinated and screened by our fourteen core organizers."

"Where did you get the fourteen core organizers?"

"I just sent out an e-mail saying we need volunteers who can give at least fifteen to twenty hours a week. I got 110 applications. And I picked the best fourteen."

When I left his house, my head was spinning. A brave new world was opening up that might allow organizing on a scale I had never imagined possible.

We needed something like MoveOn for the hip-hop generation. Hmmm . . . I thought. Hmmmm.

Everything That Rises Must Converge

There's a famous story by Flannery O'Connor called "Everything That Rises Must Converge." It's not my favorite story. It's about people riding on the bus in Alabama. To be honest, I didn't really understand the story. But the title. The title! Everything that rises must converge. What a perfect way to articulate what is happening in our world and our movement right now.

After 2000, a funny thing started to happen. All the separate conferences I went to during the '90s started to discover each other and cross-pollinate. The largely white adult conferences like Bioneers and Take Back America started inviting more people of color and creating youth-oriented tracks. The youth organizing and activism conferences became more sophisticated.

Integration is inevitable. We're all more connected than we realize. We're going to become even more connected. This is one of the human dynamics that gives me hope.

Imagine how much more integrated we can be in ten to twenty years if we play our cards right.

The Accidental Political Organizer

For someone who was so invested in politics with a small p, it's amazing how little interest I had in Politics with a big P.

When Bill Clinton was elected president in 1992, I was a twenty-year-old college student in Ohio. I was totally uninterested in electoral politics. Not only did I not vote, I literally didn't even know it was election day. I remember sitting in my dining hall late one night and someone busted in and announced that Bill Clinton had won. I remember people being happy. I remember something about a saxophone. Ross Perot having big ears. George Bush losing because there was a recession. Not much more than that.

Actually, I do remember being happy about Bush losing. I knew how terrible Reagan and Bush had been. I knew that Reagan had cut funding for education and social programs. I knew that Bush was a CIA guy and that both of them had done all types of scandalously illegal things in Central America and the Middle East. But I was also very cynical about Democrats. They didn't seem all that different to me. And growing up in hypocritical Hyde Park, I had zero faith that white liberals were going to lift a finger for black people or poor people any more than any other politicians. My main memory of Clinton was that he had criticized rap artist Sista Souljah in an unnecessary and disrespectful way. And because hip-hop was the main lens through which I judged everything, I automatically didn't like the guy.

The mere thought of a twenty-year-old college student in a battleground state like Ohio not knowing it's election day sends chills up my spine. Yet I was that dude.

I got my first taste of electoral politics in 2000 when I was twenty-seven years old. I was living in Raleigh, North Carolina, helping run a small community organization. One of our interns, Bryan Proffitt, was messing around on the Internet and said: "Hey, did you know there's going to be a vote to expand the Wake County jail?"

"There is?" I said looking over his shoulder.

"Yeah. There's a bond issue on the ballot to expand the Wake County jail by two hundred beds."

"When is the election?"

"It looks like it's November 7, which is . . . next week."

We both looked at each other: "Shit!!"

"Is there polling on it? Who's behind it? Is there any opposition? This is craziness! Why didn't we know about this??"

Looking around online, we quickly learned that the Wake County sheriff was behind it—which was a bad thing. Sheriff Baker, the most popular black elected official in Wake County. He had strong support from the church community. There hadn't been a lot of media or polling on the issue. There was no organized opposition.

That night we had an emergency meeting of fifteen people, mostly North Carolina State students. We instantly formed a group called Citizens for Safety and created a slogan: *Schools? Yes. Jails? No.* (There was another ballot issue on schools.) We allocated $1,000 from our budget to run a week-long surprise campaign against the jail to sow the seeds of doubt, in hopes that the proponents would get caught off guard and wouldn't have time to hit back.

Our campaign had five tactics:

1) Blitz Raleigh with posters and fliers.
2) Call people we know and tell them to spread the word.
3) Hold a press conference.
4) Flier church parking lots the Sunday before election day.
5) Flier voters at polling places on election day.

In one week, with a budget of $1,000, that was about all we could do. First we put up the posters to create a buzz. Every lamppost on Hillsborough Street and around downtown read "Schools? Yes. Jails? No." in huge block letters. We recruited a crew of poets at a local spoken word event. Then we held a press conference downtown in front of the court building. Everyone had seen our posters so all the local media showed up. One of our interns, Angela Traurig, spoke, representing Citizens for Safety, along with Ajamu Dillahunt, an old-school organizer from Black Workers for Justice. We were all over the TV news and newspapers. It doesn't take much to get on TV in a midsized city.

On Saturday, we did training with twenty students for GOTV (get out the vote). My roommate Everette worked for the North Carolina Democratic Party, and his friend Reverend Romal Tune trained us in how to conduct GOTV: "You go to the white churches at eleven a.m. You go to the black churches at noon . . ." He had us all pray together.

On Sunday, we were able to flier thirty church parking lots. We fliered the projects and around NC State and Shaw University. And we had people stand outside of a dozen polling places on election day and hand out fliers.

In the end we lost by a few points. The sheriff unleashed a major blitz in the last few days and outspent us more than 100 to 1. We got crushed in the black precincts by voters loyal to the sheriff, many of whom were directly affected by crime and probably saw the jail expansion as a way to create jobs.

As we sat around at our victory party on our couch watching the results come in, I learned some powerful lessons: Electoral campaigns are awesome—even a local ballot issue can inspire incredible energy. Though we lost, none of the kids seemed ultimately discouraged. We had convinced lots of people to vote against the jail.

I had gotten the bug for electoral organizing, but I didn't know what to do with it.

We were so focused on our local campaign that we didn't even pay attention to the national election results. We didn't even notice what was going on in Florida.

It didn't hit me until two years later, actually.

If I had my life to do over, there is one glaringly obvious thing I would go back and change. In 2000, I would have moved to Florida to convince 538 more voters to vote for Al Gore.

Florida was decided by 537 votes. This was the margin of victory that made George W. Bush president. I missed the greatest opportunity in a generation for one ordinary person to alter the entire course of world history. If only I had known what was going on and understood the implications! I could have moved to Florida and organized 538 more voters. There would have been no Iraq war. No hundreds of thousands of lost lives and trillion-plus dollars wasted. No tax cuts for the rich. America would not be in debt.

The thought haunts me to this day. I vowed never to miss an opportunity to change history like that again.

I Had to Admit: The Beauty of Elections

Like most cynical young people, I had no great love for elections or big-P Politics. But the more I got into it, the more I liked electoral campaigns. They were at least a partial antidote to the problems of the social justice movement.

Top eight reasons for people who hate politics to love elections:

1) Bridge barriers: Elections force us to work together across our barriers: race, class, issues, and ideology. Women, gays, environmentalists, people of color, students, and labor—we are all getting screwed by the same folks. Elections are a very concrete way to bring us all together.

2) Talk to regular people: Elections necessitate us to get out of activist bubbles and communicate with everyday people who don't agree with us. This can only be a good thing.

3) Include the whole country: Elections force us to focus on the entire country, especially suburban areas and Middle America, not just cities and the coasts. The movement desperately needs to become more inclusive.

4) Data: Elections make us get serious about data. We claim we represent "the people." But who are these people? Maybe they show up at a rally. But do we have their names and phone numbers? Can we contact them? No!

5) Think big: Elections encourage us to think large-scale. They force us to consider how to build majorities and win.

6) Money and . . . money: Elections open up a whole new stream of money for community-based work. Two streams, actually—the money it takes to win elections, and the much bigger stream controlling government budgets and what our tax dollars should be spent on.

7) Ease: On top of all that, elections are an easy thing to organize around. Unlike most other movement activities, the media actually wants to cover you. Regular people are more invested in what you are talking about, and think you are addressing something practical, not some pie-in-the-sky fantasy. There are very clear deadlines, and very clear results. Compared to "saving the planet" or "fighting racism," elections are satisfying, practical, and simple. That makes it easy to get more people involved.

8) Winning and losing: Oh yeah. That. Winners get to hire and empower a bunch of people who share their values. And they get to vote on things that affect us all.

Why, then, do so many of us have such big problems with elections?

How the Hell Am I Supposed to Vote?

It was fall 2002. Republicans had just crushed Democrats again in the midterm elections, playing on the fear of Middle Eastern terrorism, and now controlled a majority of the House and Senate. Republicans had won control of the U.S. Senate by a total of 109,000 votes spread across two states: Missouri and Minnesota.

I was living at the time in San Francisco, in an activist house on 14th and Valencia. My friends Jené and Kayana took me in off the street out of pure generosity. Jené made her living working at dance clubs, and Kayana was a documentary photographer who also had a job as a bartender. By night they made money off of San Francisco's nightlife. By day they did their real work: high-risk direct actions that involved climbing buildings and hanging banners against corporate bad guys. Jené and Kayana had a little crew of women actionistas who weren't about to let the boys have all the fun climbing things, hanging signs, and getting arrested. It was amazing living with them.

One night I came home at midnight and ran into Kayana's boyfriend at the time, Han Shan, who was coming out of the building as I was going in. Han had always been a bit of a wild man. He had movie-star good looks and resembled Harrison Ford in *Star Wars*. He had been the program director of the Ruckus Society, was deeply involved in Students for a Free Tibet, and had pulled off all sorts of daredevil banner hangs and actions. Tonight he was wired. "You ready to go on a mission?" he asked, sounding slightly manic.

"Sure. What is it?"

"Don't worry, just get in the truck. You're gonna like it."

We got in Kayana's pickup.

"What do you know about Gavin Newsom's Care Not Cash?" he asked me.

"Nothing." I shrugged.

"Okay, well Gavin Newsom is a pretty-boy rich kid on the city council. He wants to be mayor, so he's put a stupid issue on the ballot called Care Not Cash (Prop N). It basically takes away benefits from homeless people under the guise of reform and he's only using it to make a name for himself as tough on spending."

We pulled the truck alongside an abandoned couch on the sidewalk. Han got out, produced a can of black spray paint, and started writing. It came out crisp—black paint against the tan back wall of the couch. In plain letters it read: *Gavin Newsom's idea of a homeless shelter.*

Brilliant.

We hoisted the couch up onto the truck and drove it over to Gavin Newsom's house in the tony Marina district. Somehow Han had managed to get his home address. We off-loaded the couch and placed it in front of the politician's house. A photo of it appeared in the local paper the next week.

This was a clever little stunt. I started carrying a fat magic marker around with me and writing *Gavin Newsom's idea of a homeless shelter* on every random piece of junk furniture people left out in the street: refrigerators, cardboard boxes. Apparently, Gavin Newsom was very creative when it came to homeless shelters. It probably wasn't even illegal to write on stuff people were throwing away.

This little game got me paying even more attention to local politics. A week before the election, I picked up a copy of the local *Guardian* newspaper. It featured a lively endorsement slate on the front cover: *Prop N: No No No.*

How clever, I thought. You could tear off the cover of the newspaper and take it into the polling place with you. I had never seen a paper dramatize a local election like this. I knew for a fact that the weekly papers in D.C., Chicago, New York, and Raleigh didn't do anything of the sort. Smart idea! I read the endorsements, felt like I understood the local issues, and for the first time in my life I was actually excited to vote.

However, when I arrived at the polling place, I forgot to bring a copy of the *Guardian* with me. The poll worker gave me a ballot, which was eight pages long, in three languages. I looked at it and felt overwhelmed. How the hell was I supposed to know how to vote on all these confusing-ass ballot measures? I walked around the polling place, asking people if I could borrow a copy of the *Guardian*. Finally, I fished one out of the trash can and used it to vote. The process was still confusing, matching up the format in the newspaper to the format on the ballot, and it took me close to an hour. But I felt good afterward. I walked down the street happy and satisfied with myself for having cast a somewhat informed vote for the first time in my life.

Then I started to get angry.

If I, as a highly educated, politically aware thirty-year-old had had trouble figuring out how to vote, what about all these nineteen-year-olds we were asking to go vote for the first time? What if they didn't live in San Francisco and no one gave them a copy of the *Guardian*? What if they lived in Raleigh or Tulsa or a small town in Missouri, or a suburb in Arizona? We were setting them up to go into the voting booths, feel totally disempowered, gamble on voting the wrong way (or else leave most of the ballot blank), and then leave and never want to vote again!

A month after the election, I was still angry.

I had started reading up on the 2000 and 2002 elections. And I started to have an epiphany. Holy shit. Elections were not this big thing up in the sky that were controlled by faceless politicians. They were things where the whole fate of the country could be decided by less than a thousand votes in one state. Holy shit. These were not big, scary, intimidating numbers. This was not something where you needed to affect millions and millions of people or be able to spend millions and millions of dollars on TV ads. This was a game that could come down to a couple thousand people here, a couple thousand people there. This was a game I could play.

The hip-hop generation! What if we could get a couple thousand people to vote in a key swing state? We could swing a Senate seat. We could win a national election. We could win a House race, a governor's race. I thought of Lisa Sullivan. She got into organizing through electoral politics in New Haven. But she never taught us how to do it.

Why weren't we jumping up and down screaming about what an incredible opportunity this was? How come nobody told us that a few thousand pissed-off kids who no one expected to vote could show up at the right place at the right time and alter the leadership and direction of the world's most powerful country?

League of Young Voters team photo, 2008

The League of Pissed-off Voters

In a fit of angry inspiration, I composed the following e-mail and pressed send.

Subject: League of Hip-hop Voters. Say Whut?!
Date: Monday, December 2, 2002, 1:48 AM
From: "Billy Wimsatt" <billywimsatt@gmail.com>

Peace everyone,
I hope this finds you well.

I've been talking with a few people and it seems like others have a similar idea: Creating Local Voter Guides for the Hip-Hop Nation & Young Voters for the 2004 Elections.

Warning, everyone: I am fired up about this. Let me tell you a story. I voted early in San Francisco this year and guess what? I DIDN'T KNOW WHAT TO VOTE FOR on 80% of the candidates and ballot initiatives!!! Lucky for me, someone gave me a Bay Guardian Voter Guide and it saved my life. Still, it took me an ENTIRE HOUR to vote and FILL OUT the eight-page confusing-ass ballot that was written in three languages.

As far as I know, the Guardian is the ONLY high-circulation newspaper in the country which prints progressive candidate endorsements on the cover before the election. Without the Guardian, I would've left 80% of the choices BLANK and I would've left the polling place feeling completely disempowered.

Me—an educated/politicized person who is on the advisory board of Rap the Vote.

I'm all for registering young voters. But unless we give kids voter guides, we're setting them up to feel stupid! Ballot initiatives are worded confusing as hell. You can't tell the good initiatives from the bad ones. No one knows who most local candidates are.

Then, a week ago, I got an e-mail from Darby, an 18-year-old hip-hop activist who is creating a voter guide in his hometown, Pittsburgh, PA.

So I wonder: how many others out there want to create progressive hip-hop voter guides in their hometowns for the 2004 elections??? This is a strictly non-501(c)(3) activity. Which is okay—we can do this for very little $.

If we get enough cities, we could start the League of Hip-Hop Voters (what!) and Davey D and OKPlayer and other non-501(c)(3) hip-hop e-newsletters could put it out to hundreds of thousands of hip-hop kids nationwide. Then hip-hop activists in each city could print them out and make copies.

Then eventually we can create the League of Punk Voters, Latina Voters, Rave Voters, etc. There are many ways to cut the cake. One thing at a time.

But if you want to see what this could become, check out the League of Conservation Voters (www.lcv.org). They are not fucking playing.

You want to talk about hip-hop flexing its political power? You want to stop prisons? Fund education not war? Talk to me about copying LCV.org!!

Is something like this already going on in your area? I'm very ignorant. Let me know.

Is anyone else fired up about creating voter guides in your city in 2004? I'd love to be part of a team that compiles a local voter guide!

A SIMPLE voter guide. I'm talking ONE page. With pictures.

Let me know.
billy

I sent this e-mail out to 120 people I knew around the country. In the next few days, I received sixty responses, several from people saying they wanted to make voter guides in their home cities and states.

My friend Wendy Day from Rap Coalition forwarded my e-mail to her friend Kyle Stewart, a lawyer at USA Networks in L.A., who had been ranting and raving about how we needed to mobilize the hip-hop vote to get Bush out of office.

So Kyle calls me up. "Put me to work," she says. "I'm ready to quit my job. I'll do anything you want. What do you need me to do?"

I was like: *Whoa!* I told her, "Honestly, I was just pissed off the other day and I sent out an e-mail. I mean, yeah, I want to do it, but I'm not a real organization. I'm literally just a person who sent out one e-mail. I'm going to Brazil next week for the World Social Forum and I was thinking about doing international work. I hardly know anything about voting. I didn't even vote myself until a few years ago. There are all these progressive organizations and youth voting groups. The first thing we should do is call them all up and ask them why they're not already doing this. Maybe one of them is already doing it. Or maybe they'll want to do it if we give them the idea."

I gave her a list of groups and a list of questions to ask. And then I flew off to Brazil. I told everyone at the World Social Forum that I wanted to start doing international work. Most of the people I talked to politely suggested that I please go back to my own country and do something about President Bush.

When I got back from Brazil, I called Kyle.

"I called all the groups you gave me," she said. "I called more than thirty groups. And they all said the same thing: 'We're not doing this. We're not planning to do this. No one else we know is planning to do this. You should do it.'"

Wow. Okay . . .

It's astonishing to think of how little connection there was between voting and any other form of activism back then. Nowadays it seems like a no-brainer. But in 2003, there was still a huuuuuge disconnect. The people who organized against sweatshops and prisons and the WTO and the war and every other political issue were largely disconnected from voting. For the past ten years, young people had voted at the lowest levels ever and we were not seen as progressive. Remember, in 2000 we had voted in almost equal percentages for Al Gore and George W. Bush.

We needed to do more than start a website with a voter guide tool. We needed to catalyze a friggin' movement!

I was an unlikely person to start a youth vote organization, since I myself had not voted until the age of twenty-seven.

I sent out a second e-mail to three hundred people. Again, it got a 50 percent response rate. People told me: "Go for it." They voted on the name. The top choices were: League of Hip-hop Voters, League of Pissed-off Voters, and League of Young Voters, in about equal numbers. They signed up for hundreds of hours of volunteer work.

All my other plans went out the window. When I decided to start the League, I wanted to do it all the way. It was quite a commitment, especially for someone like me. I had spent my twenties hopping from one project to the next. Sleeping on couches. Usually working on five different projects at a time.

I jumped in with both feet. I committed to do the League whether or not anyone else came along, and whether or not we could raise any money. I committed to run it for the next five years, until 2008. Our constituency was ages eighteen through thirty-five. My thirty-sixth birthday was two weeks after the 2008 election.

Five years. It was a profound commitment.

A Grassroots Electoral Renaissance

I wasn't the only one with this idea.

In 2004, every week there was another creative new organization launching to register voters or shoot spitballs at the Bush regime. There were literally three different Bike the Vote projects that weren't connected to each other. There was a project to row a boat down the Mississippi River from Minnesota to New Orleans to retrace the path of Huckleberry Finn and register voters in the swing states along its shores. There was Rock the Vote, Smoke the Vote, Fuck the Vote, and Votergasm. Yes, there were two different vote-for-sex initiatives. There was Music for America and Punkvoter and Concerts for Change and Bands Against Bush, Drinking Liberally, and two separate groups of Moms Against Bush. Run Against Bush organized meet-ups for anti-Bush joggers who wore matching T-shirts. They sold 20,000 shirts online and raised $250,000 for the Democratic Party. Then there was Operation Bubbe, which transported young liberal Jewish New Yorkers to get out the Jewish grandparent vote in Florida. (In 2008, this was revived as The Great Schlep, and comedian Sarah Silverman did a hilarious YouTube clip about it.)

Everywhere you turned, there was another creative idea.

There was Swing State Spring Break, which evolved into Swing State Summer Break, which by fall became Swing the State: Your Anti-Bush Travel Agency. Not to be confused with the Swing State Project, which was urging Democrats to move to swing states. Or Driving Votes, which arranged rides and carpools to swing states. Or Downtown for Democracy, which did the same thing for New York artists.

There was only one thing all this activity reminded me of. It was so spontaneous, so improvisational, so energetic and vibrantly purposeful. I had only witnessed one thing like it in my entire life: hip-hop.

Speaking of which, there were four major hip-hop voting efforts. Russell Simmons's Hip-hop Summit Action Network was eclipsed by Puffy's Vote or Die. There was the union-bankrolled Hip-hop Civic Engagement Project which registered 350,000 voters, not to be confused with the National Hip-hop Political Convention which brought together thousands of young activists in Newark and spawned a network of local organizing committees (also known as LOCs) in more than a dozen states.

The biggest funding went to a group called ACT, America Coming Together.

Young voter organizing was suddenly fundable (at least in the ten to fifteen states that were considered battlegrounds). The Pew Charitable Trust gave the PIRGs $8 million to run a huge nonpartisan voter registration and turnout campaign. And a couple of major partisan funders arrived on the scene and invested more than $5 million in this cohort of emerging groups.

Politics 'n' Pancakes

We needed a simple way to get the League network going, to see who was serious about organizing a local voter bloc and who was just blowing hot air.

So in May of 2003, we organized our first national action. It was called Politics 'n' Pancakes. I always believe in organizing around food and culture. The idea was to organize brunch—because, after all, who doesn't like brunch?—and to talk about the potential to create a young progressive voter bloc in different cities. We had about twenty people commit to be brunch organizers in different places. It was a pretty diverse group, mostly women. And people freaked the concept in every which way.

In New York alone there were five different varieties. We had Politics 'n' Coconut Chutney in Brooklyn. We had Politics 'n' Pizza in Jersey. Politics 'n' Adobo in Queens. Politics 'n' Apple Martinis in Manhattan. And a Pissed-off Potluck in the Bronx, at the home of Maricruz Badia, a young environmental justice organizer who was nine months pregnant (and gave birth to her son the next day).

Keep in mind, all of this was created out of thin air. So leading up to the launch, I was going out to every conference and event I could, recruiting people. Outside a fundraiser at a club called SOBs in New York, I ran into my old friend Adrienne Maree Brown. Adrienne Maree Brown! She had been involved in hip-hop and work on prison and drug laws. Charismatic as hell, she was a natural organizer and just starting to develop a little following. For her birthday, she got a bunch of Virgos together and they threw a Virgo bash with over one thousand people. She was exactly the sort of person the League was designed to recruit.

"What's up, Adrienne!" I said, pulling out my little xeroxed survey. "I'm starting a group called the League of Hip-hop Voters . . . Will you fill out one of these?" I handed her the survey.

She wrote her name, e-mail, and phone. And then, in big letters: *Sorry. I have no time.*

Little did she know.

I put her on my e-mail list and started sending her e-mails. Intrigued, she began editing them and sending them back to me with feedback. I told her I was pulling together a book of case studies on young people who had won or swung elections. Soon I had convinced her to become my official coeditor. Before she knew it, she had fallen into the project hook, line, and sinker, and was spending twenty hours a week on the League.

First she decided to go to a Politics 'n' Pancakes brunch in New York. Then she decided to organize a Politics 'n' Pancakes brunch in New York. Then she was helping organize all five brunches in the New York area and was cochairing the national brunch organizers conference call. She got her friend Dani McClain into it in Cincinnati. And she got her friend Hallie Montoya Tansey into it in San Francisco. Between her friends and my friends, we had a little network rolling in ten to fifteen states.

Meanwhile, our book of case studies was starting to take shape. We had great stories to tell. Alisha Thomas Morgan was a twenty-two-year-old black woman who ran for state representative in suburban Atlanta in a 77 percent white area—in Newt Gingrich's old district!—and won by knocking on every door, putting her personal cell phone number on every piece of campaign literature, and returning every call. Nick Tilsen in South Dakota helped swing a Senate race by turning out voters on the Pine Ridge reservation. Amazing stories! And I had an even more ambitious plan of how to distribute it: we would have twelve coauthors who would double as regional organizers and build chapters of the League in their respective parts of the country and networks.

Michael Moore had just come out with a book titled *Stupid White Men*, so we titled our book *How to Get Stupid White Men Out of Office*. Another one of those titles that Nonny probably would've thought of a better name for.

We had no money for the first year, but the momentum was tremendous.

My friend James Bernard from the *Source* had gone to work for Service

Employees International Union (SEIU) on the security guards campaign—organizing mostly young black men from the hip-hop generation to form unions. He convinced SEIU to give us some start-up money and hooked us up with a meeting space at the AFL-CIO headquarters in D.C.

In the fall of 2003, we had our first two big meetings back-to-back. The first was a gathering of the entire youth field at AFL-CIO headquarters. We felt like big shots, sitting around the table where the heads of all the big labor unions sit. We called the meeting PY-VOSS (Progressive Young Voter Organizing Strategy Session). It was organized by myself and two new friends: Malia Lazu, who had build a new model called Mass Vote in Boston, and Meighan Davis, who ran the Sierra Student Coalition.

Voter organizing—we had coined a term. Not just registering voters. Not just robotically turning out voters on election day, or having rock stars make public service announcements. But actually organizing young voters into smart, informed, empowered voting blocs at the local level—all across the country. This was a quite a concept at the time.

We were starting to get the sense that most of the other youth groups had no real plans to do much of anything for the election. We wanted to create a space early on to bring everyone together to build momentum around shared strategy and action.

PY-VOSS worked pretty well. We had a lot of the traditional players there like the United States Student Association and Black Youth Vote. We also invited a bunch of groups that had never done voting work before like the Radical Cheerleaders, Third World Majority, Choice USA, and the National Hip-hop Theater Festival. We invited representatives from each of the top thirteen major swing states, with the idea that local organizers needed to shape the conversation of how national organizations were going to play in their states.

The meeting was productive. We did an exercise where everyone used colored stickers to put their field networks up on a map. We did another exercise where everyone wrote up their assets and what they needed from other groups. A lot of amazing people were there who no one knew about yet. A guy named Jefferson Smith, a quirky genius from Oregon who ran a group called the Oregon Bus Project, came and introduced an idea he had been thinking about called Trick or Vote—a mass canvass on Halloween, in costume. Everyone was like: *Wow, who's this crazy guy?* He would later go on to become a state representative in Portland, and his organization the Bus Federation would expand and become the standard bearer for youth-driven field organizations in five Western states. A young environmentalist named Billy Parish was there who later went on to create the Energy Action Coalition. And Malia was about to be cast on a reality TV show called *American Candidate* which would catapult her into the national spotlight.

A lot of enthusiasm and trust was built. It reminded me of the hip-hop meetings we used to throw in the park in Chicago. But it was profoundly disappointing as well. It was clearer than ever that no one aside from us was trying to take leadership on a national level to build a serious progressive youth voter effort. In creating the League, we had set out to build a niche in what had looked to us from a distance like a very crowded young voter field. After the meeting, we realized, it wasn't a niche we were filling. It was the Grand Canyon.

The next week, in October 2003, the League held our own founding retreat at the Omega Center in upstate New York. We were gaining momentum like a snowball rolling downhill. We took over the old Active Element office on 135th Street in Harlem. In January 2004, we hired four full-time staff with benefits. By the end of 2004, we would raise and spend more than a million dollars.

Karl Rove vs. Octavia Butler

The 2004 election looked to me like a huge life test with my name on it. I was still reeling from the missed opportunity in Florida in 2000. I worked one hundred hours a week and I didn't even feel tired. Everywhere I went, I was recruiting people and putting up stickers. I felt like I was born to do this. It seemed like the absolute most important thing anyone in the world could be working on. As one of my idols Gloria Totten, the head of Progressive Majority, told fifty of us at PY-VOSS: "The 2004 election could look a lot like the 2000 election. It could come right back down to Florida or Ohio and end in a recount." And if it did, I was going to personally make sure we encouraged every single young person I could get my hands on in Florida and Ohio to get everyone they knew out to vote.

The League for me was the culmination of everything I had ever done or cared about. It brought together every aspect of my life: hip-hop, writing, philanthropy, and youth organizing. And it added a new dimension, electoral organizing, which I knew nothing about, but which I was cocky enough to think that I could figure out pretty easily.

Every little step seemed like a huge victory which I would write breathless e-mails about to our growing list.

At the time I had just started reading a series of science fiction books by Octavia Butler.

Octavia Butler is a pretty unique figure in the literary world. A black female science fiction writer, she created terrifying scenarios that rang intimately true. Her book, *Parable of the Sower*, takes place in fortressed suburban Los Angeles, twenty years in the future, when civilization, short on water and oil, has descended into armed mayhem. The streets are run by savage gangs of junkies who burn down suburban enclaves, ransack the homes, and kill the inhabitants. Our protagonist is a fifteen-year-old black girl with a birth defect. Her enclave gets torched, and she must fend for herself outside the gates. She learns to take care of herself, builds a movement among the castaways, and develops a profound and pragmatic religion based on her lived experience. The second book in the series, *Parable of the Talents*, is really about building a progressive political movement in the face of an authoritarian regime. Christian fundamentalists have taken over the U.S. government, promising to restore order. But they turn out to be wicked and authoritarian. Our heroic little band of castaways must fight for their lives and build a movement by, let's see . . . recruiting and managing a team, knocking on doors, raising money, drawing media coverage, and speaking at colleges and universities.

Sound familiar? In the America of 2004, it rang all too true. I was really, really scared of Bush and the vast right-wing apparatus he represented. The Democratic establishment was asleep at the wheel. They had brought a plastic knife to a gun fight, and they were getting mopped across the floor. The 2000 presidential election in Florida had been stolen through the manipulation of voter databases and the disenfranchisement of black voters. Bush had clearly lied about Iraq. The Democrats clearly weren't up to the challenge. But maybe me and my thousand closest politics-hating friends were.

I had been reading about Republican ownership of voting machine companies and books about Karl Rove and how he had masterminded the right-wing takeover of Texas. Now he was on the path to securing permanent rule over all three branches of government, while Democrats stood by whining and progressives were marginalized as outcasts. It was a scary political moment.

It sounds naïve to say this now. By 2006, the tide of public opinion shifted, and the Republican political machine turned out to be not quite as disciplined and effective as it had once appeared. But in 2003 and 2004, it was a different story. It seemed entirely possible that if Bush were to win again in 2004, the country could go in a direction foreshadowed by Octavia Butler.

A Waitress From New Orleans:
Shana's Voter Guide for the Pissed Off

At this point, we had a theory that people could make their own local progressive voter guides. But no one had actually done it. We needed someone to try it out.

In late 2003, a waitress in New Orleans named Shana Sassoon created the first League voter guide for a September local election.

Shana was married to Abram Himelstein, coauthor of a book called *Tales of a Punk Rock Nothing* with my friend Jamie Schweser. Abram had a homegrown publishing house called New Mouth from the Dirty South which had published the *Future 500* and *Another World Is Possible*. I was chatting with Shana one day when she realized she had never voted in a local election. She decided to make a voter guide.

She did three weeks of research, basically asking people she respected and trusted about candidates and issues. She spent $118 to print five thousand copies of a one-sheet voter guide, complete with cartoon illustrations cut out and pasted zine-style.

It was called *A Voter Guide for the Pissed Off*. She handed out copies at the restaurant where she worked, to her friends and neighbors, and put them up in neighborhood bars and coffee shops. It created an instant sensation. People were running off extra copies at work. They were all over the place, and Shana was transformed into someone people came to with questions about New Orleans politics and elections.

She made voter guides with a growing group of savvy friends during the next five elections, involving about thirty other people who together built the League chapter in New Orleans. The League partnered with a local juvenile justice coalition to elect a new sheriff for New Orleans Parish who had signed off on a reform platform. And Shana used the skills she was learning to help organize her own neighborhood efforts, holding tough but cordial meetings with Mayor Ray Nagin.

Election Night 2004

In less than a year, we built more than sixty local League groups in twenty-one states. In July 2004, we organized three hundred leaders to come to a mass training session called Smackdown 2004 in Columbus, Ohio, where we trained kids to use ninety-day planners, which laid out in precise detail what they needed to do every single day leading up to the election on November 2.

We didn't swing the election in Ohio. But we did print and distribute more than 350,000 copies of 147 voter guides from thirty-one states. We had eleven local voter guides in Florida alone, twelve in Ohio. Our efforts accounted for a significant slice of the margin of victory in seven state and local races, including the election of Governor Christine Gregoire in Washington State, who won by 129 votes—one of the few bright spots in the 2004 election.

At eleven p.m. on election day 2004, we got on a conference call with a bunch of other national voter groups. Everyone else was ready to concede and move on. The League was the only group that had our Ohio organizers on the call. Our people told stories of massive voter suppression and invited everyone to a protest they had organized the next morning at Republican Secretary of State Kenneth Blackwell's office in Columbus.

In the days that followed, while the rest of the progressive movement sat around feeling sorry for itself, the Ohio League went into overdrive organizing public hearings at a church in Columbus to document instances of voter suppression. They recruited lawyers, elections experts, hired a court stenographer, and collected sworn affidavits. As League organizer Amy Kaplan writes: "With no help from the Kerry campaign, the Democratic Party, or the 527s that had already left Ohio, we pulled together more than six hundred people to attend hearings on November 13 and 15, and collected more than one hundred affidavits of people who witnessed violations of voting rights and systemic voter suppression. The hearings model was then replicated by the election protection coalition in Cleveland, Cincinnati, and Toledo. The hearings were nationally broadcast on Pacifica radio and attracted the attention of Reverend Jesse Jackson, who came to Ohio several times to shine a national spotlight on the investigation, litigation, and documentation. The evidence and testimony gathered at these hearings formed the basis for a report issued by Congressman John Conyers Jr. entitled, 'Preserving Democracy: What Went Wrong in Ohio?' On January 6, 2005, three dozen representatives, led by Representative Stephanie Tubbs Jones and Senator Barbara Boxer, initiated an unprecedented constitutional confrontation that challenged the legitimacy of the Ohio vote."

The investigation also significantly damaged the credibility of the Ohio Republican Party, Secretary of State Ken Blackwell, and set the stage for Democrats to sweep in 2006, winning elections for governor, the Senate, and other contested offices in the midterm elections.

When we debriefed from the election with eighty of our top local organizers in New Orleans, there were incredible stories from all over the country. The progressive movement as a whole went into a coma for the first six months of 2005. (We barely woke up in time to stop Bush from privatizing Social Security.) But the League network was alive and kicking. We had a vision to go deeper and build power at the state and local level for the long term.

League 2.0

My father is a philosopher of science. I grew up with him always talking about the "conceptual foundations" of this or that scientific notion. I think this planted in my head a fascination with the history of ideas.

In its initial vision, the League had three conceptual foundations that fused together into one big idea. First was the notion of online voter guides for the hip-hop generation. Second, the model of Albuquerque, New Mexico, where young people who were fighting on a local environmental justice issue had accidentally swung their state in the presidential election—by 366 votes. It's like, hey, if Native American and Latino youth in New Mexico can swing a state election without even fully intending to, how many other people could be doing the same thing? Third, there was the model from MoveOn: using a national e-mail list to trigger local groups to take action in the real world. We needed something like MoveOn for the hip-hop generation. I thought the League just might be it.

Over time the vision began to evolve.

A few months before the 2004 election, our Western regional organizer, Hallie Montoya Tansey, called me up, concerned.

"Am I going to lose my job after the election?" she wanted to know.

"Well, honestly . . . yes," I said. "There isn't money for after the election. Funders are giving us money for the election, not for afterward."

She thought about it for a minute.

"What if I raise my own salary for 2005, can I keep my job?" she asked. "I think it's important to organize people after the election. We're telling people we're building a movement and helping them build power to change their communities in the long term. We can't just leave after the election is over."

I agreed with her. Hallie was living in San Francisco at the time. She rallied her friends and they began madly organizing house parties and selling T-shirts on top of the organizing she was doing in swing states. By the time election day came, she and her friends had raised an extra $35,000 to keep her job funded.

She became our field director. Under Hallie's leadership, the organization transitioned to a new model we called League 2.0. Instead of starting chapters all over the place, we would go deep in a few key states and work to transform them. We analyzed the country and chose six states which were sure to be perennial battlegrounds and where we had developed the strongest organizers: New Mexico, Wisconsin, California, Pennsylvania, Ohio, and Maine.

At its best, the League 2.0 model worked out beautifully. In Maine, for example, the League grew into a political powerhouse. In its first six years, the Maine League helped win or swing twenty elections, and helped pass or block nineteen pieces of legislation, including the passage of three completely unique laws that the chapter essentially invented from scratch.

The first law, Opportunity Maine, makes it so students who go to college in state and choose to stay there after they graduate get their student loans almost completely paid off over time. The second law, Rent Green, requires landlords to disclose their average monthly heating bills, thus incentivizing landlords to weatherize their rental units. The third law is a tax credit that benefits local artists. All three of these laws were dreamed up by young people, and the League pushed to make them happen. On top of all of this, the League's Maine director, Justin Alfond, who had no previous political experience, ran and won a state senate seat. Another of our organizers, Jenna Vendil, won a seat on the Portland school committee.

There were trade-offs to going deeper in fewer places. But the greatest benefit was that it allowed the League to focus on building power and leadership in low-income communities of color.

Robert "Biko" Baker is leading this next phase of the League's development. Biko grew up on the North Side of Milwaukee and found a niche as a hip-hop entrepreneur and writer for the *Source* magazine. In college, he studied the civil rights movement and won a scholarship to a PhD program at UCLA. In 2004, he moved back home to Milwaukee to work on the presidential election. He ended up sticking around to help the Poets, who were well-known local spoken word artists, build the Campaign Against Violence (CAV). They organized festivals, rallies, and taught an intensive form of conflict resolution and self-love to kids in the hood and in the juvenile detention center. We recognized Biko's talent and recruited him, first as a local organizer. He worked his way up to national staff, and in 2008 I passed the torch to him as executive director.

"At first when I became executive director, I was scared," Biko reflected two years into the job. "I had to raise so much money and I had people depending on me to feed their families. I have learned so much at the League. It has been such a blessing. When I first got involved, I was basically a cultural organizer. I knew how to give speeches and build relationships, but I didn't really understand the political process, or what it takes to run an organization.

"Young kids who are caught up in street life, they can see that I come from the same place, so they trust my leadership. A lot of kids we work with start out like: *F— voting*. In the absence of jobs, education, or a proper society to plug into, young people are acting out of desperation. We show them not only how to get voter registration cards, get people out to vote, and use a database. We develop them as leaders. Then they get invited to conferences. They meet with politicians. They get invited to the White House. They feel empowered. Coming from a community with a lot of oppression, you grow up with an 'us vs. them' mentality. But over time you get to know all different types of people. You realize it's just *us*. I tell young people: When the ultimate principle is democracy and love, you can feel confident being 100 percent authentic talking to anybody, whether you're talking to a White House aide, a senator, a funder, or a community member. For me, the League is about doing more than getting young people to vote. We're trying to change the culture in a deep way. For urban kids, that means letting go of judgment and pain so we can learn new things. Like how to build a green economy. I've learned so much about retrofitting homes and weatherization. I know how to build a worm bed compost pile that you can turn into $4-a-bag fertilizer! That can create jobs. We don't have to be afraid to learn these things. We constantly have to keep becoming more and more sophisticated."

It has been a joy to watch the League under Biko's leadership, as it continues to evolve.

The Evolution of a New Progressive Movement

"Progressive" was a term we reclaimed in the 1990s to mean something in between "liberal" and "leftist." It was supposed to be less squishy and hand-wringy than "liberal." It was supposed to sound more pragmatic and less dogmatic than "leftist." But it was definitely to the left of the Democratic Party—populist and forward thinking. Not stuck in the past.

The evolution of the word progressive mirrors the evolution of the movement it describes. Kind of like the word "hip-hop."

Hip-hop, as a term, was coined in the 1970s to describe four elements of New York City youth subculture—breaking, rap, deejaying, and graffiti—and to unite them all under a common banner that had vague political undertones. In the early '90s when rap blew up, and the other three elements took a backseat, mainstream America started using the terms "rap" and "hip-hop" interchangeably.

"No!!!" the hip-hop purists shouted. "Hip-hop is not just rap. It's a whole culture. It includes all four elements."

"Hip-hop is a whole culture," came corporate America's reply. "It's not just rap. It's also: fashion, movies, video games, and R&B. Basically, it's anything with a black urban influence that we want you to buy."

In the popular imagination, this is what hip-hop became.

In the 1980s and '90s, insurgent leftists had started to call themselves progressives as an homage to the progressive reform movement of the early 1900s. They were ready to fight and be bold and win and not just yell from the sidelines. They sought to form a broad populist movement based on economic and social justice. They saw themselves as more progressive than the liberals who they considered to be compromised and spineless.

At the same time, liberals were looking for a new word. The "L" word brand had been severely battered by right-wing taunting. "Liberal" was framed as the pathetic weakling kid who nobody wants to play with, not even other liberals. Democrats were looking for a new word too. They wanted to be sexy and forward thinking again, not stuck in the past. So liberals and Democrats grabbed the word.

And conservative Democrats grabbed the term as well. They embraced the term progressive to mean "not as liberal as liberals."

So under the big tent of "progressiveness" an uneasy alliance was formed of leftists, liberals, and conservative Dems.

Progressive was a powerful word and every group seemed to embrace it, define itself against it, and put their own spin on it. LGBT folks sometimes use it to mean progressive on gender and sexuality. Racial justice advocates sometimes use it to mean progressive on race. And sometimes each group distinguishes and distances itself from progressiveness for not being progressive enough on their issues. People of color sometimes talk, often justifiably, about progressives in a similar fashion to "white liberals"—a group that was supposed to be an ally but was actually just a fair-weather friend.

How the Progressive Movement Got a Brain

Up until about 2003, the progressive movement was mostly a bunch of random disconnected pieces, lacking a shared identity, working in silos on issues and policies, holding protests and rallies, but rarely coming together in a deliberate way. There were high points like Seattle. But these were mostly flashes in the pan. Voter data was kept on Excel spreadsheets, and not upgraded from election to election.

Meanwhile, the right wing had managed to organize itself as a powerful new movement. In reaction to the movements and mayhem of the 1960s, four distinct segments of conservatism had joined forces into a new right-wing alliance: cultural conservatives, libertarians, wealthy Republican business elites, and a growing number of working-class white Democrats who were alienated by how friendly the Democratic Party was supposedly becoming with black folks. In short, the People of God joined in an unholy alliance with the People of Money, the People of Guns, and the People of Resentment to form a powerful new governing coalition. By the early 2000s, there were a number of alarming reports detailing this new right-wing movement, and how well-organized and effective they were.

By late 2002, still reeling from the thumping Democrats had received in that year's midterm elections, several of the major progressive groups in D.C. began organizing a response. They held a series of meetings in anticipation of the 2004 elections and decided to form two major alliances: National Voice, a coalition of major nonprofit groups, and America Votes, a coalition of major labor unions and advocacy groups (Sierra Club, NAACP, NARAL, and others).

Meanwhile, the Campaign for America's Future (CAF) was developed as a progressive response to the more conservative DLC (Democratic Leadership Council) which had run Democratic politics since the election of Bill Clinton. CAF's goal was to unite the progressive movement around bold visionary ideas and get the Democratic Party to stand for more than just becoming Republican-lite. At its first Take Back America conference in D.C., thousands showed up, including a who's who of the progressive movement at the time.

The importance of these three new entities—National Voice, America Votes, and Take Back America—cannot be underestimated. They created a broad platform—an underlying superstructure—for alliance-building in the modern progressive movement to flourish.

National Voice helped raise tens of millions of dollars for nonpartisan groups to do vote work. They ran a campaign called "November 2" (election day 2004) and made T-shirts, posters, and TV spots reminding people to vote. After the election, many of the partner groups thought National Voice should go away (which was the original plan), so that it wouldn't be in competition for funding with its partner groups. It went away temporarily, but was later revived on a more low-profile state-by-state basis as State Voices, which now operates nonpartisan coordinated issue- and voter-engagement tables in sixteen states that link over six hundred state and local organizations.

America Votes was parallel to National Voice, but more political.

Meanwhile, a former Clinton staffer named Rob Stein created a famous PowerPoint presentation, "The Conservative Message Machine Money Matrix," about the rise of the right wing and began showing it to big Democratic donors. This led to the formation of the Democracy Alliance, whose goal was to bring together major Democratic and progressive donors to invest long-term funding to create a new political infrastructure.

Democracy Alliance focused its funding recommendations in four buckets: ideas, leadership, media, and civic engagement (voting, field organizing, and advocacy), and developed a portfolio of old and new groups which were to become anchors in a revitalized progressive field.

What was profound about all of these developments is that previously (during the Clinton years) there had been a huge divide between four camps: the Democratic leadership, which was totally out of touch with the grassroots; the D.C. advocacy community, which was frustrated, disempowered, and out of touch; the social justice movement, which was vibrant and consisted of many small organizations, but was considered by everyone in D.C. to be marginal and irrelevant; and artists and creative communities, from Hollywood to the hood, who decided they needed to plug in with this impressive new array of progressive political movements.

We Realized We Needed Each Other

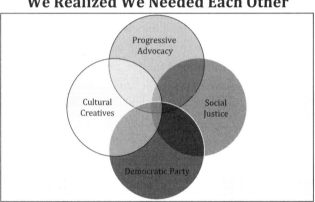

During the Bush years, these four groups began to meet in the middle and realize they needed each other. Very badly. Like, they couldn't afford not to work together anymore. They needed to form a new unified progressive movement. Thank you, George Bush! Social justice groups grew more savvy. The D.C. groups became bolder, more movement-oriented, and more interested in connecting with the grassroots.

The Seven-Part Creative Explosion

From 2002–2010, in rapid succession, there were at least seven major explosions of creativity across the progressive movement:

1) Online Organizing Explosion: Kicked off by MoveOn, popularized by the Howard Dean campaign, and spread like wildfire in countless forms.

2) Vote Explosion: In a few years, the majority of progressive groups began including voter outreach as a core strategy.

3) Blog Explosion: Building on the success of DailyKos, a universe of influential bloggers and blog sites mushroomed almost overnight. In late 2004, Matt Stoller and others recruited them into an influential network, BlogPAC, which organized calls and raised millions of dollars for progressive candidates. In 2006, the bloggers held a convention,

Netroots Nation. Bloggers became so influential that major progressive institutions struggled to keep up.

4) Democracy Alliance Explosion: The significance of the Democracy Alliance cannot be underestimated. For the first time, a critical mass of major progressive donors got organized to strategically build the progressive movement. In the process, they seeded major new leadership development groups like the Center for Progressive Leadership and Young People For; media shops like Media Matters; and think tanks like Center for American Progress as well, strengthening and connecting several anchor organizations.

5) Plumbing and Wiring Explosion: Democracy Alliance donors also invested heavily in progressive infrastructure, the plumbing of a functional movement. This included an alphabet soup of behind-the-scenes projects and groups, from Catalist, a shared voter data bank; to Atlas Project, a shared political targeting service; to New Organizing Institute, which trained online organizers and field operatives.

6) Obama Explosion: Much has been written about the great strides of the Obama campaign. What is not popularly understood is how much the Obama explosion built on the progressive organizing explosions that preceded it. From talent to tactics to policy ideas, many of the assets of the Obama campaign were wisely derived from little-known streams and tributaries of the progressive movement.

7) Translocal Alliance Explosion: This explosion of creativity is the least known. Local grassroots social and racial justice groups were also making a play. Seeing hundreds of millions of dollars spent on the election in 2004, several of the major independent community-based organizations got together to form a new entity. They called it Pushback Network. These were groups like SWOP (SouthWest Organizing Project) in New Mexico, Southern Echo in Mississippi, and Kentuckians for the Commonwealth. Pushback Network was a way to connect across state lines, share best practices, and position the network of state-based groups to be recognized on the national stage.

Several parallel, connected, and overlapping translocal issue alliances also formed: Right to the City (opposing gentrification), the National Day Laborers Organizing Network (NDLON), the Domestic Workers Alliance, and Grassroots Global Justice. In 2008, several of these groupings got together with Jobs with Justice and Pushback Network and began to form a loose alliance of alliances which called itself the Inter-Alliance Dialogue.

The Inter-Alliance Dialogue debuted at the U.S. Social Forum in Detroit under the banner "Enough is Enough—Basta Ya!" The Social Forum attracted 15,000 attendees in an amazingly well-organized event that showed the grassroots social justice movement as alive and kicking. Many traditional leftist and grassroots social justice groups got leapfrogged by the shiny new progressive movement train. Some of these smaller groups had been saying and doing many of the same things for years, laboring in obscurity, without catching the eye of media or big donors. They found themselves gasping for breath, struggling to catch up in the twenty-first century progressive marketplace. But the Social Forum and the Inter-Alliance Dialogue evidenced signs of renewed life.

In addition to these seven innovation explosions, several of the major national groups got infused with fresh blood as well. Ben Jealous, a contemporary of Lisa Sullivan, took the helm at NAACP and hired a bunch of young dynamos. Deepak Bhargava became head of the Center for Community Change and brought a torrent of bold energy and vision. Mike Brune, who ran the scrappier and more radical Rainforest Action Network for many years, became head of the Sierra Club. Mary Kay Henry was named the first female president of SEIU, the country's largest labor union.

After bumping up against old-guard leadership for decades, a slightly younger, slightly more diverse, slightly more collaborative generation was starting to gain institutional control of the progressive movement.

The Generational Alliance

In 2005, youth groups decided to form our own alliance, with America Votes, National Voice, and Pushback Network as models. We called it the Generational Alliance. Our goal was threefold:

1) To connect four sectors of the youth movement: campus, community, civic engagement, and culture.
2) To push a united youth policy agenda and organizing strategy.
3) To create an integrated youth leadership pipeline.

The leadership pipeline idea was this: A kid starts out in juvenile detention. She gets connected to a poetry workshop in jail. Once she gets out, she connects with the spoken word scene via Youth Speaks. Through spoken word, she hooks up with a local organizing group. She learns skills and finds a mentor who helps her finish high school and get into college. In college, she earns a fellowship from Young People For or Generation Change, which exposes her to the national progressive movement and millions of mentor and internship opportunities. She uses her leadership skills to get elected to student government where she becomes a member of United States Student Association, and learns about federal lobbying and education policy. Then, after college, she gets involved with the League of Young Voters and helps build a local progressive voter bloc. With further exposure to leadership opportunities through the Center for Progressive Leadership, she helps wins elections and brings a whole new set of people into the political process.

The Generational Alliance was started by four people: Val Benavidez and myself from the League; Iara Peng, who founded Young People For; and Taj James, who created Movement Strategy Center, an alliance-building hub for community-based groups. We were supported by a visionary funder named Grant Garrison at Rockefeller Brothers Fund who saw the potential of our vision and helped us get it off the ground.

The idea of connecting these four pillars of youth organizing (campus, community, culture, and civic engagement) was hard. For the most part, these subsets of the youth movement didn't connect, talk to each other, or even know about each other.

Community groups were usually small, local, and focused on teenagers. Groups like Southwest Youth Collaborative in Chicago, InnerCity Struggle in L.A., and HOMEY in San Francisco could take a kid off the streets, give her a place to go, politicize her, and give her organizing skills working on local issues in the community. But what happens after she leaves the program?

Campus organizing was its own insular world. Most campuses had chapters of national groups like the Sierra Student Coalition, United Students Against Sweatshops, NAACP, and/or their own homegrown groups. But they tended to have little connection to life either before or after college. What happened to campus activists after they graduated?

And then there were cultural groups: Youth Speaks, the Hip-hop Theater Festival, the spoken word community, the hip-hop community, youth media organizations. They were making political songs, poems, movies, art, and media, but they weren't connecting to any organized action or concrete political agenda.

The Generational Alliance was a way to join these disparate pieces into one integrated youth movement. It has been a slow process, but it's starting to bear fruit. We passed on the leadership to Christina Hollenback, who cut her teeth organizing around affirmative action at the University of Michigan, and then worked at the League and United States Student Association before becoming head of the Generational Alliance.

"In terms of straight-up politics, we're finally starting to have an impact," says Christina. "The White House and leaders in Congress are starting to consult us and want to know what we think. But the trust that we have built between organizations has been as transformative as anything else we've done. This is a generation that responds as much to 'us' as to 'I.' That's a big shift. Collectively, we know we can achieve more than any of us can achieve individually. We're getting each others' backs on issues. But deeper than that, we're bringing the heart and the spirit back into this work. There's a lot to be healed. We're looking not only at how to win on legislation, but how to do community transformation and self-transformation at the same time."

In 2010, along with historic health care legislation that extended health benefits to six million young people, Congress passed SAFRA (Student Aid and Fiscal Responsibility Act), which cut the predatory loan companies out of the student loan process. This was a quadruple win because it: 1) saved tax payers $87 billion over ten years; 2) invested more than $40 billion in additional Pell grants for students; 3) cut the interest rate on student loans; and 4) cut billions from the debt.

There is nothing not to love about this bill. Unless you're a student loan company.

When Democrats in Congress were passing this bill (every single Republican member of Congress voted against it), Senator Harkin of Iowa gave two thank yous: he thanked his family and he thanked the United States Student Association.

"I still can't believe it," reflected USSA President Gregory Cendana. "We realized it was going to be up to us—up to students—to lead the campaign. And it was going to be one of the biggest fights of our lives. It was amazing to have been at the signing with Obama. The White House gave us forty tickets to acknowledge the leadership of students in passing this bill."

What does it do?

"It's finally going to eliminate the middleperson in student lending. Lenders have been getting subsidies of up to $10 billion a year to provide loans that the Department of Education can do more efficiently. We're already hearing from students about the changes on their campuses. One of the biggest things people will notice: if you have a Pell grant, you'll see that figure increase. More people will be getting Pell grants. And there will be an increase in Perkins loans—the lowest interest loans. What people won't notice is that critical programs won't be cut from state budgets, especially at community colleges and minority-serving institutions. And folks who are graduating will be able to get some relief too in the form of greater loan forgiveness and better terms for repayment. Our state student associations have also been fighting budget cuts at the state level. California was able to organize a huge mobilization to fight for funding for the Cal grant, which was slated for elimination. Governor Schwarzenegger put it back in the budget along with some funding for education and acknowledged it was because of student organizing."

Billy Wimsatt

Generational Alliance team photo, 2007.

Who Are the Top 100 History-Changers of Our Generation?

I've never told anyone this before. It's going to sound f'd-up. Terrible. There has never been a Top 100 for activists. Maybe that's because we don't have our own magazine. Maybe because there are only about three people who would give a crap anyway. Maybe it's because we're not supposed to have egos and it would be considered bad form to rank people pound for pound on who is having the greatest impact in making the world a better place.

I understand why it's distasteful to rank activists. But I actually think it could be good to inspire healthy competition. Shit, there are annual rankings for every other damn thing. Why not have rankings for who is doing the best job of changing the world that year? Obviously it would be impossible to measure in an objective way. But you could look at criteria like: How many policies did you help change? How many people did you help elect? How many hearts and minds did you help shift? How many leaders did you develop? How much new money did you move? What did you contribute to alliance building, organizational infrastructure, the idea landscape, and a positive movement culture? What was the real impact and significance of each of these actions in the world? And what was your personal added value?

So here's the part I never told anyone. I do these rankings in my head for leaders of my generation. Not an exact ranking. But I generally want to know who's in the Top 10 or Top 100 for my generation. Back in the '90s, there was Julia Butterfly, the young woman who sat in a redwood tree for two years. There was Van Jones in the Bay Area doing his police and prison work. There was the Coup and Dead Prez, politicizing rap music. There was Ocean and Michele Robbins organizing the YES! Jams community. There was Jon Sellers and the Ruckus Society doing creative direct action.

There was Malika Sanders and 21st Century Youth Leadership Movement in Selma, Alabama. There was Eli Lee and the Albuquerque, New Mexico, crew. There was Erin Potts working with the Beastie Boys and Lhadon Tethong from Students for a Free Tibet. There was Taj James and Lisa Sullivan from the Black Student Leadership Network/LISTEN, Inc. crew. There was the United Students Against Sweatshops crew, the United States Student Association, and the SLAM crew from Hunter College. There was Alli Starr, David Taylor, and the direct action crew that organized to shut down the WTO in Seattle. There was the Indymedia.org crew that democratized media online. There was Blackout Films which made movement videos. There was Julia Cohen and Ryan Friedrichs from Youth Vote Coalition. There was Robin Templeton, Asha Bandele, and Marianne Manilov from the Center for Commercial-Free Public Education. And a whole bunch of other people and groups—literally hundreds—we profiled in the *Future 500*.

Some time around 2004–06, the bar for effectiveness in the movement was raised dramatically. Before 2004, there were very few effective young national movement leaders. So pretty much all you had to do was show up, run an innovative organization, and you were somewhere high in the ranking.

Around 2004 and 2005, the revolution in progressive technology-driven organizing increased effectiveness by a factor of one hundred and blew everything that came before it out of the water. Hands down, Eli Pariser from MoveOn was the single most effective young history-changer of the decade. MoveOn was the most effective organization of the decade, raising more than $100 million, helping swing hundreds of elections and policies, shaping the agenda of the Democratic Party, and pushing Barack Obama over the top in the primary. It also spawned, incubated, or inspired dozens of other efforts, including AVAAZ (the global version of MoveOn), the New Organizing Institute and RootsCamp (which trained a generation in technology-driven organizing), ColorofChange.org, Presente.org, and half a dozen national coalitions such as Win Without War and others. Its staff went on to start and run dozens of entities like the PCCC (Progressive Change Campaign Committee). And it set the standard for the entire field of online organizing, which was mimicked by the Obama campaign on down. Eli is a humble guy but he's probably had more positive impact in the world than any young social change leader since Martin Luther King Jr. Probably a controversial thing to say, and Eli is going to hate me for calling him out. But honestly, folks, who else has had an impact on remotely the same scale?

By 2008, most of the staff of MoveOn and AVAAZ were more effective than almost anyone else, not because they were inherently more capable but because they had found a better organizing model and operating system. Ditto for the Top 100 bloggers. Ditto for the Top 100 young political organizers on the Obama campaign. Ditto for the Top 100 climate and green jobs organizers. Ditto for a new generation of political appointees, elected leaders, and non-profit, social enterprise, and technology leaders. People in my generation were struggling to keep up with kids who had interned for us only a few years before.

In his book *Outliers: The Story of Success*, Malcolm Gladwell talks a lot about successful age cohorts. For example, the ideal time to be born to become a wealthy tech baron was within a few years of 1955. Vinod Khosla (Sun Microsystems), Steve Jobs (Apple), Eric Schmidt (Novell/Google), and of course Bill Gates were all born in 1955. Microsoft's other two bigwigs, Paul Allen and Steve Ballmer, were born in 1953 and 1956 respectively. What's so special about 1955? Universities started having computers around 1970 that were powerful enough for determined students to begin to access and play with them. If you were too old in the early 1970s, you graduated from college without access. If you were too young, you came along after the first big wave of computer companies had already been created.

Similarly, the best time to be born to become an effective twenty-first century political organizer was after 1977. People born in 1978 got to college around 1996, just as e-mail was becoming the norm on college campuses and activist groups were figuring out how to use it. When I went to college in the early '90s, we didn't have e-mail, and when it finally came along, it was really clunky. The ideal time to have been born as a twenty-first century political organizer was around 1980, the year Eli Pariser was born. Much of the new progressive movement leadership was born around the same time: Billy Parish, Jessy Tolkan, Ricken Patel, Heather Smith, Phaedra Ellis-Lamkins, Jackie Bray, Lenore Palladino, Anna Galland (half of the MoveOn staff actually), Molly Moon Neitzel, Hallie Montoya Tansey, and many, many more.

I would speculate that the cohort of people who are even younger are going to end up being even more effective. People born around 1984 or 1985 were graduating from college just as Barack Obama's primary election campaign was heating up. A couple hundred of them got the full experience of twelve to eighteen months on the campaign trail, and began early enough to establish some seniority on the campaign to land jobs in the Obama administration. This group of young leaders will enter their thirties as an extremely savvy and experienced group of young progressive insiders. They will be prepared to take major jobs in government, nonprofits, and the private sector, or to move back home and run for Congress with the backing of the most powerful progressive political network ever created.

Old-school heads from my age bracket are working to adapt to twenty-first century reality. We feel like Cutty and other members of Avon Barksdale's gang in *The Wire* who are forced to confront the superior strategy and organizational culture of Marlo Stansfield.

Part IV

We Elected Obama. Now What?

The Obamas and Hyde Park

In Chicago, especially in Hyde Park, everyone seems to have some sort of a personal connection to the Obamas. Last fall, I went to visit my friend Amanda who works at the Audy Home. It's in the same building as the juvenile court where I had to go when I was fourteen. On the train, I run into GQ, an old friend who has been rapping on the train lines in Chicago for the past fifteen years.

GQ puts me on the phone with Chris Golden, another old friend who is a hip-hop impresario and happens to work at a barbershop near my house. That afternoon, I stop by to see Chris and get my hair cut. Come to find out Chris works at Barack Obama's barbershop, and one of the other barbers there is friends with my old friend Kevin, from back in ninth and tenth grade. Kevin's mom used to work at the Baskin Robbins on 53rd Street where Barack and Michelle went on their first date and had their first kiss. Chris has a seven-year-old son now. We go to watch his son play basketball after school. He tells me about how he used to work for Michelle Obama at Public Allies and how Michelle was trying to convince him to apply to Stanford, but he decided to cut hair instead. He said that even after Obama was in the Senate, Michelle would write him e-mails telling him he needed to go to college.

Knowing the Obamas as neighborhood folks has given me a profound perspective on how people can go from ordinary good people to extraordinary world-changing people in a matter of years. The story of the Obamas is one of the greatest stories of our time. Barack Obama has written his own best-selling books about his journey. But it is easy to forget: this is a black man who admitted to doing cocaine in his autobiography. Chris remembers him in the '90s as Michelle's somewhat ordinary husband who struggled to quit smoking and didn't appear to be in any way her equal. My friend's brother went to high school with him in Hawaii as a teenager. He said: "No one would have believed that Barry Obama would go on to become president of the United States."

This was someone who one night slept outside on the streets of New York City. This is someone who went door to door in the projects, who spent time collecting petitions at a community college. Who started a youth organization in a high school on Chicago's South Side. Who witnessed a shooting on the streets of Hyde Park. Who built coalitions of low-income community groups and business owners to create economic development on the South Side.

It's incredible to think about a young black couple doing neighborhood-level work, and ten years later they're in the White House. My friend Ludovic Blain told me the story of how a small progressive foundation in New York, the Jewish Fund for Justice, gave Barack Obama a $5,000 grant back in the late 1980s for grassroots organizing with low-income residents. "That's part of why I respect this brother so much. He's stayed up late at night writing a grant proposal for $5,000 to organize poor families. He's been through everything we've been through and more. He's seen everything we have and more. He's read everything we've read and more. He's had all the same conversations we've had and more. He *is* us—but he's like us 4.0 or 5.0."

But What About When They Disappoint Us?

Ludovic has his own Barack Obama story: "In 1991, I was a student activist with NYPIRG (New York Public Interest Research Group), organizing students at City College of New York for environmental justice in Harlem. I remember one day I was speaking with some professors about how white the environmental movement was. They told me, 'Oh yeah, there was another black guy with NYPIRG about six years ago.'

"Turns out it was Barack Obama! He doesn't write about this in his book, but before he went to Chicago, his first organizing job was working for NYPIRG at City College in New York. Barack Obama had the same job I had six years before! And he was on the board of another organization I worked for. I'm telling you, Barack Obama is one of us. He's stood out on the street in the rain trying to sign people up. He's had the exact same conversations about strategy and power and race that we've had. And since his organizing days he's been in seven levels of conversations we haven't been in yet."

I try to keep all of this in mind when Obama does things I don't agree with. Why is he giving away all these handouts to oil and coal, insurance companies, Wall Street and military contractors? The reality is that no president—no matter how good or powerful they might be—is allowed to simply do what they think is right. Their actions must reflect the landscape of organized interest groups with power. Those interest groups still have way, way, way more power than we do.

How do we become more powerful? Simple: organize more people, move more money, change more hearts and minds, transform more industries and institutions, develop more leaders, invent better ideas, win more elections, and keep winning, year after year after year. It's just that simple. Just that hard.

As Van Jones says: "Hope is thinking: *I can lose twenty pounds.* Change is losing the twenty pounds and keeping off the weight. Going from despair to hope is a huge step. In some ways it's the most important step. But going from hope to change is one hundred times harder. So what's happening is that people got hope. They started to believe they could lose twenty pounds. But then it didn't happen on the first try and they got discouraged. And they lost hope. But the paradox is that you need the hope to stay motivated to do the long hard work to get the change. We need a new and deeper hope narrative. The lesson of 2009 is that hope is not just about electing one person. That's a good step, but it really has to be about all of us stepping up. We need Hope 2.0."

Tear Down the Leader

I realize it's kind of risky to stick up for the Obamas and hold them up as examples right now. As I complete this book in the summer of 2010, little more than one year into their first term, it has become fashionable in many circles to hate on the Obamas, or at least to be extremely skeptical and disillusioned with their leadership and the Democratic Party. So let me acknowledge that I get why people are upset and angry and disillusioned that the Obamas aren't governing in a more progressive way.

I too wish Obama had said: "Hey America, we're in an economic meltdown. We can't afford to send more troops to Afghanistan. BP, you're cleaning up every last drop of that oil or you'll never do business here again. ICE, you gots to chill. We're doubling the stimulus to get the economy going. Gay folks can get married. Period. Geithner and Summers, you had your chance. I'm bringing in Warren, Krugman, and Stiglitz. Senator Lieberman, if you so much as breathe the wrong way, I'm locking you in your room with no dinner until you behave."

It's a nice fantasy. There are a million things I would have liked to see resolved differently: immigration, health care, LGBT equality, climate crisis, economic justice. But at the end of the day, the idea that you and I are going to Monday-morning quarterback the Obamas is complete bullshit. We are not in their shoes.

I want to emphasize a distinction here. It is good, absolutely necessary in fact, to push Obama and the Democratic Party to be more progressive. But we need to have a grown-up understanding of how to play the game. Too often our thinking about politics is intellectually and emotionally immature. So we love Obama, then we hate him. We get starry-eyed with hope, then depressed and demoralized when he doesn't turn out to be a savior.

Look, I was never a hope person. I never had stars in my eyes about Obama. Everything he's doing is pretty much exactly what I expected. Change is a long-term game. The way you make real progress and change is the same way you raise a child or maintain a marriage: by patiently sticking with it for decades, enthusiastically celebrating every little victory, intensely supporting your people despite their shortcomings, and working hard to understand their experience so you can be a better partner. That is what is required to make deep transformative change. People want to have one-night stands with politicians or the political process, and wonder why they're not happy in the morning. It's because true change, like true love, requires steadfast commitment and realistic expectations.

But there's something else going on, something deep and dark and hard to talk about. It has to do with the way we treat our leaders. Yes, I said it. How *we* treat our leaders. Not how they treat us. How we treat them. We don't seem to grasp the concept of supporting them. We know how to criticize leaders. We know how to protest them. We know how to grumble and complain. But for some reason, supporting leaders doesn't come as easily to us. Why is that? Maybe we have a fear of leaders abusing power and becoming demagogues who oppress us. As a Jew I get that. Maybe we feel like we trusted them and they let us down. But come on! Do we really want to play the role of powerless victims? That's a little too easy. We have a dark side too.

What if it's jealousy? We feel powerless and less than. It makes us feel important to cut them down a notch. Maybe that's what makes us feel powerful. Or maybe it's our fear of power. Having real power and responsibility is scary. The responsibility of electing someone is a big deal, someone who we feel connected to, someone who is kind of similar to us. It raises our hopes and expectations and trust and fear in a deep, visceral way. Being part of a governing coalition is a hard job. It's scary. All the responsibility is on us.

Or maybe it's all of these reasons mixed together.

Ultimately, I don't know why. I'm not a psychologist. All I know is that supporting leaders is necessary to win. We depend on our leaders. They depend on us. And supporting them through hard times is something we're going to need to practice diligently if we want to make real change. True, there has to be reciprocity: our leaders need to support us too. It's a two-way street. And true, many of our leaders aren't good enough and need to be replaced. We need to make difficult choices and hold our leaders accountable. But that's not what's going on here. What's going on is an extremely good leadership team (about the best we were going to get) making difficult, honest choices in an extremely toxic political climate and the worst economy since the Great Depression. First and foremost, they need our support.

No one who isn't in the Obamas' inner circle truly understands the constraints they are facing. Joe Lieberman could declare himself a Republican at any moment. Same with Ben Nelson from Nebraska. He doesn't have to do shit for the Democratic leadership. What are they going to do? Find a more progressive Democrat to run against him in Nebraska? Yeah, right. For decades, progressive folks have abandoned places like Nebraska and clustered in big cities on the coasts. Now we're paying the price.

The medium-term solution over the next decade or two—as people of color inch toward majority status—is to organize our asses off and help Democrats win sixty-five or seventy votes in the Senate, with similar majorities in the House. That way we don't have to rely on the Joe Liebermans or Ben Nelsons. Then we can buy ourselves wiggle room to take a risk and primary them. And then a president like Obama can pass all the progressive legislation he or she wants. We might even have a prayer of passing real campaign finance reform and other systemic changes in Washington which would really begin to level the playing field. People think we can pass real campaign finance reform without a Democratic super-super-majority. I hope they're right, but personally I kind of doubt it.

So yes, it is important to push the Obamas to be better. But we have to walk two very fine lines: we need to make sure we're *expanding* their political space to create progressive change, not tearing them down, and we need to realize just how damn good they are under the circumstances.

I have no illusions about their shortcomings. And in part because of that, I am deeply inspired by who they actually are, what they have achieved so far, and how we can build on their progress. It's our job to learn from and support them, create more political space for them, and draw on their success so that our generation can do even better. No time to complain. We're up next, on deck, coming out of the dugout . . .

As this book goes to press, we are in a scary political moment. The right wing is organizing up a storm, exploiting the insecurity of the white working class, spreading vicious lies about Barack Obama. And inciting violence against Democrats in Congress. Republicans have been borrowing directly from our playbook, reading *Rules for Radicals* by Saul Alinsky, and have caught us totally flat-footed by combining our tactics with their talent for distortion and manipulation.

Posing as a prostitute in need of tax help, a right-wing prankster with a video camera took down ACORN, America's largest community organization, which has helped millions of poor and working-class people over the years. Republicans even snagged Ted Kennedy's Senate seat in Massachusetts. Politicians are running scared of the Fox News and right wing–manufactured Tea Party. And pollsters are predicting a bloodbath for Democrats in the fall. To make matters worse, the Supreme Court decided in *Citizens United* that what is left of our fragile democracy is officially for sale to the highest bidder: corporations can buy unlimited campaign ads to destroy their political opponents.

People are freaking out. There are so many lies and accusations flying around that even well-intentioned people are getting confused. Someone wrote this very telling comment on my blog recently: *People aren't stupid enough to vote for either Republicans or Democrats any longer. Witness the travesty of the recent Supreme Court decision allowing corporations to openly buy elections.*

Um . . . no.

 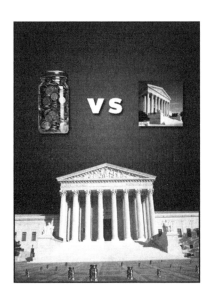

The Supreme Court's *Citizens United* ruling was a HORRIBLE decision. But it was a 5–4 decision split along partisan lines. The five Republican justices voted for the decision. The four Democratic justices voted against it and wrote a *blistering* dissent. The real lesson of *Citizens United* is that we need to stop Republicans from taking over the U.S. government and appointing right-wing extremists to the Supreme Court.

There has rarely been a more clear-cut case of the need to stop Republicans at all costs. If a few hundred more of us had voted Democrat in Florida back in

2000, Bush wouldn't have become president in the first place. Alito and Roberts wouldn't be on the Supreme Court. We would have a 6–3 majority on the Supreme Court *against* corporations buying elections.

A lot of our people don't have the basic facts so they draw the wrong lesson. It's not that electoral politics doesn't work. It's that you have to *win* and win and win and keep winning. You have to replace bad people with mediocre people. Then you have to replace mediocre people with good people. Then you have to replace good people with great people as the most diverse generation in history becomes a majority. It's a thirty-year plan.

Unity '09 Meets Confusion '09

After we elected Obama, our people became very confused. This was a very important historical moment. We had just elected the most progressive and intelligent president in at least forty years. And we elected him with a huge mandate, and with large Democratic majorities in the House (259–176) and Senate (58 Democrats, 40 Republicans, and 2 Independents). Historically, presidents are strongest when they are first elected. FDR passed the New Deal in his first hundred days in 1933. Also, historically, the president's party typically loses seats in the midterm election two years after they take office. Obama knew that once 2010 hit, it would be hard to pass strong progressive legislation because Congress would be campaigning. And after 2010, he might lose seats and never get another chance.

So Obama and his team were smart and tried to cram all his top legislative priorities (the economy, health care, energy, financial regulation, and workers rights) into 2009. They faced four big challenges: One, the Republicans went apeshit and threatened to filibuster anything Democrats tried to pass in the Senate. Two, Democrats didn't quite have the sixty votes needed to avoid filibusters. Three, the economy remained in a shambles. Four, the Democratic and progressive base decided to sit on the sidelines and throw up their hands while the Tea Party came in and ate their lunch.

This is a crucial moment in history to study if we ever want to create progressive change again in this country. We came so close. So close! We got 95 percent of the way there. We won halfway decent policies and rules. At any other time, we would've celebrated to the moon the things we won. But our expectations for Obama were so high, and we came so close to winning so much more, that for many people the whole effort felt like failure. It was not a failure by any stretch of the imagination. It is still the best progressive policy and administration in at least forty years. So it's important to understand what worked and where we dropped the ball.

First of all, we must grasp the nature of the political process and what a president can actually do.

Let's look at Obama's supporters in four categories: The first category were the passive Obama supporters. They thought the big fight, or at least their role in it, was over. They went back to watching TV and went on with their lives. These were the people who really didn't get it.

The second category got it a little bit more. They were the unrealistic Obama supporters. These were people who understood the fight had just begun, but had unrealistic expectations about who Obama was able to be as president and what he could accomplish with a highly mobilized right-wing base, and without sixty reliable votes in the Senate. They were upset that he escalated U.S. presence in Afghanistan (one of his campaign promises), and began turning off to the political process.

Then there was a third group of active and loyal Obama supporters, mobilized through Organizing for America's thirteen-million-person e-mail list. For those who missed it, after the 2008 election, the Obama for America presidential campaign transitioned into Organizing for America (OFA), which became a part of the DNC (Democratic National Committee). It was an unprecedented breakthrough to transition a presidential campaign into a permanent grassroots field and communications operation to push policy as well as elections. In 2009, they rebuilt their state field operation and advocated on issues like passing the president's budget, health care, and energy.

The process wasn't smooth. A lot of grassroots activists felt like they got dropped for several months after the election while OFA Part Two got up and running. And OFA was sometimes out of sync with its grassroots base because it had to exist within the political limitations of the DNC. But it was without question a huge step forward, and it did a lot to keep 2008 election volunteers engaged in the important 2009 and 2010 policy fights. It was extremely important to have so many grassroots supporters stick by the president's side, and continue to donate, door knock, and fight for health care and a mainstream progressive agenda, despite apathy on the left, attacks from the right, and the worst economy since the Great Depression.

OFA was joined by other large inside-the-beltway progressive, labor, and environmental groups, who dutifully pressed on in the most difficult time. They formed a new alliance called Unity '09. Unity '09 was supposed to be to policy what America Votes was to elections: a strategic hub for all the major progressive groups to coordinate their policy, communications, and field operations in key battleground states. At the table were big labor groups like the AFL-CIO, SEIU, and Working America, and big green groups like the Sierra Club and the League of Conservation Voters. As well as other usual suspects: U.S. Action, Center for Community Change, NAACP, Planned Parenthood, and National Council for La Raza.

After the election, I went to work at Green for All, whose main policy goal was to pass green-jobs legislation as part of the energy and climate bill—and to make sure it was beneficial to workers and included opportunities for low-income people. During the summer of 2009, I represented Green for All at the Unity '09 table. They held weekly meetings at a hotel in D.C. focused on each of the hot legislative issues: health care, climate and energy, immigration, etc.

The first challenge Unity '09 helped overcome was me-first-ism among the major progressive groups. Even before Obama and the new Congress were elected in 2008, they had received holiday wish lists from every progressive group under the sun about the legislation they wanted to see passed in the first one hundred days of 2009. Every group wanted their legislation to go first. But legislation takes a long time and it's messy. The reality was that most groups would have to wait their turn. Obama and congressional leadership would select the top priorities. And if we wanted to have any chance of passing anything, it was important for every group to get behind whatever happened first—we needed to establish a winning streak. To pass strong progressive legislation, you need to create momentum and confidence. If the first big bills didn't pass, the entire agenda might be dead in the water.

The second problem Unity '09 addressed was lack of coordination. They held weekly in-person meetings to coordinate state strategy for each issue in battleground states. Their sister group Progressive Media held 8:45 a.m. daily meetings to coordinate media strategy. A sister organization held weekly meetings to facilitate open dialogue between progressive groups and the Obama administration. Unity '09 also helped administer funds from major progressive donors to support needs of the table as a whole, and to address gaps in key states. They thought at first that they were going to have $20 million but they ended up with more like $5 million.

Unity '09 had its bumps and limitations, but overall it was a pretty impressive baby step forward for progressives. When Fox News found out about Unity '09, they brought Karl Rove on TV to try to make it all sound like a sinister left-wing plot.

While most of the large progressive groups in Unity '09 coordinated to support Obama's agenda, a growing number of groups began pushing the president and Congress to be more progressive—to "support AND strengthen" major legislation. MoveOn walked a fine line here. They played hardball with the administration. They fought valiantly for a public option on health care, and they refused to support the compromised climate and energy bill. In general, aside from MoveOn, the groups pushing for a more progressive approach like Greenpeace, Friends of the Earth, and the universal health care groups were not nearly as organized or effective as the insider groups. But they still had an important impact by counterbalancing the right-wing message. Although they were not always appreciated by the Obama administration and the more mainstream groups (who were afraid they would derail legislation from the left), they played a key role in keeping the legislation from being watered down and yanked even further to the right.

For many of us, the experience of Obama as president and a Democratic majority in Congress was a profoundly confusing one. Our whole lives, our entire experience of politics had been about stopping bad things. Our entire movement was based around fighting and critiquing people who were abusing power. Now, suddenly, we were part of the governing coalition of the world's greatest superpower. Now, suddenly, to some degree at least, we could actually exercise state power, turn good ideas into laws, and use the tools and resources of government to help people.

What a crazy idea! It was completely disorienting. Most of us were wholly unprepared for it. The main people who had experience were veterans of the Clinton administration like Rahm Emanuel and John Podesta, and they figured prominently into Obama's transition team and the new administration. Those of us who grew up on the oppositional and symbolic politics of the '80s and '90s were slow to adjust to the new reality of Internet-fueled practical politics of the twenty-first century. We were caught flat-footed and had no idea how to play a constructive role in this new political moment. As a movement, we needed to quickly shift gears and, as Van Jones had been saying for years, "move from opposition to proposition."

Unity '09 died a swift death. In 2010, its funding was cut and in a formal sense it went away. But it planted an important seed of an idea which will likely blossom again in a more twenty-first century form.

20th Century vs. 21st Century Organizations

I'm back in the barbershop getting my hair cut by my friend Chris. His seven-year-old son is wandering around the shop asking when he can get on a laptop to play video games.

"Go play on Facebook," Chris tells him.

"Your seven-year-old is on Facebook?"

"Yeah, his mother and I didn't help him. He went on there by himself, lied about his age. Made up a birthday! Now he's on Facebook, MySpace, and Twitter."

The younger generation, born in 1980 and after, is highly professionalized and tech-savvy. And they better be. Unemployment during the Great Depression topped out at 25 percent. Youth unemployment in April 2010 hit 27 percent overall, 41 percent for black youth, and much higher in the hardest-hit communities. Like never before, we need a movement to fight for jobs and opportunities. To build such a movement we need to create streamlined organizations that can survive in the twenty-first century. Let's look at the characteristics of these new organizations:

20th Century Organization	21st Century Organization
Tech phobic	Tech savvy
Old-media focused	New-media focused
Staff-intensive	Volunteer-intensive
Tries to do everything	Focused on best strengths
Competitive	Collaborative
Empire-driven	Partnership-driven
Big and prestigious	Small and effective
Grow grow grow	Leverage leverage leverage
Physical office	Virtual office
Slow slow slow	Fast fast fast
Focused on annual programs	Pivots focus in real time
Layers of management	Empowered teams
Paper-heavy	Paperless
Centralized strategy	Crowd-sourced strategy
One to many	Many to many
Opaque	Transparent
Charisma/personality-driven	Results/systems-driven
Directs the grassroots	Empowers the grassroots
Fights against problems	Changes the game

MoveOn is the prototype of a twenty-first century organization. They don't have an office. They have a tiny board of directors. They have twenty-five staff and they organize more members than the NRA, which has a staff of five hundred (five million members vs. four million). They don't do strategic planning (too slow—what's the point?). They have a budget above $10 million but they have never applied for a foundation grant. They don't have huge donors. In fact, because they are a PAC, they don't accept donations over $5,000. No one, not even the executive director, has a secretary or an assistant. Their overhead is practically zero. They don't have interns. They don't even have a mission statement! The most effective progressive political organization of the twenty-first century so far does not have a mission statement. I'll let you digest that one for a second.

In traditional thinking, one would imagine that an organization with that description would be extremely unaccountable. How can you be accountable without a mission? How can you be accountable without a large, representative board of directors to guide you? How can you have an accountable staff if there are no in-person staff meetings?

In fact, MoveOn is probably *more* accountable, at least to its membership, than any other major national organization. They are constantly monitoring and tracking member feedback, open rates, click-throughs, response rates, donation rates, and many other feedback loops. The entire orientation is based on anticipating, day-by-day, and even hour-by-hour, what its members most want and need from MoveOn, and then giving it to them very quickly.

MoveOn isn't the only organization moving in this direction. Nearly the entire social change movement is headed the same way. It's unclear exactly where this is all going. It's unclear exactly what nonprofit and advocacy organizations will look like in another ten, twenty, or fifty years. It's unclear what will become of twentieth century organizations that are unable or unwilling to adapt. And it's unclear how to build twenty-first century organizations to effectively organize and represent the most disenfranchised members of our communities.

One Million Mini-Obamas

How do we build a movement in the age of Obama? It's challenging because Obama sucked up a lot of the movement energy. But the movement he built was a relatively shallow, electorally driven one focused on electing a single person. When he got elected, the movement—although much bigger than anything that had been created before (bravo!)—was somehow not substantial or deep enough to keep people's hearts engaged. A lot of the drop-off was the natural cycle of ebb and flow. But also, after the election, there was no clearly compelling place for everyone to go. Some energy went into the administration. Some of it went to OFA. Some of it went into MoveOn local councils. Some of it went into a thousand other organizations and efforts. But a lot if it dissipated and didn't know where to go.

So what do we do now? What is our vision for the next ten to twenty years? Here is a provocative way to think about it: we need a million mini-Obamas.

To be specific, we need a million people who are willing to do their own version of what Barack and Michelle did.

What catapulted Barack Obama from a troubled adolescence to president of the United States in thirty years? How did Barack and Michelle go from being a community-oriented neighborhood couple in their thirties to running the country in ten years or less?

How did they do it?

I want to know because I believe to save this country and this world, we need millions of new leaders who are roughly in the mold of Barack and Michelle Obama. Each of us will look different. Not all of us are called to be politicians. Some of us will have ordinary-sounding names like Robert Baker or Laura Vazquez. Some of us will be teachers, professionals, farmers, nurses, computer programmers, social workers, or community organizers. But we all have an important role to play as leaders in this society. I'm not saying that the Obamas are perfect role models in every way. But they're the best damn nationally recognized role models we've had in my lifetime. It would behoove us to study them and learn from their example, whether or not we choose to follow it.

Nine Ingredients that Made Barack Obama

Let's focus on Barack for a moment, although in a parallel universe Michelle could have made just as great a president. What makes someone a Barack Obama? Let's break it down. Here are nine characteristics:

1) He was an ordinary kid.
2) Who had a bumpy childhood, with insecurities and weaknesses as well as gifts.
3) Who believed in himself and in other people.
4) Who read a lot of books, and asked a lot of questions.
5) Who was disciplined at work and school.
6) Who married his personal ambition with the public good.
7) Who built great partnerships.
8) Who embraced mainstream America.
9) Who got VERY lucky.

Now I have a question for you. Let's go through the list one by one. How many things on this list can you do? I bet you can do most of them. Do you believe in yourself and other people? Yes or no? Do you read a lot of books and ask a lot of questions? Yes or no? Are you disciplined at school and work? Well, could you become more disciplined? Could you read more books? Could you ask more questions? Could you believe in yourself a little more? *Well, can you?* The only thing on the list that you can't control is LUCK. Everything else is pretty much in your hands.

Most things on the list are pretty straightforward. Numbers 6, 7, and 8 are some of the trickier ones.

Marrying personal ambition to public good is pretty rare. Many people who are personally ambitious aren't focused on doing good. And many people who are doing good work aren't focused on being personally ambitious. These dynamics operate in tension with each other, so it's easy to fall off the rails in either direction.

Building partnerships is hard and takes years and years of practice. You have to be self-aware. You have to be aware of others. You have to keep things in perspective. You have to be mature enough to communicate and to hear, to see and be seen, to give and receive, to respect and expect respect, to ask for support and to support without being asked, to lead and be led, to love and be loved, to change and be changed. Partnership is a learning process with few road signs. For most adults it takes decades, longer if extensive healing is involved.

Embracing mainstream America! For many progressive, creative, urban people, people of color, gay folks, and anyone else who was teased in junior high, who was made to feel different, weird, wrong, ugly, less than, disliked— this is one of the most difficult. Learning to hate/fear the popular/normal kids, and by extension mainstream America, is a defense mechanism, and for many good, sensitive people, it is buried very deep.

But you can work that out over time.

So, I have a question: are you going to become Barack Obama 2.0?

Maybe you are! Yes, what if you are Barack Obama 2.0? What if Barack Obama is just like you and me, except he did the stuff on this list with a little bit more intensity. He got himself on an upward spiral, and *poof*, he went straight to the top. Is it possible you could do your own version of the same thing?

If you were suddenly made president tomorrow, imagine how disciplined you would become. Imagine how respectfully you would treat yourself and everyone you met. Imagine how you would prioritize your time. What if the whole world was depending on your every move, and every word you uttered was reported in the press? Imagine what a good and responsible person you would have to be all the time! Imagine how you would greet strangers on the street. Imagine how much you would have to know about and love the world and every single part of the United States. That's the part of being a politician

I actually think is cool. You are forced to interact with everyone you meet in a very real life-or-death way. Immigrants and cops. Landlords and evicted tenants. The uninsured patient and the HMO CEO. You are forced to hear all sides of a story. Forced to visit every neighborhood, suburb, small town, parade, and place of worship. It seems like the most amazing learning experience one could ever hope for.

Maybe you're not Obama 2.0. Maybe you're only 50 percent there. Maybe I'm only 10 percent. What if you could become 60 percent? What if I could become 20 percent? What if we could get ourselves on an upward spiral? What if we could take one more step, and another step, and another? Imagine if tens of thousands of us did it together. (There's of course only room for one president and 535 members of Congress at a time. And we don't want to get into power or ego battles with each other. Luckily, there are more than 500,000 elected leadership roles to fill in the U.S.—and those are just the elected ones.)

Imagine what we could change if millions of us, inspired by the Obamas' example (or inspired by whoever we're inspired by), stepped up just a little bit and took on greater leadership and responsibility. Imagine how profoundly we could transform this country.

To be specific, we need a million more people to follow some version of Michelle and Barack's four-part formula:

1) Lifetime commitment: Make a lifetime commitment to strategic change no matter what.
2) Go deep locally: In your own community, on your own block, in your own neighborhood, precinct, rural route, or apartment building.
3) Commit to learning: Humbly commit to being the best organizer, leader, and partner you can be.
4) Connect beyond local: Connect your local community work to the larger movement.

Picture Barack and Michelle following this formula on the South Side of Chicago twenty years ago. This is exactly what they did. Try this thought experiment: Picture yourself doing this in your community. Picture what this could look like in your everyday life.

Can you picture it?

Field 5.0: The Future of Organizing

Let's start out by defining our goal.

Let's say, for the sake of this book, that our goal is to have a sane country, run by sane people, making sane decisions (instead of an out-of-control country run by right-wing extremists and unaccountable corporations).

How do we get there?

Some people think our best silver bullet is to pass comprehensive campaign finance reform to get money out of politics and allow regular people who aren't ultrarich to run for office without being bought off by lobbyists. As silver bullets go, it's a pretty good shot—if we could only get Congress to pull the trigger.

But the truth is that the entrenched culture of corporate corruption is so deep and powerful that it is almost impossible to pass or maintain public financing laws unless you have one thing: a highly educated, organized, and motivated electorate.

How do you get a highly educated, organized, and motivated electorate?

There are three ways to do it, and we need all three:

1) Fix our education system.
2) Fix our media.
3) Build a mass movement.

Radically improving our education system would be a game-changer. It is also the most expensive strategy. It would probably cost hundreds of billions of dollars and multiple decades to have a major effect. Yet we absolutely must do it. We need to do it. The problem is that we almost certainly will never do it until we fix the other two pieces. As it stands now, a majority of American voters don't want to pay to educate "other people's kids."

The second way to develop a more informed and engaged electorate is through a major national TV network like Fox. Or you need a national radio network like Premiere (which carries Glenn Beck and Rush Limbaugh). And you need a crew of progressive talk show hosts who are as talented and popular as Limbaugh, Beck, and company. Otherwise, anything good you try to do—expanding health care, saving the economy, creating green jobs, fixing immigration, you name it—will be overpowered by the right-wing noise machine: *Conspiracy! Conspiracy! Liberal elites! Socialism!* Air America tried but didn't have enough money, and they had a lot of internal challenges so they eventually went under. This is probably the simplest strategy. It's a no-brainer. If I were a billionaire, I'd create it in a heartbeat. But billionaire I am not.

That leaves only one strategy: building a movement.

And that's where the million mini-Obamas come in. But what would we do with those million mini-Obamas even if we had them?

And why one million? That's the minimum number of organizers we would need (spread out across every neighborhood, town, and precinct), to have at least a semipersonal relationship with every single person in the United States (300-to-1 ratio).

Obviously, it would be nice if we could have *three* million organizers who only have to know one hundred people each. Or six million organizers who only have to know fifty. But one step at a time.

If we could build and sustain a million-person organizing team, in every precinct in the United States, it would be truly game-changing.

It would be the movement-building moon shot of our era.

If we could succeed at creating an integrated national movement that had a permanent local field presence in all 300,000 precincts in the United States, we could alter the political life of our nation, permanently, deeply, profoundly. On every key issue. In every election.

How do we build a unified progressive movement that operates in sync at the local level in every precinct in America?

Organizing for America is sort of trying to do it as a political party. MoveOn, the only other organization that could even come close, is gradually moving in that direction, but they haven't stated this as a goal and in any case they'd have a long way to go. 1Sky has a stated goal of doing it for the climate movement—by having a climate precinct captain in all 300,000 precincts. A bold and inspiring vision. But it has an extremely long way to go. The local foods movement is organizing people to get involved in community gardens and food justice. There are hundreds of twentieth century–style community organizations that have density in particular communities. But they all have slightly different organizing models and they tend to be pretty territorial.

So there are bits and pieces of a precinct-based field strategy. But they are fragmented, have different tax statuses, and are often in some level of competition with one another.

What we eventually need is simple: progressive neighborhood or precinct-level organizations in every community that perform the following five functions:

1) Bring together progressive-minded people of all ages, races, and cultures to form a beloved community at the local level.
2) Work on local, state, and federal issues together.
3) Mobilize around elections.
4) Raise money locally.
5) Coordinate with one another.

This is a humongous idea. It's not quite on the scale of creating the Internet, or creating a space program that puts people on the moon. But it's definitely up there. Achieving it would require the entire progressive community to come together on an unprecedented scale toward a shared goal: to recruit, train, and support one million volunteer organizers. (And by the way, they would need to be volunteers. To pay them all a salary would cost $40 billion a year—that's how big this thing is.) Can you picture this? Is it exciting? Do you have your 3-D glasses on yet?

We have most of the ingredients right now to make it happen. We just haven't connected the dots yet. We have progressive organizations with lists of people in every neighborhood, precinct, and probably most major rural routes in America. We have Internet tools to connect us. We have shared values for the most part. We have activities for local groups to do. A decent percentage of us are already connected to each other through existing organizations and social networks. We have combined e-mail lists of more than fifty million people who might be interested.

It is physically and theoretically possible to create this type of field organization. But at the current moment, we have not yet figured out a way to make it structurally and socially possible. The main challenges are structure, management, coordination, and trust.

How to overcome those?

Movement Sci-Fi: Anything that Can Happen Probably Will

Now take a deep breath. Go back in time ten years and try to remember the progressive movement before we had all this stuff. Up until about 2003, the progressive movement did not really appear to have a brain.

Today, the progressive movement does have a brain. But it's sort of like the brain of an emotionally disturbed child. We need the progressive movement to have the brain of a mature, highly-experienced, and strategic grown-up.

Slowly, we are putting the pieces in place to build a coordinated and integrated progressive movement to scale. Slowly, we're putting together the ingredients: the vision, the values, national and local community, national and local leadership, the issues, the coordination, the infrastructure, the money, the communication, the distribution channels, the critical mass of people, and the potential to create a governing majority.

We'll get there.

When we created the League of Young Voters, our original tagline was, "A progressive governing majority in our lifetime." When we came up with this idea back in 2003, it seemed extremely farfetched. Republicans controlled all three chambers of government, including 5–4 control of the Supreme Court, and they had wind in their sails. They were systematically kicking the legs out from under the Democratic Party: destroying the labor unions, defunding the trial lawyers, controlling the money from lobbyists, peeling off blacks, Jews, Latinos, and killing us in the media.

It was truly a stretch of the imagination to think of a progressive governing majority in our lifetime.

Five years later, on election night 2008, as we stood at the victory party in Columbus, Ohio, our eyes glued to CNN, watching the results come in, Biko, the new head of the League, sent me a text message: *progressive governing majority in our lifetime.*

It was surreal to see those words flash across my phone. As we soon learned, we had not actually achieved a *progressive* governing majority. We had come a few Senate votes short of a Democratic governing majority. Not all Democrats were progressive and five to fifteen of those Democratic Senators (as well as thirty to forty House Democrats) were weak-kneed when it came to tough votes to support President Obama on climate, health care, and economic justice.

But at least it gave us a taste of what is possible over the coming decades if we play our cards right. As Marianne Manilov from Engage Network says: "Organizing is like media. The old model of media was broadcast, one to many. The new model is many to many. With organizing, the old model was one to many. And there's no reason why organizing won't go the same way as media, to a more decentralized user-driven model."

MoveOn revolutionized advocacy and fundraising by making it possible for users to contribute twenty-five dollars to help pay to run a specific ad in a specific newspaper or media market. This is only the beginning.

The advances with data alone are staggering. Imagine what our data and handheld devices will look like in another ten years. Our handheld devices will be so hot, they'll make today's iPhones look like play toys. Imagine the way our handheld devices will integrate voter data with consumer data, opinion data, volunteer data, donor data, barcode scanning, Google Earth, and Facebook profiles on the spot. It's kinda scary how little privacy any of us will have—but it will make the technical side of organizing unbelievably cheap and easy.

Think of the advances in microtargeting via online social networks. Think of the advances in behavioral marketing and profile modeling. Privacy is dead. Everything we do online will be used to build a profile of us that can be used to communicate with us in a customized way. Who needs the FBI anymore?

In a few years, a canvasser coming to my door will know everything about me before she even knocks.

Brian Komar at the Center for American Progress explains: "It isn't a matter of whether all of these incredible advances are going to happen. It's a matter of how we maximize the opportunity, and who is going to get there first, our side or the right wing."

Take the advances in data, handhelds, microtargeting, and social networking; advances in organizational coordination and infrastructure. Put it all together in your brain.

Presto. What do you get?

A whole new way to do politics. Much more powerfully. For a lot less money.

It's probably going to happen one way or another. I went to Brazil in 2003 for the World Social Forum. Someone took me to a café and ordered me an acai smoothie. I had never heard of acai before. It was like nothing I'd ever tasted. A black-purple fruit—intense, tart, sweet, and addictive, like blueberries on crack—straight from the Brazilian rainforest. And it cost a buck! I was hooked. I literally drank five acai smoothies a day while I was there. I hadn't been back in the U.S. a month when I passed a smoothie stand, and holy shit. They're selling acai. It was watered down, but still delicious. Smart idea, I thought, to bring acai to the States. Next thing I know, in a matter of two years, acai is everywhere. Every product in the store, you can buy a version now with acai. Acai water. Acai ice cream. Acai candy. Acai trail mix. Acai with mango. Acai cereal. Acai powder. Acai pills. On and on. Our cracked-out capitalist society works like that. Anything good or cool or interesting from any corner of the globe is now for sale in supermarkets. Any good name you can think of, someone else already bought the website or is about to buy it tomorrow. Have a good idea? Tomorrow it will appear in an advertising campaign. Next week there will be a reality show about it. The following year a car is named after it. And the year after that it will have its own cable network.

Then twenty years in the future, some "visionary risk taker" in the philanthropic community will have a breakthrough and realize it's probably something they should be funding, but not until after they convene a gathering to discuss it, hire a consultant to study it, prepare a white paper on the topic, and then have a series of meetings to get approval from the board.

I'm only teasing, foundation execs! Even the foundation world is speeding up, and Twittering its way into the twenty-first century. Everything is moving faster and faster. We are rapidly moving from the twenty-four-hour news cycle to the one-hour news cycle.

As coordination and movement consciousness builds, the division of labor between organizations will grow clearer. Organizations may take on more specific roles.

Right now, everyone is trying to do everything and it's inefficient. Everyone is trying to build and maintain an e-mail list. Everyone needs their own operations and administrative back end. Every group needs to organize its own conference. Every group needs a communications person and a website. Every group needs a fundraising arm. And needs to write proposals to foundations, and needs a human resources person. It's a vibrant marketplace. But it's messy and inefficient too.

Over time, these inefficiencies will tend to get ironed out because donors won't want to pay for them. Groups that become more efficient and effective and tell their stories better will tend to outperform other groups and attract more people and resources.

In the future, online social networks will become interoperable. It will just be your identity which lives online, and you will keep all your photo albums there and your friends and contacts and your calendar and blogs and videos and whatever else. People will be tagged as friend, professional, public, or blocked, and will have different levels of privacy access. The progressive movement will exist as a souped-up version of a community. Though it will probably not be called the "progressive movement." It will probably be a subset of Google or Facebook or Switchboard or GooGoo or Spaceship or who knows what. Or maybe it will be its own thing. Or multiple overlapping things. But it will live online and be reflected in the real world.

There will be a set of values, a vision, and an issues platform. There will be national and local issue campaigns that you can participate in online. There will be local "communities" which will connect to your online social networks. The online communities, neighborhoods, and campaigns will connect to real world counterparts. Most big progressive funders will be behind it and do their funding through it, because it will be more efficient and will track the results of the money automatically.

People will do a lot of voting. Vote for your favorite issue. Vote for your favorite message. Vote for your favorite tactic. Vote for your favorite leader. The votes will lead to money. And the money will pay for work that people want to see get done.

So, for instance, if you live near Houston and you are pissed off about a nearby oil spill in the Gulf of Mexico, you might go online to GooGoo. And among a menu of action options, you may choose to donate money to pay someone who has been vetted through the site to knock on doors of your neighbors in a key congressional district to ask them to write letters to their congressperson. One local organizer might offer to knock on five hundred doors for $3,000. Another will offer to do it for $2,500. You will read their online client reviews and click a button to donate $50 to your favorite one.

Eli Pariser of MoveOn came up with a name for these types of scenarios: "Organizing Sci-Fi." Or Movement Sci-Fi.

Technology has the potential to flatten the playing field.

It can make regular people with time and/or money as powerful politically as executive directors or ward bosses.

When you click on an issue, a map will pop up and tell you where each representative stands on it, and how many votes you are away from winning or losing. Then you will be prompted to take action to call, donate, organize, or participate in an action to impact that issue.

This all sounds great. Except for one thing. As in all great science fiction novels, there are the good guys and the bad guys. We will not be the only ones constantly upgrading our strategies.

The right wing and industry groups will spend billions of dollars manipulating the system, and running fake grassroots campaigns that look like they're coming from real people.

Our job? Out-organize them.

The Progressive Cluster Problem

One of our biggest structural problems is that progressive-minded people like to leave the small towns and suburbs where they're from and move to the big city where they tend to become politically impotent. This dilemma of progressive clustering cannot be underestimated. I speak with a glass house here as someone who owns an apartment in Brooklyn. If we could somehow blow up (nonviolently of course) the biggest progressive cluster cities (New York, Philly, Boston, D.C., Chicago, L.A., Miami, Atlanta, Houston, and the San Francisco Bay Area) and scatter the roughly thirty million inhabitants at random across the country, our overall politics would probably end up much improved. (Yes, New York and California would no longer be solid blue states, but suddenly Wyoming, Alabama, Idaho, Utah, Alaska, and many other states and districts would be in play.)

The problem is several-fold: Progressive flight leaves small towns and suburban communities politically unbalanced. Meanwhile, big-city progressives become complacent, politically irrelevant, out of touch, and often bigoted toward mainstream America. When they do get involved locally, they end up competing against each other. A recent city council race in Brooklyn pitted five pretty decent progressive candidates against each other. It became a huge fight. What a waste! What a shame! Imagine how much better off we would be if four of them had decided to build their political careers somewhere else. And what will the four losing candidates do now that they lost the election? Probably become discouraged.

As actor Danny Hoch says at the end of his show *Taking Over*: "Stop moving to New York. Stop moving to Brooklyn. Stop moving to Williamsburg. Go back to Iowa. Go back to Ohio and Michigan and Wisconsin. Wherever you're from . . . GO HOME!"

Three of my heroes who went home are Jane Fleming Kleeb, Tom Perriello, and Zack Exley.

Jane used to run the Young Democrats of America. She had a high-prestige job in Washington, D.C. She was on Fox News all the time. She left to move to Nebraska, one of the reddest states in the country. And she didn't move to Omaha (the big city) or Lincoln (the college town). She moved to a small town in the rural western part of the state. She fell in love with a cowboy named Scott Kleeb. They have two daughters and she's running for school board.

I met Tom Perriello at a house party in Brooklyn at the home of author and food justice advocate Anna Lappé. Tom was living in New York and working for AVAAZ, the global online network. He was originally from Charlottesville, Virginia, and he had an idea to move back there and run for Congress in a district that had been controlled for decades by a horrible Republican. In 2008, he ran a brilliant campaign and ended up winning by 745 votes. He is one of the Republicans' top ten battles in 2010, and he was even the target of an assassination attempt by right-wing crazies who tried to sever his gas lines but cut his brother's instead. Whether or not he holds his seat in 2010, Tom Perriello is a hero. He was one of the key votes to pass health care, student aid, and energy legislation in 2009.

Zack Exley's claim to fame was that in 1999 he bought the website GWBush.com and published the first online parody of a political campaign. George Bush called him a "garbage man," and even said, "There ought to be limits to freedom," when explaining to a reporter why his campaign was trying to shut down Zack's site. In 2002, he joined the staff of MoveOn, helped the Dean campaign with Internet activities, and then in 2004 got hired to do online work for Kerry-Edwards. After the election, Zack and Judith Freeman (who was a badass computer nerd and a political analyst at the AFL-CIO) and a team of others got the idea to create an institute to teach new online organizing principles. This became the New Organizing Institute, which has trained a generation in twenty-first century organizing, run by Judith. Meanwhile, Zack got interested in church-based organizing and he and his wife moved to her hometown of Kansas City, Missouri, where he is making common cause with radical Christians and runs a blog called Revolution in Jesusland.

If we truly want to transform this country, we need tens of thousands more like these three heroes to leave their hip enclaves in New York, D.C., Chicago, and the Bay Area, and move back to what Sarah Palin calls "The Real America."

Outside Game, Inside Game

> *"The more radical you want to be, the nicer the suit you have to wear,*
> *and the more credentials you have to have . . . if you want to be effective."*
> —Patricia Bauman

Obama's election really messed with my worldview. My whole life, I saw myself as fighting an evil or at least misguided and uncaring system. I saw Democrats, if I thought of them at all, as mostly incompetent sellouts. My heroes were people like James Baldwin, Noam Chomsky, bell hooks, Molly Ivins, Studs Terkel, KRS-One, Malcolm X, Alice Walker, Maya Angelou, and Howard Zinn.

But wait a minute. It didn't occur to me that most of the people I admired, at the end of the day, were writers, intellectuals, and social critics. None of them actually ran anything large-scale. None of them were actually responsible for conducting any type of organized institutional change. None of them ran a major organization or held public office (with the partial exception of Malcolm X, who, after a leadership role in the Nation of Islam, went on to found Muslim Mosque, Inc., and the Organization of Afro-American Unity. Tellingly, neither organization survived for long after his assassination.). As far as I know, almost none of my major role models growing up were responsible for managing a staff, developing sophisticated campaign strategy, facilitating a group process, building an organizational system, managing a budget, meeting payroll, winning an election, or getting a piece of legislation passed.

This was a startling discovery. No wonder I had no clue how to get anything done!

Careerwise, a lot of my peers were passing me up. Kids who didn't seem especially remarkable in high school and college were working their way up the career ladder to journalistic dream jobs at the *New York Times* and NPR. Other classmates were pulling down six figures from law firms and investment banks, buying houses and starting families with people they met in law school. I was like: *Whoa, I'm getting left in the dust here*. Maybe I had peaked too early. Maybe I had marginalized myself from mainstream success. Maybe I had put too much faith in the fanciful idea of building a political movement, and I was destined to spend the rest of my life feeling like a has-been.

The truth is that I don't know what is the best path for me. Or even what options will be open to me after two decades of grassroots political work. I would like to think I can still use moxy and smart moves to break through into positions of power and influence. Van Jones provided a model of how someone could rise from grassroots power to national political power, even if his stint in government only lasted six months. Who knows what will happen to me? It may be that, at the end of the day, my most effective role is outside the formal structures of power. And it may turn out that my colorful past will prevent me from ever being able to hold major institutional power.

That's why *you* need to go inside if you have the opportunity to do so. Get your inside experience. Make friends and connections in there. Learn how the machine works. Get your credentials and credibility. And keep the lines of communication open with your allies outside the gates.

It Takes Two Wings to Fly a Plane

When I was in college, I made a point to read the *National Review, Commentary, Reason,* and the *American Spectator.* Conservative thinkers make a lot of good critical points, even if I ultimately disagree with many of their moral foundations and ultimate conclusions. I have always been interested in how to reconcile opposing ideologies, how to get past the rhetoric and find common-ground solutions. And I'm interested in reclaiming language like "life" and "conservative," which I instinctively relate to. In high school, I wrote a paper about the prochoice and pro-life movements finding common ground. In the paper, I wrote that I was pro-life, meaning that I care about human life, all life really. At some point in my midtwenties, I got challenged on my political beliefs by my friend Kim, a journalist in Chicago. She said: "You don't want to identify yourself as a progressive, but that's what you are."

I told her that I actually don't consider myself a progressive because I agree with good ideas and critiques from across the political spectrum and it takes two wings to fly a plane. Why oversimplify and marginalize yourself by saying you're a progressive, when really the world is more complicated?

"Okay," she said, "but let me ask you some questions . . ."

"Okay . . ."

"Do you believe everyone should be able to have health care?"

I could see where this was going. "Yes," I said.

"Do you believe we should spend more money on education and less on prisons and war?"

"Yes," I said.

"Do you believe workers should have the right to organize a union and make a living wage?"

"Yes."

"Do you believe the government needs to protect the environment?"

"Yes!!! Kim, I get it."

"Okay, well, then you're basically a progressive, whether you want to call yourself that or not. And whether you like it or not, there are two teams in this world. One team is for the stuff you believe in. The other team is against the stuff you believe in. And it's important to know which team you're on, who else is on your team, and who is not on your team. By not taking a side, you're standing on the fifty-yard line saying: 'I'm not going to get in the game.' But the game is going to happen with or without you. And if enough people on our side are like you and they don't want to be honest about where they stand and get in the game, then our side is going to keep on losing."

You gotta pick a team and be honest about what you believe in.

So, I picked my team. I'm happy to be on the team. I like teams. I like sports. I like competition. I like winning. But it doesn't mean I have to agree with everything people on my team do. Some progressive folks, especially in coastal cities and college towns, can be elitist assholes. It's NOT OKAY to look down on people. It's NOT OKAY to call people rednecks or trailer trash, or to hate on people's religion, like, "Oh those evangelicals, oh those people in the middle of the country." That's not progressive. That's being an elitist asshole. That's straight-up bigotry and hateration, and progressives of all people should know better. It's bad morally. It's bad politically. And it makes my blood boil.

To this day, I still do not deeply identify with the term *progressive* (despite its prevalence in this book). I still *do* identify with the term *conservative*. I would rather change the game than be a player. But I also recognize that it's easier to change the game after you helped your team win the pennant than it is to sit in the bleachers while your team loses and try to convince people not to eat the popcorn.

PTMD: Post-traumatic Movement Disorder

Do you have PTMD?

No, not PTSD. No, not EPMD.

PTMD: Post-traumatic Movement Disorder.

The biggest problem in movement-building isn't recruitment. It's retention. People have f'd-up experiences and then they leave.

What happens is you get involved in a movement or an organization through your friend. Then you have a fight with your friend. She sleeps with your boyfriend. And you're hurt and angry. What a hypocrite! How could she? She likes to talk all this crap about changing the world. Then she goes and stabs you in the back. It's f'd up. It's awkward, so you leave. You never want to see her again. Ever. So you never come back. You say, *Peace out, you stupid movement!* We lose you forever.

Or you get into a power struggle. Or someone disrespects you or hurts your feelings. Or you run into bad leadership. Or someone just has issues. Issues! People have their own personal issues and they try to deal with them through their work and community in the movement. People say hurtful things. People do hurtful things. And then everybody gets burned out and no one wants to be part of the movement anymore.

I understand. I sympathize. I've been through it all before. I have personally experienced just about every movement trauma imaginable at least sixty-five times.

So yeah. The movement can suck sometimes.

What keeps me coming back? Well, first of all, every community we are part of can be traumatic. If you're in the military. If you hang out with doctors or lawyers. Academia. The corporate world. Government. The arts and show business. Retail. Farming. Real estate. Finance. Tourism. Pretty much, it's pick your poison. Any sector of life you choose to operate in, you're going to be surrounded by people with issues—emotional issues, chemical issues, addiction issues. Everywhere you go, people are going to lie, cheat, steal, undermine you, hurt your feelings, and stab you in the back. We've all experienced it. It's not unique to movements for social change.

The difference is that we expect better. The movement is a place where issues get dealt with explicitly. We have a lot of very passionate people with a lot of anger and hurt who are fighting for change in the world. But changing the world is hard. Many people in social change organizations don't have adequate tools. So we end up turning our anger and passion for change on the one arena we can easily affect personally: each other. Our colleagues, our organizations, and ally organizations in the movement often end up as the focus for our critical energies. We tear each other down, like crabs in a bucket, like kids in the hood, like family. If we're not extremely careful, the people we love most end up as the objects of our misplaced anger.

There is no simple solution to movement trauma. Here are three baby steps in the right direction:

1) Each person is responsible for maintaining respect and professional

boundaries at work. Work is a place to focus on shared goals, not on playing out intense personal dynamics.

2) Each person is responsible for developing basic emotional intelligence, maturity, personal, professional, and partnership skills outside of work.

3) There should be entities set up to support people and organizations throughout this process, to mediate conflicts, and to help people heal from trauma.

Power Isn't Just People and Money, It's Ideas

Traditionally, when community organizers talk about power, they only talk about two forms: money and people. How much money and how many people can you move? Seldom mentioned is the power of ideas. Van Jones helped me see that ideas can hold just as great, if not greater, power in the paper-scissors-rock equation than money or people. If you can change the ideas landscape, you change the game. This is what Van did with green jobs.

People had been working on green jobs for decades before he came along. People like my man Ken Dunn from Chicago have been doing it since the 1970s. Anyone who hauls your recycling or insulates your home is doing a green job. But no one ever called it that. No one ever named it and framed it and packaged it and created a compelling brand and narrative around it. Or if they did, no one cared. Until Van Jones got his brains on it.

One of my favorite stories about Van was in the *New Yorker*. Van was a young hotshot lawyer who would sue the city to deal with incidents involving bad-apple cops. The more he did that, the more he saw they were part of a larger system, the prison-industrial complex. So he and his organization, the Ella Baker Center, focused on changing the prison system. They won a few fights to close prisons and jails or keep them from being built. Over time, he started asking questions: *Where are the jobs? What jobs can a person get when they're coming out of prison?*

At the same time, he became friends with Julia Butterfly (the woman who sat in a redwood tree for two years) and he began learning about the environmental crisis. He attended Social Venture Network conferences and met socially responsible business people like Gary Hirshberg from Stonyfield Farm and Amy Domini from Domini Investment Fund. He started connecting the dots.

These people over here need jobs, but all the old manufacturing jobs are going away. These people over here are trying to create new green jobs. Aha!

So he created a division of Ella Baker Center called "Reclaim the Future," which was all about finding a way to create good green jobs and get people coming out of prison trained to fill them. He spun his wheels for a few years trying to create green jobs in Oakland. It didn't work. He was ahead of his time and people liked his ideas, but creating jobs is a whole other matter.

Finally he had a breakthrough. He went to a meeting of a bunch of local groups with House Speaker Nancy Pelosi. He only had a few seconds to make his words count. So he nailed it: "Four words and you'll have a Democratic majority for the next twenty years," he said.

"What are the four words?" Pelosi asked.

"Clean Energy Jobs Bill."

She introduced the bill. It was called the Green Jobs Act. It passed the House and Senate and was signed into law by President Bush in 2007. This was the first time anyone I know of from our generation thought up an idea, turned it into a bill, had it passed by Congress and signed by the president of the United States. That, in and of itself, was a big deal. And it forced many of us to learn about the legislative process. Just because a bill passes, and it says that $125 million from the budget is going to be *allocated*, that doesn't actually mean anything. The money still has to be *appropriated* through the budget process. So the president signed the bill, everyone celebrated, and then nothing happened for two years.

Finally, in 2009, $500 million for the Green Jobs Act was included in the Recovery Act. Then it took several months for the Department of Labor to implement the program and get the money out to local groups to create jobs.

In the meantime, Van founded an organization, Green for All, and went to work in the Obama administration as a special advisor on green jobs, until right-wing talk show host Glenn Beck became obsessed with pressuring him to resign.

I worked for Van in his last two months at Green for All, to help with the transition, fundraising, and whatever needed to be done to support the new person who would take his place. The new person was Phaedra Ellis-Lamkins. Phaedra is every bit as brilliant as Van—and several years younger. Everyone assumed it would be impossible to fill Van's shoes, but Phaedra quickly proved them wrong.

From a very young age, Phaedra understood the power of ideas. She grew up working class, with a single mom, and had to move all over California as a child. When she was nineteen years old, she and her friends decided they were going to change the government in her hometown, San Jose. Silicon Valley was generating a lot of money, but regular working people didn't get paid enough. And kids didn't have health insurance. So they went to the San Jose city council and proposed their policies: health insurance for kids and a living wage for workers. People told them they were crazy. They were still teenagers. They didn't have any political power. Who the hell did they think they were?

But the naysayers didn't know who they were messing with. Phaedra and her friends wouldn't give up. Through sheer force of will, and willingness to learn, they pressed on and grew more sophisticated. They created an official-sounding organization called Working Partnerships, built relationships with labor unions, and mobilized voters for city council elections. Over the course of five years, they passed the first local child health insurance law in the country. They raised the living wage twice. And they passed an innovative law called a "community benefits agreement," one of the first in the country, which guaranteed that big development projects had to hire local workers and pay a living wage. At the age of twenty-five, she was asked by a bunch of fifty- and sixty-year-old white guys to run the San Jose Labor Council (an alliance of all the local labor unions). She built the strongest independent political organization in San Jose, and simultaneously cofounded a national organization, Working Partnerships USA, a network of community-labor alliances across the country.

When Phaedra came to Green for All, she brought deep experience on how to move industries, local and state leaders, labor unions, private investors, and government agencies. Where Van had focused on passing federal legislation and inspiring the grassroots, Phaedra added an industry-by-industry analysis. What were all the industries that could develop green jobs? Sure, solar and wind power and weatherization are good. But what about waste management? What about manufacturing? What about services? She immediately started hiring talented people from all over the country. And in less than a year, she took the organization to a whole new level.

The power of ideas! And big, established visionary leaders shouldn't be the only ones who get to have them. My colleague Jidan Koon at Movement Strategy Center came up with the idea of "Dream Tanks"—like a think tank, but for visioning: creating spaces for ordinary people to come up with new ideas to change the world.

The Power of Alliances

> *"Can you count? The future is ours if you can count."*
> —Cyrus, *The Warriors*

When Billy Parish was a student at Yale, he and his friends started a regional student environmental network.

"It didn't work," he says. "Our group, Eco Northeast, was just another student environmental network in an already splintered environment. The lesson we learned very quickly was that what was needed was not a new group. It was alliance-building between groups that were already out there. The climate crisis is SO big, we needed to think outside of ourselves and build something bigger and more powerful than any of us could have imagined on our own." So they started the Energy Action Coalition. "We were intentional in building a coalition that was as broad as possible—from tribal groups to historically black colleges to evangelical Christians. We created a culture around being part of a movement, not just an organization."

They began organizing joint national days of action. Over time, Energy Action built so much synergy and trust that they began applying for money together and established an unprecedented new mechanism in coalition-building: a collaborative budgeting and joint fundraising process that included eighteen groups making budgeting decisions by consensus.

Un. Heard. Of.

"Working across race, class, and organizational competition, to do consensus-based budgeting and fundraising—sure, we had some difficult meetings," Billy laughs. "But it forced us to develop as leaders. We probably ended up raising two or three times as much money together as we could have raised on our own. And we were way more effective!"

After four years, Billy passed the leadership torch on to Jessy Tolkan, who took the organization and ran with it. Jessy is a force of nature. She grew up in Milwaukee and her father is a car dealer. She survived cancer. She is the only person to date who has worked for USSA, the PIRGs, *and* Young Democrats of America. She grew up in the youth voting and student organizing world. She is a moral force to be reckoned with.

Jessy used her superpowers of big strategic thinking to organize Power Shift. In 2007, they brought together six thousand young people at the University of Maryland, and got half of them to skip school and lobby the next day at the Capitol in D.C. They made history twice over with the biggest youth lobby day ever on any issue, and the biggest lobby day ever on climate and green jobs by people of any age group.

And then they did it again in 2009. Twelve thousand students. The biggest youth lobby day in history. The biggest climate lobby day in history. Again.

I went to their first lobby day. I watched in awe as their Wellstone Action trainers worked with three thousand people, who spread out around the legislative office buildings to lobby in small groups with green hard hats, carrying a powerful new message: *It's not just about the environment, it's about creating well-paying jobs in your district.*

Energy Action Coalition doesn't get the credit it deserves. To me, it is the most exciting new model and organizing effort that has been built in at least five years. To me, they get the model exactly right: bring together an entire field; include unlikely suspects; fundraise collaboratively; work on federal and local policy during a legislative session; show their power through joint lobby days. During election time, they run a program called Power Vote to mobilize students. Then they hold politicians accountable, including Obama. While most other environmental groups were either compromising or protesting, Energy Action blazed a strong middle path in a video that presented a series of demands: "It's Game Time, Obama"—a clever way to hold the president accountable to his campaign promises and demand he provide strong moral leadership.

With smart legislative, electoral, and coalition-building functions, Energy Action has the most comprehensive organizing model of any group in the climate movement. The rest of the movement would do well to follow their lead and take notes.

Why Isn't There a School for Movement-Building?

There are schools for community organizing like the Midwest Academy. There are schools for electoral organizing like Wellstone Action and the New Organizing Institute. There are schools for leadership development like the Center for Progressive Leadership.

Some master's in social work programs even have a community organizing track. There are academic courses and degree programs in leadership, public policy, public administration, nonprofit management, and philanthropy. There are black, Latino, Asian, Native American, and even whiteness studies courses. There are women's and LGBT and labor and environmental studies courses, curricula and majors at many colleges. There are courses about the civil rights movement.

But there's no formal practical curriculum on movement-building as a whole, as far as I am aware.

There is very little written on movement-building as a comprehensive field of activity. And most of what is written on "social movement theory" is academic and unreadable.

It's embarrassing and bizarre, actually, how little attention is paid to the discipline of movement-building and strategic historical change.

I have received hundreds of inquiries from all over the world from students wanting to write theses or dissertations on graffiti. I have received dozens of similar requests about hip-hop, youth organizing, race, and in particular about whiteness. And about almost every other topic I've ever written about. But I don't think I've ever gotten an inquiry from a student writing about movement-building. What's wrong with this picture?

The topic is so vast, so complex, so rich. There are zillions of case studies to do. No one has ever contacted me to do a serious case study or analysis of any of the organizations I've built, or movement-building efforts or strategies I've employed. Yet I still get requests to do interviews on graffiti when I don't even do graffiti anymore. And this is true across the board. Almost none of the major progressive organizations I know of have grad students calling them, asking for interviews to understand and research their leadership, organizing, and strategic change models.

Why is that?

It's because, as a rule, the discipline of strategic change is still not recognized or taken seriously. Part of the challenge is that movement-building is so multidimensional, it's hard to put it in a box. Which is why it's so difficult to teach. And so crucial.

The Movement Strategy Center (MSC) probably comes the closest. (Full disclosure: I have a fellowship there and am a huge fan.) As much as the term "movement" gets thrown around, MSC is the only organization I'm aware of that is explicitly devoted to strategic movement-building. MSC has been working behind the scenes for nearly a decade to make the social and racial justice movements more strategic, coordinated, and effective. With some success.

Founder and director Taj James was a protégé of Lisa Sullivan during the 1990s. "Back then, there was a lot of exciting local organizing," he reflects. "But there were some major stumbling blocks: for starters, we were disconnected from each other and internally divided. For the most part, our work was happening through an organizational lens, rather than a movement lens. An organizational orientation asks: 'What can my organization do?' A movement orientation asks: 'What can one thousand organizations do?'

"Lisa and I had studied the conservative movement. Where our folks were taking an organizational or issue approach, conservatives had a movement approach and they were cleaning our clocks with it. In California, they were coming up with one ballot initiative after another to put us in a defensive posture, divide us, make us spend a lot of money, and lose. And then they'd take it to fifteen more states and do the same thing. We were always playing defense. We couldn't figure out how to operate as a unified force.

"We needed to figure out a movement strategy that could effectively compete. Since most social and racial justice groups were local, our strategy was to build it from the bottom-up, place by place, sector by sector. So how do you build an alliance in Oakland or Wichita or New Orleans? How do you build an alliance around education or reproductive justice or media justice? How do you build it from the bottom-up like the civil rights movement? And how do you weave them together over time?

"Another big area the conservatives were better at: how do you use all the tools in the toolbox? Most social justice organizations are 501(c)(3) nonprofits. That's one important tool. But what about the other tools? You can't build a house with just a screwdriver. You actually need a wrench and a hammer too. So that's when you get into exploring 501(c)(4)s that can lobby and do electoral work. And PACs and for-profit corporations and social networks and smart mobs.

"Finally, we had to figure out how to be proactive around a strategic vision, rather than always playing defense. We were focused on protest and resistance. Conservatives were focused on articulating a bold proactive vision, getting power, governing, and winning. We didn't have a clear movement vision and strategy.

"In movements, there are four overall strategies: 1) You have people trying to stop bad things, that's *resistance*. 2) People trying to win good things, that's *reform*. 3) People trying to run things, that's *governance*. 4) People trying to create new things, that's *building alternatives*."

We use this chart (below) as a reflection tool for organizations.

Strength on the Spectrum:
Where are we strong and where can we get stronger?

The Current System			New Systems
Resistance: Stop Bad Things!	**Reform:** Win Good Things!	**Governance:** Run Things!	**Build Alternatives:** Create New Things!
Reactive ⟶ Proactive ⟶ Visionary			

"We ask social justice organizations: 'Where is your energy focused?' The answer is: mostly in the first and second boxes. Then we ask: 'Where does the majority of your effort need to be focused over the next three to five years in order to achieve your mission?' People do this exercise and realize they need to do what the conservative movement has done. They need a governance strategy in order to achieve their mission."

Movement Strategy Center is considering publishing a book and starting a program to teach specific movement-building skills (beyond the core group of leaders they already work with). I'm hoping they do. One way or another, over the next ten years, we're going to need to develop a whole field around the art and science of movement-building.

The movement is the lifeboat that's going to save us. It's our Noah's ark. We need to start giving it the love, care, and rigorous attention it deserves.

Part V

What Does It Mean to Be a Grown-up?

*"Children do what they want. Adults do what they have to.
The idea is to take the best of each. As a grown-up, you have to be
responsible. But that doesn't mean giving up your dreams."*
—Anonymous

What Does It Mean to Be a Grown-up?

What is an adult?

A deceptively simple question, but not necessarily easy to answer.

If you Google the word "adult," you will find every imaginable form of pornography. Young girls. Asian mail-order brides. S&M. Sex right now delivered to your home! Sex with animals. Sex with plastic dolls. Penis enhancement. Breast enhancement. But you won't find a lot of helpful guidance on how to be an adult.

Let's start by naming the obvious. Adulthood is distinguished from adolescence and childhood. Officially, the process begins at age fourteen, fifteen, sixteen, or seventeen in most states with the ability to drive a car, have sex, hold a job, stay out after curfew, join the military, and even in some places get married. At age eighteen a young adult is no longer under the legal control of his or her parents. The process is completed at age twenty-one, the legal age to drink.

But true adulthood is not necessarily defined by age. There are eleven-year-olds who have some characteristics of adulthood (i.e., responsibility for taking care of younger siblings). And fifty-one-year-olds who have remarkably few. Adulthood is a spectrum, a process, not an all-or-nothing state of being. And people can actually regress from behaving like an adult to behaving like a child. The twin essential defining characteristics of adulthood are: responsibility (ownership over one's life, words, actions, and decisions) and maturity (the judgment to make informed, wise, and responsible decisions).

There Are No Grown-ups Here

As my friend James Bernard says: "There are no grown-ups. When you're growing up, you think there are these grown-up people who are in charge of things, who have it all figured out. The older you get, you realize that they really don't. We are the grown-ups. We are the grown-ups we've been waiting for."

I believe being a grown-up is a multidimensional challenge. We must practice being a grown-up in four dimensions of responsibility and maturity: with ourselves; with our loved ones; with our community, government, and institutions; and with our planet and future generations.

What does it look like to be a full-fledged grown-up?

Here are four dimensions of adult responsibility:

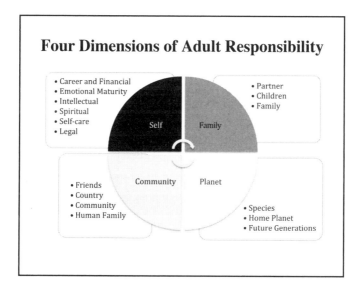

Four Dimensions of Adult Responsibility

- Career and Financial
- Emotional Maturity
- Intellectual
- Spiritual
- Self-care
- Legal

Self

Family

- Partner
- Children
- Family

Community

Planet

- Friends
- Country
- Community
- Human Family

- Species
- Home Planet
- Future Generations

That's a lot of friggin' responsibility!

Most people can't handle it—we don't even try. Or we focus on a couple of areas and give up on the rest. Whether we like it or not, taking responsibility in *all* of these areas of life, and doing it with maturity and good judgment, is what it means to be a full-fledged adult.

Are you an adult?

Take a moment and think about who you know in your life who comes closest to being a full-fledged grown-up. There aren't too many, are there? But think of a person in your life who comes close. Go through the above list and think about the various areas where they take responsibility and generally exercise good judgment. I have an assignment for you: Acknowledge that person.

Thank that person. Tell that person that you recognize and appreciate all the responsibilities they are holding. Ask them how they do it!

Emotional Maturity 1–10

I have a friend who's always having boy troubles that she confides in me about.

"On a scale of 1–10, what is your level of emotional maturity, and what is his level of emotional maturity?" I ask her.

"I'm about a 7 or an 8," she says. "And he is probably a 4 or 5. Sometimes he acts like a 7 or 8. But overall, he's a . . . 5. Yeah, 4 or 5."

"This is why you're having problems," I tell her. "You can't be a 7 or 8 and be in a relationship with someone who's a 4 or a 5. It doesn't work. He may be brilliant and amazing and fun and good in bed, and he might be ten or twenty years older than you. But at the end of the day, if his overall maturity and emotional intelligence and, most importantly, his behavior is a 4 or a 5, the relationship is not going to work. The person you're dating either has to rise to your level, or they're gonna drag you down to theirs."

I feel like I'm becoming a love coach. Another friend of mine called me recently crying because her long-term boyfriend cheated on her and broke up with her. It completely undercut her self-confidence. She had been cheated on, lied to, and rejected. She sobbed uncontrollably, and talked about how worthless she felt. This is a brilliant, drop-dead gorgeous, highly accomplished woman who has everything going for her in life. I explained the 1–10 emotional maturity scale to her and asked her where she and her ex were on that scale. She thought about it for a while.

"He's probably a 3," she said. "Sometimes he can act like he's higher, but I would say he's a 3."

"And where are you?" I asked.

"I think I go up and down. I'm definitely higher on the scale than he is. Probably in the 6 or 7 range on a good day, but I feel like I've been brought down to his level by this."

Exactly.

If one person rejects another person in a relationship, we naturally assume it is the "better" person rejecting the "worse" one. But this is not necessarily the case. I have a kind of embarrassing story that illustrates this.

When I was younger, I would go to clubs, and I would dance with a group of girls. Now keep in mind, I'm a halfway decent dancer and I'm also very respectful. I wasn't just pushing up and grinding on the booty. I would approach with a casual laid-back vibe. Sometimes they would giggle and start to dance with me. Sometimes I would get cues that they were not interested, and I would back off. Also, keep in mind, I'm not very picky about who I dance with. I'll dance with anyone. And I remember a couple times I would go dance next to a group of cheesy girls and they would practically run away from me, as if I had a sign painted across my forehead. When this happened, I actually felt bad about myself. I felt rejected, like something must be wrong with me to make them want to dis me. The reality was that these were girls who couldn't dance well, and whom I had no real interest in. Yet the fact that they rejected me made me feel bad about myself all the same.

The weird thing about emotional maturity scales is that it's often the less mature people who reject the more mature people.

Thank You, Audre Lorde

"What the hell is this, a self-help book?"

"I don't understand why you have a section on love and self-help in the middle of a book about social change."

These were comments I got from friends who read early drafts of this book. The truth is that people who are the most uncomfortable with self-help books and talking about feelings are usually the ones who need it the most. That's why I slipped it in here. If you don't like it, or you're already an 8 or above on the emotional maturity scale, cool, don't sweat it, just skip to the next chapter.

We are not social change machines. We are not movement robots. We are not political animals. We are human beings. We have feelings. We have accumulated hurts and fears.

We have emotional, spiritual, and, yes, even sexual needs and longings. The more we heal from our traumas, the more we take care of ourselves—mind, body, and spirit—the more whole we can become. The more we get our emotional partnership, trust, and intimacy needs met outside of our movement work, the more we are able to bring our best selves to the work. Therefore, *it is a moral imperative to take care of ourselves and find joy and fulfillment in our personal lives.*

Several years ago, my friend Rhea Vedro and her friends Sarah and Divine organized a spa day for a bunch of movement folks living in New York City.

Ha! That seems pretty self-indulgent, I remember thinking to myself when I saw the invite. As if reading my mind, the organizers included an Audre Lorde quote at the end of the invitation: *Caring for myself is not self-indulgence. It is self-preservation, and that is an act of political warfare.*

Whoa. Self-care as political warfare! Interesting. I went on that spa date.

Modern culture moves so fast, we often don't have time to slow down and remember who we are or our purpose in life. We spend so much time busy busy

busy. Going deep with ourselves can seem like a terrifying experience. We have messy, complicated feelings and stories down there. Fear! Trauma! Ego! Anger! Blame! Judgment! Self-loathing! Hunger! Ambition! Jealousy! Naked desire!

On the inside, we are like the emotional equivalent of Times Square. We all have a garbage dump inside of us. Who knows how half of it even got there? And we all have a radiant sun of love and light, passion and wisdom. Every one of us is *enough*. Every one of us has a purpose. And it's never too late to begin the journey.

Most of us are shut down emotionally much of the time. No one ever taught us in school how to be emotionally self-aware and resourceful. Few of us learned it in our families. In fact, most of us learned the opposite: emotional numbness is how we've learned to survive. Emotional shutdown is the major way of being that most of us have been taught in our families, in school, in work, and in relationships. For many of us, it is all we have ever known. Life feels safer that way. Emotions are dangerous, scary, unpredictable. They can jump out of a word or a look or a memory, and hit us somewhere painful, worse than being kicked. Feelings can be radioactive. We bury them under layers like nuclear fuel cells. Otherwise, they might riot. It is safer to keep them locked down.

Or is it?

The Greatest Love of All

The road of life can be cold and lonely sometimes. I've been there. During my saddest month last year, I felt like a heartbroken failure and I listened to Whitney Houston's "The Greatest Love of All" a hundred times a day. After a few weeks, I started adding in "Golden" by Jill Scott, followed by Jay-Z, M.I.A., Eminem, and Kirk Franklin. Who knew Jay-Z and Eminem wrote self-help songs? I began to feel better.

The hardest lesson I keep having to learn: there is no substitute for loving myself, respecting myself, and being true to myself. There are no shortcuts. You can't use anything external to substitute for inner-love. It doesn't work.

Have you ever fantasized to yourself: if only I could meet the right person, or get the right job, then I could be happy and it would bring out my best. Wouldn't it be nice if life worked like that?

But as Marlo told the security guard on *The Wire*:

"It's the other way."

"Huh?"

"You want it to be one way. But it's the other way."

The security guard looked at him in disbelief. Then he was dead.

Hard times forced me to look inside myself and ask hard questions: What is my purpose? What do I really want? How do I want to live?

I am a visual learner so I drew a Venn diagram for myself to map out the life I want:

Diagram of Life Goals

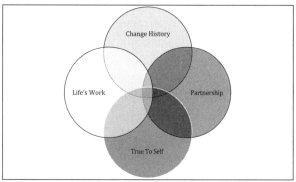

See that square in the middle? That's the sweet spot. My goal is to live as much as possible inside that zone.

Where do you live in relation to the Diagram in your life?

1	2	3	4	5	6	7	8	9	10
Outside the diagram				**Inside the diagram**				**Inside the square**	

Almost no one lives inside their sweet spot. Most people don't even live in the diagram. I would honestly put myself in the 6.5 range right now because I've made a huge leap forward recently while writing this book. I've got a foothold in my life's work. I've got a foothold in being true to myself. A foothold in life partnership. And a toehold in changing history. After twenty years of trying! Progress is not always linear and it's definitely not automatic. You have to work smart to make progress over time. I reached 7 about ten years ago, and then again maybe seven years ago. Since then and I have actually slid backward. A year ago, I was in the 3, 4, 5 range. Writing this book has helped me climb back up.

Wherever you are inside or outside your diagram right now, you are where you are for reasons, many outside your control. Your job is not to judge yourself. Your job is to be honest about where you are (wherever that is), to be gentle with yourself, and to daydream possible paths to get where you want to be.

Growing Up is Not a Right-Wing Conspiracy

Right-wing pundits have hijacked the narrative about growing up. They love to call progressives and liberals childish, idealistic, immature, naïve, wrong-headed, dangerous, stupid, and unpatriotic.

They love to lecture us. "We conservatives are the real adults. The rest of you are irresponsible children."

I'm going to go right for the jugular here.

There is a connection between growing up and understanding the government. It has become fashionable for right-wingers to bash the government. It's kind of like saying you hate your parents when you're thirteen. They're the worst parents ever. You don't need them. You never did. And you hate them hate them hate them, because they're ruining your life. But let's be specific. Which part of the government do you hate? The fire, water, and sewer departments? The highways and bridges? The national parks and coast guard? The publicly funded hospitals and state colleges?

I know: the post office! Everyone hates the post office. But guess what? You try running the friggin' post office! You try operating 35,000 retail outlets (more than McDonald's and Starbucks combined in the U.S.). You try delivering half a billion pieces of mail every day, many of them wrongly addressed, with water-based ink, poorly sealed, with not enough postage, from every country on the globe. And make sure you simultaneously pick up mail from millions of locations, to and from every remote corner of Wyoming and Alaska, through blizzards and floods, power outages and car accidents. You try doing that. Because that's what the U.S. post office does every day. And try doing it without a dime of taxpayer money (the post office is mandated to be revenue-neutral).

We can hate the government or our parents all we want. The thing is: they're ours. The grown-up approach is to understand them, work with them, and pitch in to help make them better. But the right-wing ideologues want to throw a tantrum. Just like being a teenager; what could be easier than hating your parents?

What could be easier than hating the government? It's not like some big professional wrestler dude is going to get in your face: "What did you say about the government??? You best not be talking about *my* government. I'll come over there and F you up!"

And then it's almost comical how right-wing ideologues talk about how everything Obama does is socialism.

Fine, if you don't like socialism, then don't call the socialist police and fire departments. Don't drive on the socialist highways. Don't live in the socialist-financed suburbs or turn on the socialist water and electricity. Don't use those socialist wires, pipes, Internet, or mail service. Don't support the socialist army, navy, air force, and marines. Or the socialist VA hospitals for our troops when they return from war. Don't let your parents use socialized medicine, a.k.a.

Medicare. And most of all, when you're older, don't leech off of the most socialist, commie, pinko, welfare-loving government program of all, Social Security.

Learning from My Parents

There is a photograph of my family standing outside the Wimsatt cabin in Ithaca, New York. Six or seven of us, on a hot summer day. My father is standing with his shirt off, looking at the ground, one hand on his hip, the other hand scratching his head. And I am standing directly across from him, in exactly the same stance, shirtless, looking at the ground, hand on my hip, scratching my head: a chip off the old block. We couldn't have choreographed it any better if the photo had been staged.

It is sometimes startling how much we are like our parents. I spent a lot of my young life trying not to be like my parents. Growing up, I viewed them with critical eyes—typical white liberal academics. All around our neighborhood, on the South Side of Chicago, black people were living in third world poverty. The world was going to hell in a handbasket. We were wrecking the environment. There were nuclear weapons pointed at Chicago. We lived in an unfair and segregated world that was setting my friends up for failure. And what were my parents doing about it? Nothing! Living in their self-satisfied university bubble. They were part of white adult society, part of the system that was benefitting from keeping black people down. In other words, they were part of the problem. And on top of all that, they led boring middle-class lives. Not the exciting, courageous life that I wanted to lead. I saw how they had accepted a way of life that was less than their potential. I was afraid I would turn out like them. I was afraid I would be unable to do something about the problems I saw around me. I was afraid I would fail to live up to my potential. I didn't yet know what living up to my potential looked like. I had no idea how to stop the problems of the world. I was angry and frustrated and I knew that whatever I did, it had to be different from them.

I didn't necessarily think this consciously. Even then, I knew that rebelling against your parents just for the sake of rebelling was kind of stupid and moronic. But I had a deep intuition that I had to try something different. They were disorganized; I had to be organized. They liked to accumulate junk; possessions seemed like a burden to me. They both had PhDs; what did I need a degree for?

Yet the more I learn about myself as the years pass, the more interesting it becomes to visit my parents. My mom struggles with anxiety. I do too. My mom struggles with insecurity. I do too. My mom sometimes comes across as too critical. I do too. My dad sometimes gets hyped up and oblivious to what's going on around him. I do too. My dad paces around when he's excited. I do too. My dad rubs his head when he's thinking. I do too. My dad's a workaholic. I am too.

And now I am able to appreciate the good things I got from them. I'm interested in psychology, mentorship, and career paths. My mom got her PhD studying gender and career paths. I'm fascinated by the history of ideas and the evolution of social movements. My dad studies cultural evolution and the conceptual foundations of science. I'm extremely social; my dad's extremely social. I'm hyper; my dad is hyper. I'm extremely caring and empathetic; my parents are both extremely caring and empathetic. As much as I like to think I'm special and different, and, well, better than my parents, the apple didn't fall too far from the tree.

And in fact, the older I get, the more I am humbled by how impressive they are. By the time he was my age, my dad had a four-year-old son. I am just starting to think about kids. My parents both had established careers. I am still trying to figure mine out. My mom was into health food way before her time. She gave up her career to raise me. She overcame growing up with a widowed single mom who didn't think girls should go to college for more than one year (to get their Mrs. degree), in a society that didn't take women's aspirations seriously. My dad grew up wanting to fly fighter planes and would have ended up in Vietnam if it weren't for his diabetes.

My dad was politicized when he lived in Pittsburgh in the 1960s by seeing a police officer fire a gun above the head of a black man in front of his eyes. My mom grew up on the South Side of Chicago and was politicized by her own experience of being raised in a working-class family and by the movements of the '60s.

Both of them lost touch with politics when they were busy raising me. But they ultimately became much more politically aware in the process. When I was a teenager, my mom used to rifle through my bags and closet looking for spray paint and markers. Among the contraband, she would find copies of the *Nation, In These Times,* and *Mother Jones.* Then she started calling up the local NPR station, and correcting the hosts with information she read in the alternative press.

My dad started finding ways to make the University of Chicago more connected to the larger world. He began incorporating more political analysis into his courses, and he created a new program called "Big Problems" which brings together faculty from different disciplines to teach courses which tackle the large questions of our time, like empires (ancient and modern), war, energy, and sustainable development.

My hope is that a whole generation of parents will get politicized through their kids. An average American family spends half a million to a million dollars to raise a child over its lifetime. Even the very poorest family will spend at least $50,000 to $100,000. And wealthy families often spend several million. Families make enormous sacrifices for their children because they love them and would do anything to help them be happy, healthy, and successful.

What are we willing to sacrifice to make sure they grow up living in a sane society on a healthy planet? Or more bluntly, what are we willing to do to make sure they don't inherit a hot, crowded, flooding, dying planet? Middle-class families shell out tens of thousands of dollars a year to support each individual child. Imagine if they strategically invested a fraction of that into building a better world for that child to live in.

Facing the End Game: I Am Scheduled to Die in 2048

Did I lose you? I know it's scary, but stick with me here. It's gonna be okay. Nobody likes to talk about this. It sends people into a depressing downward spiral which in turn leads them to start smoking weed and watching *Family Guy* and *America's Next Top Model*.

When I was in eighth grade, I got sent to the office one time and a school counselor sized me up: "It's hard for kids who are insightful at a young age, because you can see through the smokescreens."

We lose a lot of our best minds every year because a lot of people start thinking about the end of the world and they can't handle it and go crazy.

It got me thinking. Everyone wants to have kids, but most of us don't really think it through all the way. We all know we're going to die one day, but I've never bothered to calendar out exactly when that might occur.

It seems like an important date to have in the calendar.

I was born in 1972, and since the average life expectancy for white American males is seventy-six years, I am scheduled to die in approximately 2048. Shit, that's right around the corner! I might be able to extend my lease through 2055 or even 2060 if I'm super healthy and super lucky. But it basically means I have a good forty years left, God willing. That means my life is about at the halfway mark.

I am scheduled to die in 2048, but if I have kids, my kids could live until 2100 and my grandkids could live to see 2140.

This is the real fight for the rights of the unborn. The antiabortion movement is interested in the rights of the unborn for a brief nine-month period before they are born. I'm mostly interested in what happens to them *after* they are born—for the next seven decades of life.

What does it mean to grow up in twenty-first century America? The rules of middle-class American adulthood appear to work—but for how much longer? We are part of the most robust system of social organization ever developed. We are barreling ahead at one hundred miles per hour in the biggest, baddest, fastest car ever invented. It's an all-terrain Hummer tank, with bulletproof everything. No one can stop us. Indigenous people, protesters, environmentalists, plants, and animals try to get in our way. We run right over them. No one can stop us. We leave them crushed in our wake, bleeding and dying by the side of the road. We're going faster and faster, bigger and badder.

According to scientists, we are headed for a cliff.

A book came out in 2007 called *Peak Everything*. The obvious point it makes is that we are nearing the limits of everything the Earth has to offer. Not just peak oil. But peak water. Peak soil. Peak forest. Peak fish. Peak population. Peak wealth. Peak pollution and garbage and toxicity. People may argue whether we are at the peak, past the peak, or whether we are twenty or fifty years away from the peak for any given trend. Technology and innovation can buy us a few extra years or decades. But sooner or later, all the trend lines predict that we smash into a wall. We go over the edge of a very steep cliff. We hit an iceberg. We have a reckoning. We hit a point at which we either change course very radically in our values, our beliefs, our systems, and our patterns of life, or else we as a civilization will be *forced* to change course because we have driven the human food chain and ecosystem to the point of collapse.

We are the real conservatives.

We are the real pro-life.

I don't know what to do about this. I don't know what I can do. And I don't know what I want to do. Some days I want to do something. Some days I just want to curl up on the couch in a big warm comforter with some pillows, eat ice cream and cookies, drink wine, watch episodes of *West Wing*, read novels, and play on Facebook.

I want to find a way to stop the Hummer. But I also want to live a normal, happy American life . . . inside the comfort of the Hummer world. I have the privilege and good fortune to do so. And CarbonFootprint.com tells me that if everyone on the globe were to live with my lifestyle, we would require five planets to survive. This leaves me conflicted and not knowing what to do. I mean, sure, I'm doing a lot of good stuff. I'm doing as much good stuff as I can. But the good stuff I do never feels like enough. I am trying to live a balanced life. But I keep feeling like there are more effective strategies. And I am trying to figure out what they are.

I am trying to think about the next forty years. About how to be effective and also not broke. I feel like it is related to doing what I love—but bigger, smarter, deeper. So I'm trying to figure out what I love and what I'm good at so I can unlock the mystery. I know I love writing. I love interviewing people, understanding people, knowing (and keeping) people's secrets. I love telling the truth about scary things and being close to people and having honest conversations. I love organizing people, developing strategies, making smart moves, and winning. I love being resourceful and figuring things out. I love cross-pollinating and introducing people. But what do I do with all of this? I don't know. I feel like there's something more.

I need to figure it out quickly because I only have around forty more years to play this game called life—God willing.

What year are you estimated to die? The average U.S. lifespan is seventy-seven. Add a few years if you're a woman. Subtract a few years if you're any of the above: a person of color, male, poor, or have health issues. You can also test yourself on RealAge.com to add or subtract a few years based on your health.

What year are you expected to die?

Part VI

Management for the Movement

Organizations . . . Ugh

Okay, so clearly we have big things to do. We have a *lot* to change. A lot. Not just on a personal level, but also on a structural level, a political level, an institutional level, a social level. And the main vehicles we use to create change are these bizarre, clunky, compromised structures called . . . organizations.

This is a big deal. This is where everything breaks down. As a movement, I'm sorry to say this: many, if not most, of our organizations are somewhere between slightly and totally dysfunctional. They are dysfunctional mainly for five big garden-variety reasons: dysfunctional vision and strategy, dysfunctional structure, dysfunctional leadership, dysfunctional funding, and dysfunctional relationships with allies.

I am far, far, far from an organizational or management expert. But I have been around the block enough times by now that I've fallen in just about every pothole at least three times. I've read a lot of books. I've done a lot of coaching and leadership workshops. There's some management wisdom that nooooobody's going to teach you that I had to learn the hard way. I have the lumps to prove it. This section is important to read even if you don't consider yourself an "organization person," because somehow we have to crack the code of what makes organizations functional. And then we have to use that wisdom to code the crack that organization leaders, boards, and staff have been smoking all these years.

In this section, we're going to talk about the secret, sad life of executive directors. We're going to talk about power, race, management, visionary leadership, burnout, founder's syndrome, funding madness, and other fun topics. I'll share my stories of learning these lessons the hard way and how I got help through coaching, books, and peer support circles.

Confessions of an Executive Director

I was talking with a mentor of mine who used to run a prominent national organization with affiliates in all fifty states. One time I asked her a provocative question: "How many of the state affiliates are really well-managed, and have really good leadership?"

She thought about it for a while with a pained look on her face. "One," she said finally.

Wow. I began asking around among senior well-respected leaders in the movement, and I got a similar response.

What the F was going on?

From my own experience, I don't think most people understand what it's like to be the executive director of a nonprofit organization, especially a start-up.

Managing an organization can be so difficult, it is a wonder that I was ever able to succeed at it. Over the course of my five years as executive director of the League, members of my board almost got rid of me twice. Members of my staff tried to overthrow me twice. And it wasn't like I was doing a terrible job. I was a generally well-regarded head of a relatively successful organization. I never missed a payroll. We never got in any legal trouble. We never got bad press. I didn't make any huge outwardly obvious mistakes. Some of the people who tried to overthrow me were my friends and respected colleagues whom I had recruited to the organization. Luckily, every time there was an attempted coup or oust-Billy movement, a critical mass of staff and board stepped forward to stop the madness.

To be sure, I did make a lot of mistakes. My gift and my curse is that I am extremely ambitious and willing to take risks. So I always tried to do way too much. I hired staff who were too inexperienced and I let them run all over me. I didn't understand how to manage. I was afraid to fire people. And worst of all, I knew I was in over my head so I disempowered myself and didn't trust my own instincts. On top of that, I recruited too many board members. Why do people think large boards are good? If I had it to do all over again, I would have had *three* board members, the legal minimum, who I trusted completely. Instead, for most of my five years as ED, we had eighteen board members from all over the country and it was basically like having a second staff to manage. So I was always waaaay overextended. It always felt like I was a domino catcher. Any time there is a perceived crisis, or even one person is unhappy or thinks it's okay to undermine your leadership, you have to address the situation *immediately*. Otherwise, domino one hits domino two. Domino two hits domino three. And pretty soon the whole organization is on the brink of implosion. I learned all of these lessons the hard way several times over.

Finally, after five years as ED, I was ready to pass the torch of my own volition and I worked closely with the staff and board to carry out a very thoughtful and deliberate leadership transition. We did a huge external search but ended up hiring the best fit for the job, an internal candidate, Robert "Biko" Baker, who I had originally brought in as a local organizer in Milwaukee, and who had risen up through the ranks. We had an exemplary transition process. Biko quickly became a savvy organizational leader. It was a very satisfying experience. A few years later, we came full circle: he ended up hiring me back on staff to work on some of the League's special operations in 2010.

During the various coup attempts, I was under so much stress that my body began breaking down. I'm a healthy dude, but I started getting little pains in my back and wrists. Then tiny unexplained twitches in my eye and knees. My biggest symptom was eczema, an itchy skin rash which I had as a child. It appeared first on the backs of my knees, then spread to my fingers and arms, and at its peak probably covered 25 percent of my body including my stomach, patches of my feet, arms, legs, and my left eyelid.

I thought I was allergic to wheat and dairy and an ever-expanding list of foods. I didn't eat wheat or dairy for a whole year. The best antidote I could find was saltwater, so I started going to the beach every weekend and taking salt baths every night. But suddenly when I left the League, my eczema basically went away. It turned out I hadn't actually been allergic to wheat or dairy. I had been allergic to my job as director of a social change organization.

Somewhere in the middle of this process, I went out to dinner with my friend Rha Goddess and she gave me the funniest and the best advice of the year: "I say this with love. You need to take yourself out of the oven because you're crispy."

Management for the Movement

My first big management lesson came from my cofounder at the League, Adrienne Maree Brown. Adrienne was the training director at the time. She told me one day after she had been on staff for a couple months: "You need to learn how to manage. If you don't read *The One Minute Manager*, I'm quitting."

Say what? Okay. I guess I better read it. But I was skeptical.

Management? Isn't that what we are fighting *against*? Isn't that the corporate hierarchical oppressive system we are trying to create an alternative to? I didn't get it.

The One Minute Manager is an adorable little book, written as a children's story in large type. Its premise is simple: good management consists of three steps—One Minute Planning, One Minute Praisings, and One Minute Reprimands. All that means is, if you are a manager, have your people make simple plans. Go over the plans with them in detail. Make sure they have your feedback and any information they need to successfully do their job on the front end, before they dive into it. This is how you avoid micromanaging and disempowering them on the back end. Then you give them immediate specific praise when they do well, and immediate specific feedback when they screw up. And you do it consistently. That's it.

If you get that right, it's at least one-third of the battle.

Then there's the matter of hiring and firing.

The matter of internal systems.

The matter of vision and strategy.

And the matter of leadership experience and confidence.

Accountability, Responsibility, and Authority: The Holy Trinity of Organizational Clarity

Let's move to the basics of power. No one ever explained this to me. If someone had, it would have saved me years of bad leadership.

A lot of people are afraid of authority, accountability, and responsibility. The three go together like a holy trinity of organizational leadership clarity.

This is why I don't believe in collectives, most of the time.

Side note: I think collectives can work pretty well in a simple, regularized system like a college food co-op or an online community where the purpose is very simple, well-established, and has stable cultural norms. And where people have time to be superinefficient for the sake of having a deep culture of participatory democracy. Most of the rest of the time—in a large and dynamic, diverse organization with limited resources and time—collective leadership tends to be a recipe for inefficiency, ineffectiveness, unacknowledged power dynamics, confusion, and ultimately frustration and demoralization.

Before I understood this, when I was head of the League, I had an ongoing argument with Adrienne, who thought the organization should be run as a collective. I didn't think it should be a collective, but I couldn't articulate why. The idea of a collective sounds so good and nonoppressive. Hierarchy sounds so bad and corporate and patriarchal. To add to the matter, I was an older white straight male. My staff was majority younger queer women of color. So the collective vs. hierarchy issue was very loaded with race, gender, age differences—and the moral power that we ascribed to them—as well as the baggage of ongoing personality differences and vision struggles.

One week, Adrienne and I were having a particularly intense argument about it. She was making a very strong and compelling case. So she forced me to articulate why I believed having a collective model was not good for the organization.

Walking home from the office at two a.m. one night, I finally put the pieces together. It was so simple, yet no one had ever explained it to me clearly. It came down to three concepts: accountability, responsibility, and authority. People sometimes use these concepts loosely or interchangeably. They had always been abstract for me. So I had never thought very hard before about what each concept really meant and their relationship to one another.

"I figured it out," I told her the next day. "I figured out why we need to have hierarchy."

"Why?" she said.

"Because we want to get paid," I began provocatively. "If we didn't want to get paid, then we could have a collective."

(The real reason: because we want to be effective.)

"In order to get paid," I continued, "we need to get grants and tax-deductible donations, right? Follow me here on this chain of logic: In order to get grants, we need to be a 501(c)(3) charity, chartered by the U.S. government. In order to be a 501(c)(3), we need to have a board of directors. The board of directors is *accountable* for the financial and legal operations of the organization. So if something goes wrong in our chapter in Miami, or if something financial or legal goes wrong anywhere in the organization, who is ultimately accountable? The board of directors. And the board needs to be accountable or else the government could revoke the organization's tax status and shut the organization down.

"If the board is accountable," I went on, "then they have to take *responsibility* for the organization. And if they have the responsibility, then they need to have the *authority* to make decisions. Since the board is composed of volunteers, they have limited time in which to exercise their responsibility and authority. So that's why they hire an executive director, a paid employee, who can work full-time managing the organization. The board doesn't have time to manage or hold accountable a collective of three people or five people or ten people. Not only would that be inefficient, it is beyond the competency of a volunteer board. And it makes no sense to have multiple paid people reporting directly to a body of multiple people who are volunteers and barely have time for the organization anyway. That's why they hire *one* person who they hold accountable for managing the organization. That person, the executive director, is then *responsible* for managing the organization. Therefore, that person needs to have the *authority* to make decisions on behalf of the organization."

Accountability, responsibility and authority—they go hand in hand at every level. If a board delegates accountability to an executive director, then they have to delegate responsibility and authority too. The executive director in turn delegates accountability, responsibility, and authority down the line to senior staff, who then delegate it to junior staff, who then delegate it to volunteers. We call this relationship a hierarchy.

The word hierarchy has a lot of baggage. But hierarchies themselves are not good or bad. They are clear and efficient relationships between roles of accountability, responsibility, and authority in an organization.

This is also why codirectorships are almost always a bad idea. When two people are accountable, responsible, and have authority, it is almost always a recipe for paralysis, power struggle, or both.

A lot of arrangements that sound like good, nonoppressive ideas ("Let's let the group decide" or "Let's have a collective" or "Let's be codirectors" or "I don't know, what do you think?") are often failures of one individual to take responsibility, own the authority, make a good decision, and be willing to explain and take heat for it.

Every situation is different. I'm not saying collectives can never work. Adrienne went on to make her collective vision real as executive director of the Ruckus Society, a direct-action training organization that works with communities on the front lines of social and environmental justice struggles. Over a four-year period, Adrienne shifted Ruckus successfully into a collective leadership model, and passed the torch to two of her staff, Megan Swoboda and Sharon Lungo, who are codirectors in a leadership team made up of board, staff, and network members who make collective decisions quickly and effectively. Adrienne is one of the best facilitative leaders our movement has (she also coorganized the U.S. Social Forum in Detroit with 20,000 people), and Ruckus is a small, nimble, twenty-first century, decentralized, network-based organization. Maybe more organizations should emulate Ruckus.

In general, the bigger the organization, the more money involved, and the bigger the tent, the harder it is to run as a genuine collective. On the other hand, as Jim Collins documents in *Good to Great*, in high-functioning teams, the day-to-day *feeling* of hierarchy "melts away" because people have learned to trust each other; everyone performs well at their jobs; everyone understands the bigger picture; and everyone accepts their role on the organization chart. In a high-functioning organizational culture, everyone feels empowered and safe to be "hard on the issues" yet "soft on the people," not attacking anyone personally, not engaging in power struggles, and not undermining the leader or undercutting team spirit.

This is the ideal organizational culture all of us want to be a part of. But it is not usually accomplished by getting rid of hierarchy. It is usually accomplished by having the right people in the right seats on the bus, by everyone deeply buying into the hierarchy, and respecting each others' unique roles, responsibilities, and strengths.

Race and Power . . . Oy Vey

"Some say that God is black and the devil's white.
Well, the devil is wrong and God is what's right." —Common

All of the problems I was having were compounded by my analysis of race, class, gender, power, and morality. The neighborhood where I grew up had extremely obvious race and class divides. A mile from my parents' apartment in any direction were some of the poorest hoods in the U.S. I felt the pain of poverty and segregation very deeply and experienced personally the way our society set up many of my black friends to be tracked into cycles of rejection, low expectations, joblessness, violence, prison, and despair.

Looking for answers as a teenager, I devoured the works of Malcolm X, James Baldwin, Maya Angelou, W.E.B. DuBois, and other great black thinkers. In my mind, the framework was pretty clear: white dudes had created great empires all over the world by basically colonizing, exploiting, subjugating, committing mass genocide, and virtually destroying many other cultures in Africa, Asia, and the Americas.

As a Jew, I was horrified and terrified by the Holocaust, and the genocide of six million of my people. All over Europe, my mother reminded me, when the Nazis took over, many Jews were turned over to the SS by their friends and neighbors. This was proof to me that human beings had the capacity to do extremely evil things, then justify it to themselves and go on living as though everything was normal. Growing up, I thought about what would happen if there was another Holocaust; I wondered which of my neighbors would protect us and which would turn us over to the Nazis.

But as I studied history, there was a disconnect for me. My white ancestors had killed many more than six million people in Africa and the Americas, and committed unspeakable atrocities for not just a decade, but hundreds of years. Centuries. To call what happened "slavery" is really a euphemism. Anyone who has read the descriptions of black men tied up and made to watch their pregnant wives raped and having their bellies slashed open and burned with irons understands that it was concentration camp–style torture; the most hideous, sick, twisted human debasement imaginable was carried on for hundreds of years. Generation after generation of psychological warfare against the bodies, minds, and spirits of black and indigenous peoples. Yet somehow that was just supposed to be forgiven, left in the past, and we were all supposed to move on because race doesn't matter anymore. La-de-dah. The whole thing made me crazy. I felt like I was living in a nation of German Holocaust deniers. And there weren't a lot of white people who seemed to get it, to take it seriously, or take any responsibility for what had happened and what was still happening to black and indigenous people in the wake of these atrocities.

I became very angry, and I didn't find a lot of acceptable outlets for my anger. There were plenty of white liberals, but not many wanted to talk about this stuff. So it lived inside me as a boiling generalized anger at and suspicion of white America, white adults, white people—and that meant *all* white people, including myself. As the *Pogo* comic strip famously reflected: "We have met the enemy and he is us." If the other white people were continuing the problem by being comfortable, in denial, and self-satisfied, then the only right path seemed to be the opposite: uncomfortable, hyperaware, and self-critical.

It's like, whoa, my ancestors did something similar to what the Nazis did to the Jews and everybody is pretending it wasn't that bad. These people are clearly either not looking at the same facts I'm looking at, or they think it's okay, or they don't care, or they're not sane, or they're in straight-up denial. Whatever the case may be, they are definitely not on the same page I'm on, seeing this situation the same way I am seeing it, or experiencing the same feelings I'm experiencing. So why would I ever trust their perspectives, let alone their hearts?

It was a natural reaction. And it's the same type of reaction that thousands of conscious white people have when they learn the history, and experience the reality of how institutional, cultural, and psychological racism and white supremacy is alive and wrecking the lives of black, indigenous, and colonized peoples to this day. But ultimately, my reaction wasn't very helpful. In fact, in many ways it was very unhelpful. Very, very unhelpful. And there are tens of thousands of conscious and confused white people who are laboring under a faulty framework of how to be useful in correcting the wrongs of racism in America. Many of these people have read my books and consider me to be one of the OGs of the antiracism and whiteness studies field.

There is a whole cottage industry now dedicated to getting white people to deal with racism, oppression, whiteness, sexism, homophobia, ableism, and the like. It mostly exists in books, on liberal college campuses, and through a handful of organizations and workshops, but the ideology has spread pretty widely throughout the social justice movement. And on the white side at least, it tends to turn out tortured little antiracism robots, who memorize the right jargon, and who get the diagnosis mostly right, the prescription mostly wrong, and who are ultimately not as effective as they need to be to fight racism in America, for two main reasons: 1) They tend to hate and doubt and sabotage themselves. 2) They tend not to use the most effective strategies to actually defeat racism.

I know because I am that person. I've spent a lot of my life hating and doubting and sabotaging myself. And I've spent a lot of my life using not-very-effective strategies. It has bitten me in the ass more times than I care to admit. And I have met hundreds of other antiracist white people who have some version of the same disease. I am writing this to reach the tens of thousands of tortured white antiracist people out there to say: "Hey, we need to talk. We need to talk about updating our game a little bit."

The Racism 101 trainings cover the basics (which, sadly, many white Americans are still in denial about), such as: the long and enduring history of racism and imperialism; the systematic raping and pillaging of black and brown peoples and the stealing of land and resources; the invention of the white race as a means of social control; the myth of white superiority as a way to divide poor whites from people of color (because poor and working-class whites are also oppressed by capitalism); the distinction between personal racism and institutional racism (racist schools, banks, companies and job networks, government, religious institutions, police and prisons, media, polluters, unions, etc.); the myths of colorblindness and meritocracy; the myth that white people don't have a culture; the reality of white-skin privilege in modern-day America; the wealth, education, pollution, arrest, and incarceration gaps; the myth that whites whose families came over after slavery aren't part of the problem; the "my grandfather was poor too" fallacy; why affirmative action programs barely scratch the surface of addressing racial disparities; the reality of white power; the damage caused by the imposition of white cultural norms; the impact of racism on kids and their psychological development; why people of color see racism and white people don't; the connection of racism to sexism, classism, homophobia, ableism, and most other kinds of oppression; how white people should address racism (acknowledge and learn about it, fight racism within white communities, and be an ally to people of color, both individually and in political movements); and what white people should not do (appropriate, a.k.a. steal, from other cultures, deny or perpetuate white privilege, try to take over, impose, or lead in communities of color).

For white people who grew up sheltered and who were generally raised on the myth of the color-blind, merit-based society, all of this can be a huge revelation, and it takes some time to absorb. It's like, holy shit, everything we were taught or assumed growing up is a lie and a product of the most diabolical and destructive system of control and oppression ever invented. Our teachers and parents are in on it. Who can you trust?

Learning the basics of racism tends to rock the world of privileged white people to the very core. This is why most privileged white people dread hearing about it and avoid it at all costs, or invent a different story to make it go away. It makes us feel extremely angry, powerless, guilty, stupid, motivated, and confused. Frankly, it is supposed to, and if we have a pulse and an ounce of heart, it should. Racism is really, really bad and huge and we are part of it; we have benefited from it materially; and our society is structured around maintaining it and keeping the big lie going. All of this is basically true.

However, it is only part of the story.

The Racism 101 ideology creates its own set of problems. It tends to generate white people who feel generally bad and self-doubting and are obsessed with thinking and talking about race all the time (because people of color don't have a choice except to deal with race all the time), so they compensate for the color blindness myth by viewing and talking about everything in terms of skin color. Which is kind of like going through life viewing everything through the lens of division and fuckery. One of the trademarks of this phase is feeling like you *have* to identify yourself and everyone you talk to or about by their race during the course of a day. This white person. This black person. This Asian man. It can be awkward and painful to watch. And it can even be degrading. Definitely not the best starting place to build relationships from. I should know. I probably spent fifteen years doing it, never quite feeling good about it, but when in doubt sensing that it was "more honest." I don't feel that way anymore. Life is about a lot more than race race race race race all the time.

At the end of the day, does anyone really want to be interacted with on the basis of race? It's very two-dimensional. It's spiritually and emotionally draining. And ultimately it's dehumanizing. This is where I have to admit that the color blind philosophy is partially right. The truth is that for most people, most of the time, life actually works a lot better if you don't focus so much on race race race race race, yours or anyone else's. At best, race is only one aspect of life and, as aspects go, it's an extremely divisive and loaded one. As Winston Lofton from Weatherize DC says: "In casual conversation, I say the white man this, white folks that. But mostly I mean it as a *proxy* for Western civilization, the system, and people in power in general."

My old friend Kofi Taha explains: "The paradox we have to live with is that racism is real, but race is not."

What is most real about race is culture. Culture is rich, deep, meaningful, connecting, edifying. And this is one of the problems of the antiracism ideology. It's all about power and oppression and fighting against bad things. But people also need joy. People need to laugh. People need to dance. People need to celebrate. People need connection, spirit, and culture. This is not just icing on the cake. It's central. It's a deep human need.

But what is white American culture? Is it Home Depot and Hollywood, lite beer and fast food containers, football and prom, Disneyland and plastic surgery, Times Square and Silicon Valley, country music and pickup trucks, bowling alleys and office parks, the Constitution and drone missiles, highways and subdivisions, Harvard and the CIA? When people think of white American culture, we tend to imagine modern, superficial things. If we think about it historically, we tend to think about the last few hundred years.

But what about before that? The part I never think about is that modern "white" Americans are descended from traditional cultures in Europe several generations back. I remember calling up an old friend, Najma Nazy'at, a hip-hop activist in Boston, and her mother answering the phone. "Where does your family come from?" her mother asked me, catching me off-guard.

"I don't know. I'm white. We're mutts from all over Europe. My mom's family is Jewish from Eastern Europe."

"What kind of name is Wimsatt?"

"It's Welsh."

"Ohhhhh," she said. "The Welsh are fierce anticolonialists."

"Really?" Up until this point, I had never though twice about being part Welsh.

"Yeah, they were colonized by the British empire and they fought back. Similar to the Irish. To this day, if you're English and you're traveling in Wales, they say you need to watch your back because some Welsh still hate the English for colonizing them."

Wow. What a concept. Our ancestors were indigenous too—all of our ancestors at one point or another. They lived off the land in harmony with nature. Our ancestors were colonized too—they were conquered and assimilated into Western civilization. Every one of us, at one point or another.

I believe people of every race need to heal from the trauma and programming of modern society—our alienation from nature, from each other, and from the divine. White people need it too, just like black people need to connect to historical stories that aren't just about slavery and Jim Crow. That doesn't mean I'm about to start wearing a kilt. And it doesn't mean I am going to walk around saying, "Wow, dude, I have indigenous ancestry too." But it's helpful to have in the back of my mind a more textured story about my ancestry and identity. It's helpful to have a story that makes me feel good about my roots.

Does antiracism *have to* make white people feel bad about themselves? Does it have to be this way? Is there a way to turn out self-confident, fun white people who are not afraid of our own power and are ultimately more effective at partnering with our peers who are people of color to address systemic racism? Antiracism trainings very soberly emphasize that white people need to be "allies" to people of color, not leaders, and that we need to "interrupt" racist jokes. Okay, true that. But can we tell some jokes too? In addition to allies, what about being friends? What about joy and celebration? What about food and drink, music and dancing? What about spirit? What about love? What about laughing on the floor until the milk comes out of your nose? That's not usually in the curriculum. I believe we need to add it. It's hard to make things more okay in the world if you don't feel okay about yourself. You can't be an "ally" to people of color if you've only learned how to "interrupt" white privilege, but not how to proactively use your privilege for good. It's important to be able to follow, but sometimes it's important to lead too. We need all the tools in the toolbox to turn this world around. We need more empowered, emotionally intelligent folks of all races in the movement. Not more tortured, disempowered, self-sabotaging ones.

The other thing that gets lost a little bit is the idea that people of color have agency (the power to act). One of the orthodoxies of antiracism is the idea that anyone can be "prejudiced" but only white people can be "racist," because racism requires power and only white people have the power to back up prejudice. While in general it is true that white folks and white-dominated institutions in the U.S. have a lot more power than most others, it is obviously untrue to suggest that people of color have no real power. And in a growing number of cases, individual people of color actually do have more power than individual whites. Sometimes a lot more power. And while the distinction between prejudice and institutional power is important, trying to apply an antiracist framework on a day-to-day interpersonal basis in the context of a multiracial organization is actually not very helpful (and bordering on ridiculous). You can't think: *Our program director is a young Chicano guy so I will think of him in this way, and the communications director is an older white lesbian so I'll think of her like this.* Sure, you have to be sensitive and aware of who each person is—and racial identity is part of that. But at the end of the day, we need to focus on the individual and the role each person is playing, more than their racial identity.

Another unspoken and underlying foundation of the story is that white people are fundamentally oppressive and people of color are always victims of racism. This belief has truth to it. It explains a lot about why things are the way they are. But it is the *wrong* story to make people feel empowered to change. The reality is that people of color do have agency. And white people do have the capacity for good.

This might seem basic. But for me, as a leader of social justice organization, I had an underlying idea that my role as a white male leader was to "create space" for younger people of color to lead in the organization, and then "get out of the way." Which is partly true, though I had an equation in my head that I never articulated, which was that in order to empower my staff, I needed to disempower myself. And that the morally correct way for me to lead was to not impose on or "oppress" my staff with my white male power.

This unarticulated belief system of mine almost wrecked the organization. In essence, the way that it played out was that I failed to take responsibility for doing my job as executive director, which was to manage the organization, manage my staff, exercise my own best judgment to lead us, and make decisions to forward our mission.

My "aha" revelation, at the end of a very long, painful process, was that my entire worldview had been backward. That what I needed to do as executive director is what anyone of any race in any job needs to do. And that is simply this: To do my job. To play my role. To be fully empowered in doing it. To use my own power and judgment to make decisions. To lead the organization. And to empower the people who reported to me. Instead, I succeeded in disempowering us all.

I'm not blaming my anti–white racism ideology for my failings as an executive director. And I'm not blaming my anti–white racism ideology for blowing myself up in the *New York Times*. But the antiracism story I told myself, on top of my already deep sense of self-doubt and self-loathing, combined to form a nasty brew. Drinking it, I learned my lesson the hard way. Hopefully you won't have to.

Can Rich People Save the World?

One of the biggest myths that shattered as I grew up was the role of rich people in the movement. When you read about social movements—especially radical movements led by poor people of color—you rarely read about the wealthy funders, philanthropists, patrons, and foundations.

But the more you understand social change, the more you come to appreciate the role that very wealthy individuals have played and can play. After more than four decades of fighting the system, Ralph Nader wrote a novel toward the end of his career called *Only the Super-Rich Can Save Us!*

In the late '90s, a handful of visionary philanthropists decided to fund a new set of leaders to change the world. There were really just a couple of them operating at the national level.

The first and most generous was Ed Cohen, an eccentric Wall Street tycoon who created the Echoing Green Foundation, which awarded $30,000 a year for two years, plus health insurance, to cohorts of emerging social entrepreneurs. Echoing Green mainly funded mainstream social entrepreneurs to start programs such as Teach for America, City Year, and Public Allies. But they also funded a handful of explicitly progressive efforts including those from a young lawyer named Van Jones, who had an idea to start a criminal justice organization in the Bay Area, as well as a young staffer named Gita Drury who had worked in women's prisons in California. Together, with Angela Davis and Cassandra Shaylor, they envisioned organizing Critical Resistance, the first major national conference to challenge the prison-industrial complex.

A second major funding stream came from a young actor named Andrew Shue who appeared on the TV show *Melrose Place.* Shue put up funding to help create Do Something, which held annual "Brick Awards" for young social entrepreneurs. They mostly went to mainstream service projects, but Van Jones won one of those too, as did a handful of social justice activists.

A third was Rockefeller Philanthropy Advisors, which Lisa Sullivan went to work for and helped run a program to assist "next generation" leaders, including, again, the ubiquitous Van Jones.

Finally, there was the Funders' Collaborative on Youth Organizing, which was a small group of community-oriented foundations that came together to assist community-based youth organizations, mostly with grants of around $10,000.

I've watched wave after wave of visionary funders come and go in the youth sector. The pattern is usually the same: excitement and major investment, followed by loss of interest and scaling back. Many of them attempt to document and tell the story of the work so that other funders will get interested. But usually that doesn't work and they eventually bounce. The funding bubble bursts, most of the organizations in the sector die, and the youth leaders move on to the adult world, often without a backward glance.

FYI: Rich People Are in Charge of "The Movement"

I once had dinner with a very unusual man named Rodger McFarlane, who is a legendary hero for people with HIV/AIDS. In 1981, before the virus even had a name, Rodger set up the very first hotline (on his personal phone!) for people with a mysterious and deadly new illness. He built the biggest AIDS organization in the country, Gay Men's Health Crisis, and cofounded ACT-UP.

I didn't know any of this about him at the time. I just knew he was a big-shot funder who lived in Denver, so when I was passing through town, I called him up and he offered to take me out to dinner. He brought me to one of the fanciest restaurants in downtown Denver. I started telling him about the work we were doing. He interrupted me and proceeded to deliver the most candid and hilarious diatribe I have ever heard on the true nature of social change.

"Look, sorry to burst your bubble, kiddo, but grassroots organizations don't actually change policy. They don't win elections. Bullshit! You guys are the hired help. Rich people hire organizations. We give you grants. When foundations give grants, we're hiring you to do the work! When we're trying to get something done, we hire TV stations. We hire organizations. We call our elected officials who we helped elect. There are a handful of big progressive funders. I could count them on one hand, maybe two. They're the ones who create the strategy. Then we fund groups to carry it out. This is a class society, kiddo. Like it or not, rich people rule the world. The world is run on money. And policy and elections are no different . . ."

This is my paraphrase of what he said, not his exact words. It was so funny, I should have written it down at the time. Rodger was one of a kind. Tragically, a few years ago he decided to commit suicide in the town of Truth or Consequences, New Mexico.

As over the top as it was, his diatribe rang all too true. People think that executive directors of organizations are in charge of the movement. But in reality we're often more like program directors. The real leaders of the movement are the biggest funders who get to dictate how the game is played. There are notable exceptions, like MoveOn, which only takes grassroots gifts up to $5,000. But executive directors of progressive organizations usually work for the funders.

This isn't quite as bad as it sounds. A lot of the big funders share our goals and values and they are very smart and strategic, and/or they hire people who are, and they appreciate the fields they are funding and take a lot of cues from their grantees. At their best, funders form close partnerships with grantees which are two-way learning and strategy relationships. They are your biggest supporter, your best friend, and they understand that in order to do your best, you need to be empowered, respected, well-resourced, and given a level of autonomy.

But since this is a taboo topic and isn't normally the framework through which either the funder or the grantee thinks about the relationship, there is a mythology on both sides that prevents everyone from being honest about and maximizing the relationship. Typically what happens is that the funder doesn't know that much about the groups they fund, or the landscape in which they are operating. Typically they talk a few times a year, read proposals, and cut a check. Most funders are not intimately involved, and for the most part, organizations like to keep it that way. They want to get the check, focus on the work, and not be bothered too much by the funder. The funder in turn feels like they are respecting the group by being hands-off and not taking up too much of the group's time. They also don't want to feel like the group is overly dependent on them. It's sort of like the funding equivalent of casual sex: no major commitments on either side.

The funders want to keep their options open and the groups want the money, but they don't want the funders meddling, telling them what to do, or trying to control them. By and large, this professional arms-length arrangement is what both the funders and the grantees think they want. Like casual sex, it definitely has its upsides. But ultimately it is no way to build a strong and strategic movement, just like random hook-ups are no way to build a relationship or a family.

The downside is that although funders actually own the movement and can pull the plug at any time, they are sometimes absentee managers—extremely hands-off to the point of negligence. By the same token, they don't always feel very responsible for the organizations or the field they are building. Next year they might decide to put their chips somewhere else. And they often do, without having a deep and real connection to either the old work they are abandoning, nor the shiny new object they are picking up.

So much of the movement is driven by funding. Similar to the '90s, the entire youth voting movement of the past ten years was driven almost exclusively by four major funding bubbles. The Pew Charitable Trusts really deserve a lot of credit. During the '90s, the overwhelming perception was that young people didn't vote. The perception created a vicious cycle because politicians didn't speak to young voters or youth issues, so young voters felt even more alienated from politics and saw even less reason why their votes would matter. Pew invested more than $20 million over a fifteen-year period to figure out how to get young people to vote; to scientifically document and study what worked; to change the reality of young people; and to change the perception of young people as voters at all levels: in the media, to politicians, and to young people themselves.

It was a big, hairy, audacious goal. It took fifteen years. And overall it worked. They invested in creating a research center called CIRCLE, which has an amazing website of studies on youth voting. Leading up to the 2000 election, they invested in creating a Youth Vote Coalition, which unfortunately imploded a few years later. But before it imploded, it conducted valuable control group experiments proving that simply asking a young person to vote face-to-face at their door, and giving them basic information about voting (polling place, day and time of the election, etc.) increases their likelihood of voting by 5–10 percent. In 2004, they invested about $10 million into the PIRGs to run enormous youth vote experiments in five states. In 2006, Pew supported one of the leaders of the youth movement, Heather Smith, to create an institute called Young Voter Strategies housed at the Graduate School of Management at George Washington University, which regranted $3 million for voter registration experiments, and served as a hub to share best practices and convince the political community (candidate campaigns) to invest in young voters. They then helped Heather take over and revive Rock the Vote in the 2008 election. After that, they basically stopped funding youth voting efforts. The Pew bubble mostly ended at that point, but had a wildly successful track record and created a huge body of knowledge, experience, infrastructure, and a terrific model for future funders to boost youth voting work.

The only problem was almost no one picked it up.

In 2004, two other major players got in the game: the Rappaports and the Lewises.

Andy and Deborah Rappaport are a maverick Silicon Valley couple that wanted to shake up the Democratic Party and help create a vibrant new progressive movement. They were inspired in part by the Howard Dean for America campaign. One of the many Dean spin-off groups was Music for America, which organized artists, rock groups, and rock audiences for the candidate. It was an all-volunteer group of recent indie rock- and politics-obsessed college grads. The Rappaports flew four of the leaders out for a three-day retreat and essentially said: We want to give you $1.5 million and free office space to move Music for America to Silicon Valley and make it big.

Over the course of 2004, they invested $8 million into a smorgasbord of innovative youth, technology, and Hispanic-focused voter projects. They funded Punk Voter, Driving Votes, and Vote Mob. They funded an online platform called CivicSpace, which was based on Dean's online platform, Dean Space. In 2005 and 2006 (when most of the groups they originally funded had died), they invested millions of dollars in three huge new ventures: They formed the New Progressive Coalition, an online network to entice political donors and venture capitalists to support a "portfolio" of innovative political projects—essentially a high-tech alternative to the Democracy Alliance. They also invested in state-based youth organizations in four states (Washington, Massachusetts, Colorado, New Mexico) using the Oregon Bus Project as a model. And finally, they created an organizational incubator in San Francisco's Mission District, where several of their projects were housed.

Sadly, very sadly, in 2007—just three years after they burst on the scene—they took a big step back and phased out most of their political projects. Part of it was losing money in the market. Part of it was their funding philosophy: give three years of seed money then get out. Part of it may have been for reasons I can only speculate on.

The Rappaports got some important things right: They invested big serious money. They took risks on crazy-sounding start-up groups and ideas. They trusted their instincts and their experiences from Silicon Valley. And they weren't afraid to fly in the face of the Democratic and progressive establishment. On the other hand, they were impatient and they didn't stick around long enough to develop a deep and realistic understanding of how to be effective over the long term. They appeared to operate impulsively, thrashing about, and their track record wasn't as successful as it could have been for a counterintuitive reason: they were visionary funders. And part of the problem with being too visionary as a funder is that you really need to find extremely strong partner organizations who are committed to carrying out the vision. Otherwise, at the end of the day, the person who owns the vision and the organization is you. The groups themselves never grow strong enough to sustain themselves. And when you stop investing, most of the groups you've been funding go away with you. This was the sad fate of Music for America, Punk Voter, CivicSpace, New Progressive Coalition, and others.

I don't want to be overly critical here. On the whole, the Rappaports' contribution was a huge net positive. Their organizations carried out all sorts of innovative and important initiatives. And they still do some funding, but the scale is much smaller.

Vote Mob field director Jeremy Bird went on to run Obama's game-changing campaign in South Carolina, and later became the deputy director of Organizing for America. Scott Goodstein from Punk Voter ran a lot of new media, social media, and text messaging for the Obama campaign (he's the one who worked with Shepard Fairey to create the Obama poster). Mike Connery from Music for America went on to create FutureMajority.com and the influential Millennial Politics listserv which have served as hubs for the youth political community. Molly Neitzel from Music for America moved to Seattle to start an ice-cream shop. But I wouldn't be surprised if she becomes a senator or governor one day. And the state-based Bus Federation organizations are still going strong: Oregon Bus, Washington Bus, Forward Montana, and New Era Colorado. There were times when many people were frustrated with the Rappaports. But overall, we are sad that they took a step back. And we hope they return in a bigger way one day.

Then there was the Lewis family. The Lewises (from Progressive Insurance) began investing millions of dollars in youth work during the 2004 election cycle. The Lewises are friends with the Soros family and they do a lot of national political projects together. Similar to the Rappaports, they weren't afraid to buck the status quo in D.C. They were willing to make bets on youth groups and invest significant money. The Lewises, however, were one step further inside the beltway than the Rappaports. They are part of the Democracy Alliance and their main strategy is to catalyze the Democratic Party and other Democracy Alliance partners to care more about youth. They almost fully funded the Young Voter Alliance in 2004. And they donated something on the order of $2 million a year to youth groups from 2004–09. But their funding has tapered off recently. No one knows exactly what the future holds. It takes deep, patient, long-term investment to truly build a field, especially one as chronically underfunded and underdeveloped as youth politics. It's a mutual fund that you have to invest in for the long haul to see real results.

Luckily, the Lewis family, along with the Soros family and a few other families, have helped to anchor a Youth Table that was developed by the Democracy Alliance in 2008. Although smaller in size than the previous funding waves, hopefully it will prove more steady, as a handful of funders have expressed a long-term commitment to it.

What can we learn from these funding waves and bubbles? What are the implications for movement-building? First of all, we can't take them for granted. Essentially, the entire youth political renaissance over the past ten years has been funded primarily by a small handful of people. And most of them have stopped doing it. That's a scary reality! What if those handful of people had never decided to take a risk on youth political work? Would Democrats have taken back Congress? Would Barack Obama have won the presidency?

A typical reaction to this: We can't rely on big donors and funders! We need to find other ways to finance this movement. We need to create earned income and sell products. We need to build a small donor base or a membership base like MoveOn. We need to find another way! And that's at least half of the solution—although easier said than done. In reality, very few social justice enterprises have succeeded at creating a small donor membership base. Very few are able to generate significant revenue from selling stuff.

The other part of the equation is that we need to recruit a whole bunch more Pews, Lewises, and Rappaports. And we need to help the next generation of game-changing philanthropists become even smarter about strategy, patience, realistic expectations, and partnering. Recruiting more cool rich people isn't a substitute for small donors or generating earned income, but it is an important part of the equation. And it's one that a lot of social justice types don't usually look at.

We like to think of change as coming from the bottom-up. From the people. From people who had it hard, people who have been most affected by injustice and who have risen up against all odds to fight for themselves and their people. It's a romantic story. It's David vs. Goliath. It's Gandhi vs. the British. It's Erin Brockovich vs. Pacific Gas and Electric. It's Mandela vs. apartheid. It's the Chinese dissident in Tiananmen Square vs. the tank. It's Nigerian fishing villages vs. Shell and Chevron. It's Julia Butterfly vs. Maxxam/Pacific Lumber. There is something about the story that feels deeply good and right and authentic to our souls. And it's true to a large extent. We need strong warriors and leaders who are most impacted by injustice to courageously step up and fight for what's right.

But the reality of the magnitude of global corporate and military power is that the most oppressed people can rarely do it by themselves. The Ecuadorian peasants whose land and waterways are being destroyed by Chevron cannot stop a multinational company by themselves. And they shouldn't have to. They need allies. The more powerful the better!

Che Guevara was an upper-middle-class kid who was studying to be a doctor. Gandhi was a member of an upper caste who studied law in London. Even Karl Marx—Mr. Communism himself—was upper-middle class. Billionaire George Soros has probably done as much to change the prison-industrial complex and racist drug laws as any other living person, and it likely required less than 1 percent of his time and money.

This is not to say that everyone who changes the world is rich or comes from an upper-class background. There are literally millions of counterexamples: Fannie Lou Hamer, César Chávez, Yuri Kochiyama, and Malcolm X, to name a few.

But the sooner we stop romanticizing any particular type of person and realize that we need to build a movement that truly includes everybody—based on goals and values—and includes all of what each of us has to contribute in terms of time, talent, resources, and positioning, the more effective we will ultimately be in achieving our goals.

Two Cheers for the Cool Rich Kids Movement

You may remember the story from my second book, *No More Prisons*, about the Cool Rich Kids Movement and "Why Philanthropy Is the Greatest Art Form of the Twenty-first Century." Well, let me tell you, I'm still waiting. I'm still hoping philanthropy is going to be the greatest art from of the twenty-first century. We have a long way to go.

When I was twenty-five, I learned that there was some hidden money in my family. I realized I could become a miniphilanthropist and I started to wonder how many other young people from wealthy families were out there who wanted to use some of our money to change the world. Not just by giving it away, but by leveraging access, investments, social power, and status for the common good.

Talking about wealth is a minefield. People immediately have feelings about it. There is the anger, the jealousy, the judgment. There is the simultaneous sneering from both the right and left: "Wish I had your problems," "No wonder you can afford to do all this political work—you're a rich kid," "If you want to save the world so much, why don't you stop whining and give it all away."

The right wing's economic ideology is all about creating wealth and worshipping rich people. Until one of them steps out of line and starts talking about fairness and equality. Then they're immediately branded as a "bleeding-heart rich liberal elitist" who is out of touch with the common man.

Progressives are supposed to be all about the value and sanctity of every person, and we're all created equal, unless you're from a rich family, in which case you're a spoiled rich kid and everything you do is suspect.

The fact is that people who are born into money don't choose it any more than people choose to be born poor. Wealth warps the human spirit as surely as does poverty. People from all economic backgrounds choose to do political activism because we all know our survival depends on it—whether in an immediate personal sense or in an overall sense of species survival. So criticizing the few rich people who do use their wealth for good is backward.

The Cool Rich Kids Movement has come a long way in the last ten years. Back then it was a new idea. Today there is an organization called Resource Generation that has organized hundreds of people into chapters in cities across the country: inheritors and young finance types; people who work in philanthropy; and young wealthy people of color.

My relationship to the Cool Rich Kids Movement has changed too. I'm not young anymore. My own family's money mostly went away; my parents now have a second home in Michigan, and they are able to buy organic foods and go on vacations. But they don't have millions socked away. I usually live paycheck to paycheck, and at the moment I don't even have health insurance.

But the Cool Rich Kids Movement has begun to do great things. After Hurricane Katrina, a handful of folks connected to Resource Generation held a conference call and said: *What should we do?* They recruited a bunch of donors and created something called Gulf South Allied Funders. They partnered with 21st Century Foundation, an African American–focused philanthropy, and raised $3.5 million over three years to support grassroots community groups in the Gulf region.

This is a good start. But it's nowhere close to the unbelievable potential this group has. What if cool rich kids got really organized? What does the next level of cool rich kids organizing look like?

If we're actually going to turn the *Titanic*, we need to play on a different level of strategy and commitment. The ingredients are there. There is an amazing community. Resource Generation has a great team of organizers who are focused on changing philanthropy from the inside out. We have the people. We have the trust. We have the skills. We have the power. And unlike most efforts, we even have the money. We've only just begun to use it. So two cheers for the Cool Rich Kids Movement. The whole world is waiting for us to get our act together and figure out the third cheer.

You Don't Have to Do It Alone

The most important thing I learned as an executive director is that you don't have to do it alone.

With help, I've gotten a million times better as a leader through years of executive coaching, peer coaching, leadership courses, and an executive director support group my friends and I started in New York.

When the shit hit the fan at my organization, I truly didn't get it. I didn't understand what was happening. And I had no idea what to do. A very wise consultant I was working with asked me if I had spoken to any other executive directors about our situation.

"No," I admitted.

"Try calling five other EDs who you trust, telling them the situation, and asking their advice," she said.

Over the following weeks and months, I ended up calling twenty EDs. The vast majority of them, especially the more experienced ones, saw my situation much more clearly than I had. They gave me the courage and insight to act decisively. I learned a lot from these phone calls. I also learned that most of them had been through similar situations and had not talked about them with anyone. Most of them felt similarly isolated, and felt they had few, if any, people they could really talk to. They were happy I had reached out.

Why are EDs so isolated? First of all, because being an ED is so all-consuming that it's hard to maintain a lot of key relationships. You're lucky to keep even one other relationship intact—and if you have a romantic relationship or kids, that's usually where the energy goes. Second, it's because we end up hiring the best people in the field or appointing them to our boards of directors. So then it becomes tricky to talk to them. What about executive directors of ally and partner organizations? Ideally, they would be the perfect people to talk to. But a lot of times, we don't want to show weakness or let them know our dirty laundry. They often have a lot of the same friends, board members, and funders. And many times we are doing business or in a coalition relationship that has its own politics. So who can we really talk to? Who else knows enough about our work to *get it*, but has enough distance to be completely safe to talk to?

I don't know what works for other people. But I know for me, there were five ways I reached out for help that saved my organization: calling twenty other EDs; forming a small ED support group; executive coaching; five or ten really good books, and the Rockwood Leadership Institute.

Here's a quick and dirty on my experience:

One of the twenty EDs I reached out to was Rha Goddess, who had started a sister organization called We Got Issues around the same time I started the League. We went out to dinner. I spilled my whole story. She did the same. And we had such an amazing conversation that we decided we needed to do it monthly. Rha suggested that we invite a few of our other friends who were EDs in New York: Clyde Valentin who runs the Hip-hop Theater Festival and Kyung Ji Rhee from the Prison Moratorium Project. All of us had been friends for about ten years, but we rarely saw each other and almost never got to have private conversations about our organizations and work.

It was intense, sort of like a Joy Luck Club for struggling executive directors. Each one of us dealt with underperforming and/or revolting staff, absentee and/or interventionist boards, clueless and/or reneging funders, shysty vendors, disappointing consultants, and the constant gun to our heads of working to meet payroll every two weeks.

We would get together at Rha's house, order Thai food, and share stories, each one crazier than the last. "Your funder did what?" "But wait until you hear this." "Okay, okay, I got one that takes the cake."

It made us feel not so alone. And more than that, it helped us to solve problems, and get the courage and confidence to make tough decisions. When we met regularly, we made dramatic improvements. We made the hard decisions. When we didn't get together for three or six months, our organizational improvement processes lost momentum. Our dinners were one of the best things we could have done for ourselves. And by the end, three of us had transitioned out of our roles as EDs.

In addition, I had *four* executive coaches in my time as ED. All four had different styles. All four at different times and in different ways saved my life. Then I went to Rockwood.

Rockwood Leadership Institute is simply the best leadership organization that the social change nonprofit sector has produced thus far. You can apply for their introductory course online. The approach they teach is called "Leading from the Inside Out." They teach about personal self-mastery, vision, healing, and power, as well as organizational leadership and management skills. Pretty much everyone who goes through it will tell you it is life-changing. And unlike some other leadership and personal transformation workshops, it does not in any way resemble a cult.

Rockwood was created in 2000 by Robert Gass and Andre Carothers, who had been leaders of multiple social change organizations. They saw the glaring dysfunctions of the nonprofit sector. They saw hundreds of unskilled visionary leaders martyr themselves, implode their organizations, burn themselves and their staffs out. Robert was an extremely gifted organizational and leadership consultant who worked with everyone from Fortune 100 companies to the U.S. Senate. But both of their hearts were in the movement for social change. And they both thought: *There has to be a better way.*

So they created Rockwood. Its main offering is a four-day intensive workshop called "The Art of Leadership" which is offered usually ten times a year. They have trained more than three thousand social change leaders and developed a cohort of master trainers, one of whom, Akaya Windwood, now runs the organization.

I took the four-day course, then I was honored to be admitted into Rockwood's year-long program for executive leaders. Each year, Robert works closely with a group of twenty-five leaders of social justice groups. It is intensely competitive to get in, and intensely challenging to complete. He basically tries to teach you through experience everything he has learned in forty years of organizational and leadership coaching. Rockwood deliberately brings together groups of social change leaders from across different sectors—from environment to labor, racial justice to philanthropy, online organizing to voting, immigrant rights to LGBT. Grassroots and established, national and local. Extraordinary leaders of all races, ages, and regions of the country. It has built trust, partnership skills, a common language and analysis, and, most importantly, deep and lasting friendships across the many sectors and miniature kingdoms of the progressive movement.

The day I came back from my first session of Rockwood, I got a phone call from the Democracy Alliance to tell me that the League would not be renewed as a recommended organization in 2007. I was almost speechless. In the course of five minutes we had lost something in the neighborhood of a million dollars—half of our budget. We had been counting on that money. We had twenty-five people on staff, and only four weeks of cash in the bank.

Okay, I said to myself, *this is a leadership moment.*

Calmly, I asked Lee, our operations director, to come take a walk with me to the conference room down the hall. I told her what had happened, and in forty-five minutes we sketched out a five-part plan to: 1) cut our cash flow in half, 2) communicate our situation to five different layers of stakeholders (staff, board, DA donors, non-DA donors, and the public), 3) organize donors in the DA to continue to support us, 4) restructure the organization to be more sustainable, and 5) use this as an opportunity to fundraise our asses off.

The plan worked. In one month, we cut our cash flow almost in half without hurting our programs too dramatically. We laid off five staff. We restructured the organization to be more sustainable. We raised hundreds of thousands from outside donors, and our supporters within the Democracy Alliance stepped up and wrote a letter on our behalf that was signed by ten DA partners. When all was said and done, we made up most of the money. Our 2007 budget clocked in at $1.7 million in a nonelection year. We won our biggest string of policy victories ever. We started 2008 with three months in the bank. And we got invited back into the Democracy Alliance through the newly created Youth Table the following year. The Democracy Alliance was criticized for deciding not to renew us as part of their portfolio. But I personally sympathized with their plight. It's *hard* to organize donors. As one of the partners told me: "You've heard of herding cats? Try herding fat cats!"

Paradoxically, the crisis strengthened our organization. Losing a million dollars is one of the best things that ever happened to us.

It is a metaphor for the challenges of leadership in the twenty-first century. The twentieth century in America was centered around an ethic of unlimited growth and more more more more more. Leadership in the twenty-first century is increasingly going to be about helping people adjust to living with less.

Part VII

Future of the Movement

200 Million More Americans and One Big Urban Planning Decision

I have seen the future and it looks like Brooklyn.

According to U.S. Census projections, the U.S. is likely to add at least 120 million more people by 2050. Right now we have 310 million. In 2050, we're projected to have 439 million, and 54 percent of us will be people of color (30 percent Latino, 15 percent African American, 9 percent Asian American). By 2100, we're projected to pass 500 million.

Where are all these people going to live? In the suburbs, of course.

The suburbs are going to become denser, more diverse, more walkable, more like cities in every way. And cities—after being decimated in the second half of the twentieth century—will rapidly be repopulated. New York City alone will add a million people. Chicago will add close to a million. Rust-belt cities like Detroit and Cleveland will be revitalized and add hundreds of thousands of people as skyrocketing land, housing, water, and energy prices drive Americans toward affordable real estate near population centers, especially ones with fresh water.

Population density will revitalize public transit. Corner stores and family farms will be able to thrive again as energy, food, and land prices rise. The twenty-first century population explosion will be a mixed bag. On the one hand, it is already causing huge gentrification and displacement of low-income people and people of color—and will push many of the Earth's resources and species to the brink of extinction. On the other hand, it will force us to become more ecological, to grow our own food, and to live in more dense metropolitan areas that are majority people of color and have vibrant public space—in short, Americas cities and suburbs will begin to look more and more like Brooklyn.

As someone who lives in Brooklyn, I can tell you this is not such a bad thing. I never need a car. I do all my shopping on foot. I live a block away from a park, a block away from a major shopping street, three blocks from the subway, and half a block from an integrated public school.

What does it look like for a metropolitan area like Austin, Texas, to add 500,000 people? Or for metro Chicago to add another two million? Cities and metro areas can grow in one of two ways—up or out. Growing out is becoming untenable. We're running out of farmland, and we're running out of gas. More and more we're going to see metro areas like Austin grow up. The city itself will become denser, as every last plot of land is developed. The suburbs around it will become more tightly knit, more diverse, and more walkable as small businesses spring up to take advantage of the growing population. Suburban-style big-box stores are taking over the cities. But at the same time, urban patterns are spreading in the suburbs as well. What we're really seeing is a convergence between cities and suburbs into massive, integrated metropolitan areas.

Okay, maybe the future won't look quite like Brooklyn. It could take another hundred years or more to become that dense. Maybe in forty years many cities will look more like Denver or Minneapolis. Half people of color, walkable, bikable, busable, not supersegregated, and obsessed with ecological sustainability. Denver and Minneapolis are beautiful places—vibrant models of what cities can be. Not perfect, but a hell of a lot more livable than the segregated West Side of Chicago or the far western suburbs. If we play our cards right, and grow our metro areas *up* instead of out, it won't just be Minneapolis and Denver in twenty to forty years. It could be all of America: Chicago's West Side, western suburbs and all.

The Opening Credits of the Movie

In 2001, I was at a rally against youth jails in the outdoor amphitheater in front of Oakland City Hall. It was a beautiful sunny day with three hundred young people in their full hip-hop activist glory. Hip-hop artists and speakers were taking turns on stage. A local singer named Goapele was blessing the audience. It was one of the best youth political events I had been to in a long time. I ran into Van Jones, whose Ella Baker Center had worked hard to help organize the event. Van and I were two of the oldest people there. He was already recognized by some as one of the most effective political organizers and thinkers of our generation but he wasn't very well known. He hadn't come up with the whole green jobs frame yet, though he was starting to sense the possibilities.

"You see this?" Van said. "This is great. This is beautiful. But soon all these young organizers are going to realize that doing all these kind of rallies doesn't actually change much, and they're going to need to go to law school. They're going to need to get involved in the political system. And once they do that, this generation is going to build a new political realignment that's black and brown and is going to include all these green progressive whites. It's going to be a black, brown, Asian, Native American, progressive white, and green coalition. You know in a movie when you see the opening credits? This is the opening credits. And over the next few decades, a whole movie is going to happen that will realign the politics of American life."

Van has always been ahead of his time. Later the same day he told me: "All this time we've been playing marbles. We have gotten really good at the game of marbles. We spend a lot of time talking about how to play marbles. What color the marbles should be. And that's all fine. The problem is, we're on a football field. And there are these other people who are playing football while we're still playing marbles. And they keep knocking over our marbles game. That's why we keep getting run over."

Okay, let's talk about the bad news. I promise I will keep this mercifully short, and then we'll talk about how to dig ourselves out of the quicksand. As preparation for this, I will refer us to the words of Jim Collins in *Good to Great*: "Confront the brutal facts. Yet maintain unwavering faith."

God's Art Project

Recently, I was invited by some friends to go to Hawaii. I was walking along the beach in Kauai and my friend Jeff asked me: "What is your book really about?"

"Can I think out loud with you?" I asked.

Sure.

"The real theme of the book is *all of this*," I said, pointing to the beauty surrounding us in Hanalei Bay. "The trees, mountains, waves, animals, and human beings . . . We're like . . . God's Art Project. I know a lot of artists and activists. Some are incredibly creative. But all of us put together—all the great art and science in human history—isn't even a fraction as creative and ingenious as what God *already* created before any of us got here. That's the first part of my thesis: God has an Art Project and we are part of it.

"The second part is that we're trashing it. We're trying to play God. As the Last Poets said: 'White man's got a God complex.' Except it's not just the white man anymore. Humanity as a whole is assimilating the white man's ways. Collectively, as a human civilization, we have developed a God complex. We are trying to play God. We are worshiping false idols. And we're in danger of seriously trashing our home planet within the next hundred years. It's as if God's Art Project is hanging in a gallery, and no one is really looking at it. People are having wine and cheese and making small talk about blah blah blah.

Meanwhile, they're bumping into God's Art Project, knocking it on the floor, stepping on it, spilling wine and crackers on it, until it looks like a garbage pile. Then people think it *is* a garbage pile and start tossing plastic cups on it. Maybe we don't know any better. Maybe we don't care. Maybe we're jealous that we will never be able to create anything as good.

"If you buy the first part that God is the greatest artist, and the second part that we are a bunch of second-rate artists trashing God's work, then the third part is a question: *Okay, GREAT, so now what are we supposed to do?* And my answer to that question is that we need to be spiritual warriors. We need to be the best spiritual warriors who have ever lived. We need to use every tool, every ounce of creativity we've got, to understand and defend God's Art Project."

Renegades for Cenozoic Age

The Cenozoic Era has been described as the most creative period in the four-billion-year history of the Earth, the most recent geological period—roughly the last sixty-five million years (since the extinction of the dinosaurs).

The Cenozoic Age is the pinnacle of God's body of work to date.

It includes God's most famous living sculptures and creations.

God had an earlier creative period called the Cambrian explosion about 540 million years ago in which every type of multicellular organism began to evolve in the seas. But evolution was slow over the next 400 million years. There were lots of mass extinctions that slowed God's progress. In terms of sheer species creativity, the Cambrian explosion is dwarfed by this brief period we live in now.

The Cenozoic Era has been the renaissance, if you will, of biological diversity. More than half of all living species, including almost all birds and mammals, evolved during the past sixty-five million years. We humanoids came on the scene about 2.5 million years ago and began to distinguish ourselves from our chimpanzee cousins.

The moment we are in now (the past few hundred years—not even a blink of an eye in geological time) is witness to the greatest mass extinction since the dinosaurs were killed off by an asteroid sixty-five million years ago. From a geological and biological perspective, it is as if an asteroid has hit the Earth.

A Catholic priest named Thomas Berry wrote famously that we are in the "terminal phase" of the Cenozoic Era. Our current age (the last few hundred years) now has its own geological name, the Holocene extinction (a.k.a. human-caused extinction). From a biological perspective, this is the age we were born into. Kind of like the Holocaust for plants and animals.

Harvard biologist Edward O. Wilson extrapolates in *The Future of Life* that the current rate of extinction is likely to wipe out most species within the next hundred years.

Can humanity find a way to survive in some form on a hot, crowded planet? Probably. We're clever little creatures. But that's missing the point.

As another Harvard biologist, Stephen Jay Gould, writes, we're used to thinking of greatness in the wrong way. We're used to thinking of greatness or excellence as the highest dot on a graph. In evolutionary charts, we're used to seeing a fish become a lizard become a bird become a mammal become an ape become a human being with a smart phone. The message is that humans are the best—we're at the top of the chart. We're the final slide in the PowerPoint. But from an evolutionary perspective, excellence is not what's on top. Excellence is *variety*.

God's Art Project isn't about the peak of Mount Everest. It isn't about the human with the smart phone. It's about *the whole thing*. The wild fish and birds and tigers alive today are the product of tens of millions of years of evolution, just like we are. If excellence is variety, then less variety equals mediocrity. God's Art Project was excellent, an A+. Now it's an A-. By the time we get finished, it might be downgraded to a D or an F. It might not even be shown in galleries anymore.

Maybe I'm just being sentimental, but I thought the Cenozoic Age was pretty good. I have half a mind to make a T-shirt that says: *Defend the Cenozoic* or *Cenozoic Warrior*. Something like that. Maybe *Renegades for Cenozoic Age* (a small tribute to hip-hop's founder Afrika Bambaataa).

Alice Walker wrote a book called *Anything We Love Can Be Saved*. I sure hope so. Whether we like it or not, it really is up to us to fight for everything we love. And the love that created us. Evangelical Christians have a name for this: the Creation Care movement. We are part of God's creation. We are lucky. We are blessed. We are grateful to have been given this life. Thank you! Thank you for this life! You created us for a purpose. It is our sacred duty to care for and defend ourselves and all of creation: Your Art Project.

It's like those scenes in *Avatar* when the Mother Tree sends its seedlings to communicate with the humans. We are part of a biological system that wants to survive. We were created with its spirit. We have a role to play in its survival (as well as our own). We just need to understand our role in creation and carry out the purpose for which we were created. I'm pretty sure it wasn't to wipe out most of the other species on the planet.

Fasten Your Seat Belts: The Train Wreck Has Left the Station (But I Think We Can Catch Up to It)

The next big crisis is coming. Or at least the next big Katrina or BP oil–style crisis that is visible to human eyes. Species extinction we could mostly care less about. The next big crisis is coming. And the next ten big crises after that. And the next thousand smaller crises. In our lifetime. These will not spell the end for humanity. But each one will be a great moment of truth. A teachable moment. A learning moment, if we are willing to learn. Each one will be a moment when, like an alcoholic, we either "hit bottom" and check ourselves into rehab, or propel ourselves ever faster toward oblivion.

It's the flip side of Naomi Klein's *Shock Doctrine* (how corporations, governments, and right-wing institutions cynically exploit crises to make money and take control). We need to prepare for the next great crisis, so that the human species is prepared to understand and respond to the next great teachable moment when it comes along. We need to build up a sane civilization that is prepared to take over when the current insane civilization hits a wall and begins to break down.

At a deep level, people know what's up. Try this experiment. Try asking a group of people: "What do you think humanity will look like in fifty or one hundred years if we keep going like this?" Most likely you will get a shrug and a blank look: "I dunno." Then watch how quickly the subject changes. Time it. I guarantee you the subject will change in less than thirty seconds.

What's going on is that we're speeding toward the edge of a cliff and people can feel it. It's a cliff called: Overpopulation + Hypercapitalism + Killing the Planet's Life Support Systems + Nuclear Weapons + Normal Human Greed and Madness = (you fill in the blank).

We are speeding toward the cliff. Whatever is on the other side of it, I don't know. Most likely we will go over a series of smaller cliffs in the next twenty to forty years, which could send us spiraling toward the big one.

Can we slow it down? Can we buy ourselves time? Can we turn the car around?

This is the greatest challenge in the history of humankind. We have faced great challenges before: the Crusades, the Plague, the genocide of the Americas, slavery and the Middle Passage, World War II and the Holocaust. If we don't turn things around, the big one is going to make them all look like a walk in the park. No kidding.

Maybe I'm too self-confident, but I think we can do it. The train wreck has left the station. But I think we can catch up to it.

I don't know about you, but I *like* challenges. Puzzles. I like to solve problems, figure things out. I like difficult situations that force me to bring out my best. I like to come back at the bottom of the ninth inning. I like to bounce back in the fourth quarter. I like to crunch it at the eleventh hour. Pull an all-nighter. I like to feel my adrenaline and survival instinct kick in. I think a lot of other people like that too. And it's a good thing, because as a civilization we may be closer than we think.

It takes courage to decide to live. It takes courage to trust yourself. It takes courage to believe in something unseen. It takes courage to look the Angel of Death in the eye, not blink, and decide to keep on living. It takes courage to fight for your children and grandkids who you haven't even met. It takes courage to make sacrifices for future generations. It takes courage to change. It takes courage to eat right and exercise every day. It requires from us everything we've got. It requires courage and strength that we don't even know we possess.

When you face all of this—even as a scenario—it can be so terrifying and disturbing and enormous that a lot of people get depressed and want to jump off a bridge and take meds and shoot heroin in their arm while they are jumping off the bridge, slitting their wrists and shooting themselves in the head at the same time. Or at the more functional end of the spectrum, people try to block it out by going shopping while texting, playing Xbox while eating a dozen donuts, checking the score and changing the channel while getting their nails done, because it feels like there is nothing we can do.

What does it feel like to you?

It's weird because some people think everything is going to be just fine. Some people think it's already too late—there's nothing we can do.

The reality is almost certainly somewhere in between. The reality is more challenging. The reality is that we have a choice: adapt or die.

I think about this reality almost every day. But it doesn't make me hopeless. In fact, it makes me *motivated*. In a funny way it actually inspires me.

It inspires me because I think we can turn things around.

Why do I think so? One, because I have studied history and I understand how fast and profoundly things can shift when the right leadership, technology, and conditions converge. Two, we don't have a choice; not having a choice is a powerful motivator. Three, we have to protect our kids and grandkids. We have to protect our home, God's creation. God's Art Project. Protecting kids, grandkids, and home is a powerful motivator. Four, I think we are gradually putting the right ingredients in place to at least have a chance at turning things around.

I'm rooting for us. I think we can do it.

Games People Play (In a Good Way)

Part of what gives me hope is that it's not that people don't care. Of course we care! And people—for all the bad and stupid things that we sometimes do—are adaptable. From an evolutionary perspective, species either adapt to new conditions or die off. Just because we do a lot of stupid things as a species does not mean we are hardwired to be stupid. We're not necessarily attached to doing stupid things. They're just the result of the patterns and games we have inherited and learned to play over generations. But patterns can be broken. Games can be changed. There is nothing inevitable about our long march toward self-annihilation.

Some people play basketball. All they think about is basketball. What's the score? How's my jumpshot? Who's on my team? Who are my opponents? How can I outmaneuver them? It's all about basketball. Other people's sport is money. How can I make a million dollars? How can I make a billion dollars? What number will I be on the Forbes 400 this year? Will I move up a notch to 285, or will I get bumped back down to 300? If only I could get in the Top 100. If only I could get in the Top 10. For most of us, having $4 billion vs. $5 billion, or even $20 million vs. $100 million, wouldn't make that much difference. But for the person playing the game, it's like any other sport. At a certain point it becomes not even so much about the actual money. It's about your identity as a player in the game. It's about doing your best and being your best. It's about competing and winning and adrenaline and self-concept and the flow experience of being good at something. It's about the game. And psychologically, at least to an extent, it almost doesn't matter which game it is.

Everybody has a game. Venus and Serena have tennis. Tom of Maine has toothpaste. Some people have art. Some have religion. For some people it's having sex with a lot of people. For some people it's finding true love. For some it's being nice and getting everyone to like us. For others it's self-sabotage, and we can play our game with the same drive and intensity as Sonia Sotomayor practices constitutional law, or a Mormon missionary rides a bike around the hood, or Wangari Maathai plants trees in Kenya.

Once you start playing one game, you begin to get good at it. You get comfortable with it. You know the rules. You know the players. You know the field of play. And everyone knows you. You have a position. You are part of a community. You have a reputation to uphold. You become emotionally attached. To switch games in the middle is scary because it means forfeiting the game you have been playing. It's risky because it means walking away from something you're good at and starting from scratch in a new arena. It means changing your identity.

What's encouraging to me is that to some extent it's arbitrary what games people choose to play in life. Adolf Hitler was an art student before he became a military dictator. If he had stuck to marking art or writing books, or perhaps gone into sales and marketing, maybe we could have avoided World War II. Bill Gates was playing the game of computers and money and now he's added the game of philanthropy, education, and global health. So the question is: how do we get more people to add to their repertoire the game of figuring out how to stop the world from getting flushed down the toilet? That could be a fun game.

This book is an invitation to play a new game, which to me is probably the greatest game of all. The greatest reality TV show of all. It is the game and the reality TV show of understanding, loving, and protecting God's Art Project.

Identity As an Organizing Principle

Why do people change?

Facts? No.

Arguments? No.

Self-interest? No.

Identity!

Tom Frank's book *What's the Matter with Kansas?* is all about why working-class white people vote Republican, against their economic self-interest. Why do they do it?

Frank spends many pages documenting it, but he never quite hits the nail on the head. The nail is identity.

Identity is more than values, more than self-interest, more than a collection of ideas and facts. It is, for each person, our concept of ourselves.

Humans are social animals. Even when we're antisocial, we're antisocial as part of a larger antisocial identity, epitomized by popular icons like Tupac, Eminem, or Amy Winehouse, who make us feel a sense of affirmation and community in our antisocial specialness.

The good news (for those of us who think that we as a civilization are headed mostly in the wrong direction) is that people's identities can change, and they can change completely. But it takes a lot to change.

The bad news is that the main people who have a grasp of what it takes to change people's core identities are religious fundamentalists and cults, which understand how to address (and manipulate and exploit) people's emotional needs, but don't actually have a viable strategy for leading us out of this high-tech wilderness.

The good news is that people can change their core identities and become spiritual warriors *without joining a cult.*

We have to figure out how to do that on a massive scale.

Reality TV: Can They Save the World?

I would like to produce a reality TV show called *Can They Save the World?*

There are reality shows now about everything else. Who can be the best singer, dancer, chef, designer, model. Who's willing to work for Donald Trump and Diddy and go on a date with Flava Flav? Who's willing to eat live spiders and wrestle in a pool of mud, Jell-O, or elephant shit? And then of course there's the classic TV show: *Survivor*. But what about *Real Life Survivor*. As in: how are we going to make sure our species survives?

Somehow that topic is booo-ring. Who wants to watch a TV show about that? Well, I do, for one.

I think the people who are trying to save the world, the Van Joneses and Jessy Tolkans; the Favianna Rodriguezes, Ian Inabas, and James Ruckers; the Phaedra Ellis-Lamkins and Mary Beth Maxwells; the Judith Freemans, Taj Jameses, Marianne Manilovs, and the Annabel Parks; the Deepak Bhargavas, Maria Teresa Kumars, Ricken Patels, and Ilyse Hogues; the Christina Hollenbacks, Iara Pengs, and Biko Bakers—these are the people I want to watch a TV show about. You probably would too. So let's create a market.

The movement needs a narrative, y'all!

We need a story. A great story. The greatest story ever told. We need a story line. We need characters. We need an epic challenge. We need a plot. I learned in high school that all stories have three defining challenges: human vs. human, human vs. nature, or human vs. self.

Well . . . this story has all three. It would be high drama.

We need to start telling our story!

The Great Transformation

The next hundred years of human society are what future historians might refer to as the Great Transformation.

Humans are evolving slowly. We're beginning to get it. We're beginning to change. Slowly. Slowly. We're beginning to have a global awakening, a new ecological age. Here is why I don't live in despair. I believe that human civilization is on the cusp of a great transformation. We are the ones who history will look back on as the heroes of a new culture who saved the planetary life support system for future generations.

In fact, we're already doing it. We're already turning the direction of the *Titanic* ever so slightly. And we don't have to do it all by ourselves. We don't have to figure out everything from scratch. There are a lot of wise people who have spent their whole lives thinking about how we get ourselves out of this mess.

Duane Elgin is an author who has been working for more than forty years on the question of how humans can psychologically evolve to a more harmonious relationship with nature. Elgin has traveled the world and everywhere he goes he asks a simple set of questions: If you were to imagine the entire human family as one person, what stage of psychological development would that person be at? A toddler? A teenager? An early adult? Or an elder? He has asked this question to hundreds of groups of people. Everywhere he goes, from groups of CEOs to remote villages, about 75 percent of people give the same answer: we are a teenager.

How remarkable is that? Almost everyone agrees. All we need to do is grow up.

There's that theme again, growing up. You really can't get around it, can you?

What Could Our Movement Look Like in 10–20 Years?

"Begin with the ends in mind," says Stephen Covey in *The Seven Habits of Highly Effective People*. What does it look like to begin with the ends in mind when it comes to movement-building?

When people do visioning exercises to plan ten and twenty years into the future, they either do it for themselves as individuals, for organizations, or for their community. So you come out with answers like: "I want everyone to have health care." "I want every child to get a high-quality education." "I want to cut crime and incarceration in half at the same time." "I want to help build the green economy and cut carbon emissions by 50 percent."

Okay great, *but how?* How do we get there? To get there, we need to create overwhelming, deep, and robust political and popular will that over time forces political and institutional leaders to change. To create popular will, we need a movement. But what is this elusive movement? What does it look like exactly, concretely? People imagine movements as magical and mysterious phenomena that pop up at certain moments in history and then just as quickly disappear.

What we need is something altogether different. Let's imagine it together.

Imagine you are designing a movement from scratch. Imagine there are no preexisting organizations. No established leaders. No websites or e-mail lists. No foundations with funding priorities. No one on payroll.

Imagine we are designing a movement from scratch and there are just three things: people—millions of us; resources—billions of dollars in assets, all the technology we can imagine; and ideas—any ideas we can think of, with no limits.

Can you imagine that? What if you were in charge of designing the movement from scratch? Could you imagine a Super Movement?

Super Movement 2020: A Ten-Year Plan

I have a plan. A ten-year plan, actually.

You can be part of it if you want to.

The plan has a name: Super Movement 2020. It is the culmination of everything in the book.

The goal: build an integrated progressive movement by 2020 with sustainable volunteer leadership in all 300,000 precincts in the United States that use a shared operating system.

The operating system would have ten principles:

1) Values-based
2) Multi-issue, multistrategy
3) Multicultural and inclusive
4) Permanent and sustainable
5) Fun, creative, and social
6) Efficient and effective, powered by state-of-the-art tools
7) Democratic and transparent
8) Strategic, proactive, and solution-oriented
9) Mission-driven, yet respects each individual
10) Collaborative with existing organizations and coalitions

Super Movement 2020 would not just be another organization, coalition, or campaign. It would function as a collaborative effort to align, connect, and maximize the people power of thousands of existing groups and networks to shape elections, policy, media, and community in every neighborhood in America. In short, it would be a *framework* for collaboration and movement-building.

Obviously, to become real this would need to be developed in partnership with hundreds of people and organizations. My sense is that if we get the framework right, it can be built for very little money using volunteer power, twenty-first century technologies, and the resources of participating organizations.

I think we can do it. Or something like it.

Or something even better.

Think about how much incredible movement-building has happened in the past twenty-five years. Now think about the next twenty-five. It's going to be just as packed, if not more so! A lot of major crises and important historical breakthroughs are going to happen. Each overnight success will require years of thousands of people pouring their hearts out, shoulder to the grindstone. It feels like things are never going to change—until they do.

What will be your role in all of it?

Love. Survival. Prosperity.

"Look, if you had one shot. One opportunity. To seize everything you ever wanted. In one moment. Would you capture it? Or just let it slip?"
—Eminem

You just got a peek at a provocative vision of how we could build a Super Movement over the next ten to twenty years.

What do you think? Are you excited? Do you have questions?

Where does this Super Movement lead? What does success look like? What is the end game?

If we had to describe the goals and values of the Super Movement in three words, what would they be?

My nominations: Love. Survival. Prosperity.

We need a movement that is focused on *loving* God's creation, being grateful to be alive and appreciating God's art project. Love is what created us. Everything we do must begin with love. God is Love. Evolution is Love. Love is what's at the heart of the First Commandment and the Golden Rule. We must love ourselves, love each other, and love God's creation. In the long run, *there is no other way* for our species to survive on this planet. There is no other way. Love is the way. Love is the origin, the path, and the destination. Love is the beginning, the ends, and the means.

In practical terms, love requires *survival*. Like Noah during the great flood, we must focus on ensuring our survival on this blue-green life raft floating in outer space. This is our calling as a species that has acquired the power of God but not yet the wisdom. We need to grow up and become mature adults so that we may survive.

But we don't want to just *survive*, do we? We want to thrive. We want to laugh, play, sing, dance, eat, pray, and, you know, have lots of great sex. We want to experience the miracle of life, the abundance and joyful *prosperity* of it all.

The good news is we can.

And so can other beings we share this Earth with.

We can have it all!

There is enough sun and wind to power our civilization without cooking the planet. There is enough land for people and other species to coexist—if we use it wisely. There is enough work. There is enough food. There is enough shelter. Enough water. There is *enough*. And *we* are enough. We are smart enough, creative enough, adaptable enough. God and evolution made us enough. They did not set us up to fail. We just have to use all the bounty God gave us and point it in the right direction.

I went to my friends' wedding recently at a mosque in Milwaukee. On the door was sign that read:

Watch your thoughts. They become words.
Watch your words. They become actions.
Watch your actions. They become habits.
Watch your habits. They become your character.
Watch your character. It becomes your destiny.

For our own sake and for the sake of all creation, we are called to be our best selves, our truest selves. We don't have to do it alone. In fact, we *can't* do it alone. To love, survive, and truly prosper, we need to build community. We need to build the beloved community Martin Luther King Jr. talked about. In every hood and every hollow, every apartment and every gated community, every prison and every suburb, every trailer park and every dorm room in the United States and in this world. *It is our sacred duty to build community everywhere we go.* It is our sacred duty to build community that reflects the values of love, survival, and prosperity, in every precinct, on every block, in every workplace, and in our homes.

So welcome to Billy's Church and Synagogue of Love, Survival, and Prosperity.

That's kind of a joke. But it's also kind of serious.

I think we can do something. Something together. Something BIG.

I think we can do it. I think we can grow up and become mature adults. I think we can connect the dots.

I think we can turn this little *Titanic* around. I think we can stop the asteroid.

I think we can change the game.

I think we can pull the Hummer over to the side of the road for a minute . . .

. . . Get out, stretch our legs, and walk around for a little while.

I think we can adapt and build a Super Movement for the twenty-first century. And I think our Super Movement can help our civilization to adapt.

Think about everything we've accomplished in the last five to ten years . . .

What if we build on that? What could we build?

History comes in waves and it may be that we're at low tide for a while. That's okay. Low tide gives us time to get ready for the next big wave.

No one said change was going to come easy. But I think we can do it.

The train wreck may have left the station. But we're the Little Engine that Could.

So everyone come on over here. Gather around. Put your hands in the middle . . .

And on the count of three, say it with me:

I think we can. I think we can. I think we can . . .

Do you think we can?

Afterword: More than a Book

Hey, I'm impressed. You read the whole book. Good job. Not many people read whole books anymore. It says something about you. So I want to share something more personal. Yeah, I can write a book about changing the world. But how do I actually put it into practice?

I'm at a crossroads in my life right now. I am making big plans and I'm going to share them with you. And then I'm going to invite you, if you're willing, to write your own stories, plans, and bright ideas either privately for yourself, or on www.billywimsatt.com.

My dream is that this book will become more than a book. My dream is that tens of thousands of people will read it, and over the next ten to twenty years we will build a bigger, better, more integrated Super Movement capable of governing and meeting the challenges of the twenty-first century.

Admittedly, it's a huge plan.

There is no rush, no need to stress. This is a long-term process, not an urgent call to action. We need to go slow to go fast. We need to take our time to do it right.

Frankly, we're not there yet. If we were to dive in right now and say, "Okay, let's go, let's build a Super Movement," we would almost certainly fail. We haven't done the proper groundwork yet. We must lay solid foundations for success over time with a lot of people and buy-in from existing groups. The process needs to go in stages.

In the meantime, we need to take baby steps. Not all of these baby steps will be as inspiring as building a Super Movement. And that's okay. We need to practice a little bit before we build Noah's ark for the twenty-first century. No one has ever done this before on this grand a scale. We are babies in the art of healing the world, so we need to begin with baby steps. Here are some of mine:

I am going on an extended book tour all over the country. I'm going to try to do a couple of hundred events in the coming years to get people reading, talking, and thinking about the kind of movement we want to build over the next decade. Almost like a political campaign, except I'm not running for office. Almost like a music tour, except I don't have any bodyguards or talent. So get your act together and invite me to your town or college. Also, I really want to encourage you to start a club to read books, watch movies, and discuss what you and your friends want to do in the coming years. My friends and I started a little group; you can start one too.

One of the immediate baby steps is to not let the progress we made by electing Barack Obama get wiped away.

So in addition to touring, I will be running a voter turnout operation in some of the most competitive Senate and House races in 2010. Traditionally, in a midterm election, the president's party loses seats. In 1994, the Republicans picked up fifty-four House and eight Senate seats, and it basically prevented Bill Clinton from doing anything good for the next six years. Conventional wisdom says that Democrats will lose big in 2010. And it's probably true. The mainstream media is acting like it's a done deal.

But there is no reason why this *must* be the case. Democrats are being stupid again, going into this election acting like they're going to lose. The right-wing fanatics are motivated and the 2008 Obama voters are demoralized. But what if we are able to somehow motivate the Obama voters again? It's a numbers game and a motivation game. We don't *have* to lose! What the F? That is not how you play the game. You don't go into an election assuming you're going to lose and let the right-wing gangsters stomp all over you!

I'm just one person. But I say F that.

If we somehow miraculously get it together, get motivated, make the wind blow the other direction, and turn our people out to vote, we could pick up two more Senate seats for Democrats in 2010. Even with just two more sucky Democrats, we'd have a whole different ball game. Obama would have the wind at his back again. The right wing would be caught off-guard. And then we'd be able to pass halfway decent progressive legislation. Not great. Not amazing. Not anything close to what we need. But baby steps in the right direction instead of going backward.

A lot of our people are talking about staying home in 2010 to punish Obama and the Democrats for not being progressive enough or not trying hard enough. On the war. On immigration. On jobs. On reforming Wall Street. On stopping climate change. On fixing our broken democracy. On all sorts of things. I understand that. I'm frustrated and upset about all the same things.

I understand the sentiment. I understand the impulse. I understand the strategy.

But at the end of the day, it's just wrong.

And frankly, it isn't very grown up.

It's like if you're married to someone and they're trying to do right but not succeeding. Do you punish that person? Do you say: "Okay, well, until you get a job, I'm not going to have sex with you"? Or: "Unless you lose twenty pounds, I'm not buying you a birthday present"? Or: "Until you cook dinner, there's no way I'm doing the dishes"?

Does anyone think that this kind of ultimatum would be motivating in a relationship with a partner? No, it would most likely lead to neither person getting what they want. So why would we think it works any better in a relationship with our elected representatives?

In order to get out of a bad place, you have to say: "Go team! We're in this together. I'm rooting for you! I know you're depressed right now, honey. I know you're having a bad day/week/month/year/life. I know you're having trouble finding a job and finding time to exercise. But let's get together, help you get a job, have sex, go work out, cook some dinner, *and* clean the kitchen. I know it's hard. I know you're trying. Let's make this work. Go team!"

That's how successful relationships work. You have to root for your team. You have to be a good partner. And you have to be patient.

The simple reality is that the more we organize voters in every election, the more power we have to create change over time. The more we get frustrated and say, "F this bullshit," the more we shoot ourselves in the foot. The more that we vote and volunteer in *every* election, the more likely we are to create real change over the long term. It's just that simple. Just that hard.

I know I'm just one person, but . . .

I'm not ready to give up on this election or any other. I'm not ready to say: "Oh, sure, let's just hand our country back to the right-wing crazies again. Eight years wasn't enough." I don't know about you, but I'm not ready to throw in the towel. I'm not ready to say: "Oh, sure, it's fine with me if every issue we've been working on is dead in the water for the next two to six years. Let's let the Clinton and Bush years repeat themselves. Let's have Obama and the Democrats become demoralized and not be able to govern. Then let's have another eight years with another incompetent right-wing ideologue in the White House. How about Sarah Palin? Let's let her screw up the country for another eight years. Let's see, that would take us to 2020 or 2024. Then America will finally be ready for another good president again. Sounds like a plan."

I don't think we can afford to wait that long.

So I'm gonna do my part. Win, lose, or draw, I'm going to be spending time in Ohio, Missouri, Nevada, Florida, New Hampshire, and other key states, working to organize young and low-income people to vote again in 2010 and every year thereafter.

If you are reading this *after* the 2010 election, then you are living with the consequences of whether or not we succeeded. If we lost some races narrowly, you can see what a difference you could have made if you had gotten involved. I will probably continue running voter programs, because impacting the balance of power in the U.S. government is about the most important thing any living person can do at this moment in history. Many huge decisions are determined by one vote, which in turn is often decided by a few hundred or a few thousand votes in one district or one state. It's a bizarre truth of the modern age. One very motivated person, who gets out voters in the right district at the right time, can actually impact the entire course of world history.

So one way or another, whatever else I do, I'm going to keep working on elections, as flawed and problematic as they are.

Shoot! Someone has to do it. If I can vent for a minute, most of the best projects I work on are like this. Super important but for some reason not on anyone's radar. WTF? Why the hell are there so many obvious gaps like this? It's crazy. There are so many thousands of talented people who care about the world and want to do something but who don't know what to do with themselves. And there are so many absolutely critical gaping holes just crying out for someone halfway competent to fill them.

My official "job" right now is that I have a fellowship with the Movement Strategy Center working on a project called the Future of Field. The project has evolved a lot since I started it. In the beginning, it was called Field 3.0 and I was thinking of it as a five- to ten-year project. As I discussed the work with others, I began to sketch out a twenty-year process with distinct stages: Field 3.0, Field 4.0, and Field 5.0.

At the same time, I am launching a new effort called All Hands of Deck (www.allhandsondeck.net), a dream organization whose goal is to get more and more groups and individuals to plan and collaborate effectively on elections and other long-term issues related to building a Super Movement.

One of the most exciting projects is a collaboration with Salsa Labs (www.salsalabs.org), the biggest online organization you've never heard of before. Salsa Labs is the progressive movement's largest online organizing platform. They have more than two thousand clients, including probably half of the activist groups you get e-mail from. Their combined database is more than thirty million people—six times the size of MoveOn and more than twice the size of OFA. They have unique e-mail addresses for close to 10 percent of the U.S. population! We're working with them to provide opt-ins for their clients to maximize their lists, conduct offline organizing, and participate in elections. We're also working with a handful of niche nonpartisan groups like the

Coffee Party, the League of Pissed-off Voters, and others to maximize their impact in target states in 2010.

Over the long term, personally, I want to work in the arenas of ideas and stories, innovation, invention, and alliance building. I am talking with folks about developing an incubator for innovative political ideas and projects. We are also looking at recycling some of the best ideas, projects, and organizations that have died over the years. Sort of an organizational recycling center and movement incubator. Eventually, I want to work in philanthropy again. After we get the operating system figured out, the flow of money will probably still be the single biggest determinant of movement success, and I want to help water the garden.

During the course of my life, I want to do five key things: 1) tell stories through books and new media; 2) recruit and develop new leaders; 3) incubate ideas, projects, and organizations that help build a movement; 4) help develop a better operating system for the movement; and 5) help develop a smarter generation of philanthropists to move billions of dollars in more effective ways to stop the world of our children and grandchildren from going down the toilet.

That's my plan. And I'm going to need a lot of help and partnerships to make it happen.

The Story that Hasn't Been Written Yet

Okay, you just devoted hours of your life to listening to my story, ideas, and plans. I appreciate that. I feel heard. I feel listened to. My greatest hope is that reading this will remind you of *your* story and you will seize this moment of inspiration as a springboard for boldly living *your* truth in the world.

If you decide you want to get more connected to the movement, there is a high probability that we will cross paths one day. You're welcome to friend me on Facebook ("Billy Wimsatt" is my Facebook name). Just write me a note so I know you're not a random stalker. I am friends with a sizable proportion of the movement (thousands of amazing amazing people) and I will be organizing events to help connect folks in local areas to create little twenty-first century movement teams all over the place.

What I ask of you: First and foremost, be true to yourself. Be a student and a *warrior* of Love, Survival, and Prosperity. Be good. Get power. And don't do anything stupid to mess up your life. Does that sound like a decent plan? Are you down? Are you down till the wheels fall off? What about after the wheels fall off? Will you still be down?

It's kind of like those army recruitment commercials. We're looking for a few good organizers. Except we don't have zillions of dollars to recruit and pay you. And you won't get a free trip to the Middle East. And you won't get to kill anyone. Your top secret assignment: write the next chapter of this book.

Write the Next Chapter

This book has four major threads: my stories, movement stories, life strategies, and movement strategies. I want to invite you to add a fifth thread: yours.

The secret to great writing is that you just have to put down literally anything that comes into your head, without censoring yourself, without judging, without even trying to write in complete sentences. If you find yourself thinking instead of writing, just pick up a pen and start. *It takes the same amount of time to think as it does to write, so you may as well write!* It takes less time, actually, because your brain will loop over and over again on the same thought for hours, or even years, until you put it down on paper. Once you write it down, you can have the peace of mind to move on and think the next thought.

1) Warm-up Questions

What are your favorite and least favorite parts of this book and why?

How does your story connect with the themes in this book?

Did you learn anything new? If so, what?

Are there ideas in here you're personally wrestling with?

Now, think about the most courageous and true things you have ever done in your life. What were they? How did you do them? How did you overcome your fears? How did you feel afterward? What, if anything, was impacted (even the slightest bit) as a result of your actions?

What are your greatest gifts and strengths?

How would you describe your calling in life? (This is a hard one.)

What do you feel moved to *do* right now, after reading this book?

2) Your Story of Self

There is a practice in community organizing called "Story of Self." It was used extensively by the Obama campaign to train volunteers to quickly tell their own story of who they are and why they were supporting Obama.

Telling your story is important because it reminds you of who you are and what you stand for. And it allows other people to quickly understand you, understand your values, connect, and share their own stories with you.

Marshall Ganz, who teaches community organizing at Harvard, says that every great political story has three components: Story of Self, Story of Us, and Story of Now.

The Story of Self has an underlying structure with four components: 1) a challenge you experienced; 2) an action you took; 3) the result; and 4) your values. I recommend that you take this opportunity to jot down several of your most important, pivotal life stories: the turning points that made you who you are. Many of the stories in this book were long forgotten until I started actively thinking about the turning points and lessons learned in my life. The more Stories of Self you have, the better; and the more you practice telling them, the better.

What's your Story of Self? Challenge? Action? Result? Values?

(Try to think of one that you haven't remembered in a while. Write. Repeat.)

3) Jog Your Memory

What were your most formative political experiences?

Who are your old friends and where are they now? How was your path similar to or different from theirs?

Who were your best teachers (in school or otherwise)? What did you learn from them?

When did you feel most alive and in a flow?

4) Self-reflection

Who are the most effective *change agents* you know personally? What makes them effective?

If you were to apprentice with any living person or organization, who would it be? What specifically would you hope to learn? (List as many as you can think of.)

5) Your Future

What do you want the next chapter of your story to be?

If you knew you were going to die in five to ten years and you could choose one big project to devote yourself to in order to make a difference in the world, what would it be?

What would a movement look and feel like that you'd want to be a part of for the rest of your life? What might your role be in creating it where you live? If you were to organize your own neighborhood or precinct in a long-term way, what would you do? How would you go about it? What would it look like? What help would you need?

BONUS

Go through every year of your life, starting as far back as you can remember. How old were you/what year was it/what grade were you in? Who were your friends? What were you thinking about that year? What were the major lessons you learned each year? (When I did this exercise, I realized that most of the people and activities I spent time on didn't end up meaning as much to me in retrospect. It helped me get perspective on my life, and find courage to make changes and focus on what was most important to me.)

The Greatest Friends of All

For my parents, Bill and Barbara Wimsatt.

For Lenore.

With huge appreciation to the Akashic team: Johnny Temple, Ibrahim Ahmad, Aaron Petrovich, Johanna Ingalls, and to my friends who gave detailed feedback on short notice: Anne Glickman, Meghan Davis, Pete Miser, Julia Day, Julia Nagle, Ian Rhodewalt, Beth Pollack, Marianne Manilov, Ryan Clayton, Noelle Celeste, Hallie Montoya Tansey, Esther Morales, Kristina Rizga, Christina Hollenback, Toni Nagy, Jamie Schweser, Tate Hausman, and Alissa Hauser.

And for my amazing community of friends, family, and touchstones over the years who have sustained me, raised me, taught me, and had my back. I'm so happy we are building this community and movement together.

Anonymous, Gita Drury, Nick Arons and Vivien Labaton, Murat Armbruster, Leigh Arsenault, Lucy and Peter Ascoli, Caron Atlas, Aniello Alioto, Ibrahim Abdul-Matin and Fatima Ashraf, Baye Adofo-Wilson, Aimee Allison, Alexandra Acker, Andrew Gillum, Nimco Ahmed, Taz Ahmed, Laurie Atwater, Alex Cotton, Justin Alfond and Rachel Weinstein, Pugslee Atomz, Alejandra Ibañez, Alain "Ket" Mariduena, Cheryl Aldave, Wyndi Anderson, Ang 13, Manuela Arciniegas, Pat and Ron Adler, Tenene Allison, Caitlin Baggot, Sung E Bai, Robert Biko Baker, Calvin Baker, Andre Banks, Weusi Baraka, Ebony and Embri Barley, Brother Abdullah, Harriett and Allison Barlow, Mustu Barma, Maria Bacha, Erika Backburg, Scott Beale, Kathy Barry and Bob Burnett, Oriana Bolden, Jumaani Bates, Thomas Bates, Patricia Bauman, Robin Beck, Mike Berg, Andy Bernstein, Josh Begley, Val Benavidez, Medea Benjamin, Max Benitez, Amanda Berger, Julie Bergman-Sender, Carmen Berkley, Shayna Berkowitz and Phyllis Weiner, James Bernard, Kiyan Bigloo, Rachel Bishop,

Deepak Bhargava, Fanny Brito, Lorraine Bieber, Jeremy Bird, Tony Blanke-meyer, Toni Blackman, Wes Boyd and Joan Blades, Dereca Blackmon, Ludovic Blain, Alison Byrne-Fields, Jeff Blodgett, Becky Bond, Heather and Paul Booth, Andrew Bossie, Sophia Bowart, Ann Bowers, Heather Box, Andrew Boyd, Melissa Bradley-Burns, Daniel Burton-Rose, Donna Bransford, Wayne Brasler, Jackie Bray, Josh Brietbart, Hunter "Toast" Brumfield, Charlotte Brody, Julianne Britton, Joanie B, Adrienne Maree Brown, Siobhan Brewer, Claudine Brown, Moni'ca Brown, Patrick Brown, Tiffany Brown, Bill Buddinger, Sam Buffington, Anna Burger, Rachel Burrows, Tracy Burt, Liz Butler, Julia Butterfly, Eric Byler, Erin Byrd, Will Byrne, Christopher Ettinger, Christopher Harris, Connie Cagampang Heller and Jonathan Heller, Eileen Cabiling, Jlove and Hector Calderon, Mahea Campbell and Alea Woodlee, Kimo Campbell, Nancy Harris Dalwin and Geoffrey Dalwin, Melanie Campbell, Esther Campos, Liz Camuti, Tony Cani, Juan Pablo Caraballo, Carol Cantwell, Jon Caramanica, Maegan Carberry, Danielle Meltzer Cassel and Pete Cassel, Eben Carlson, Dan Carol, Seiji Carpenter, Kimberley Carter Gamble and Foster Gamble, Majora Carter, Melvin Carter, Catalina Ruiz-Healy, Cat Gund, Kevin Cathcart, Everette Harvey Thompson, Ann Caton, Greg Cendana, Zoe Chace, Henry Chalfant, Noland Chambliss, Jeff Chang, Vivien Chang, Craig Harwood, Dj Chela, Eddie Chez, Farai Chideya, Andre Carothers, Charlotte Chinana, Susan Chinn, Debra Cleaver, Wyatt Closs, Eddie Codel, Michelle Coffey, Peggy Clark, Julia Cohen, Jameel Coleman, Mike Connery, Ebonie Johnson Cooper, Jason Cooper, Theo Copley, Seiji Carpenter, Sharif Corinaldi, Frank Corona, Adrianna Cortes, Ricardo Cortes, Kevin Coval, Kelly Craighead, TJ Crawford, Chris Crass, Mary Creasman, Cynthia Renfro, Tania Cuevas, Kevin Curtis, Camielle Cyprian, Davey D, Wendy Day, Meighan Davis, Kim Davis, Nicole Derse, Sharhonda Dawson, Julia De Martini Day, Eric De Bat, Sihle Dinani, Deborah Schneider, Deborah Bronstein, Leda Dederich, Gary DelGado, Joyce Deep, Mathilda DeDios, Quinn Delaney & Wayne Jordan, Gavin and Sarah DeVore Leonard, Ken Dunn, Jené Despain, Neha Desai, Ajamu Dillahunt, Paul Downs, Knicole Dominique, Joe Donlin, Amy Dorfman, Sam Dorman, Bernard Dory, Mario DeJuan, Jonathan and Adam Doster, Gita Drury, Jack Drury, Marta Drury and Kerry Lobel, Sandi DuBowski, Rachel Durchslag, Muhibb Dyer, Jotaka Eaddy, Beka Economopulos, Ali'a Edwards, Sara-Zia Ebrahimi, Ditra Edwards, Eric Rubinstein, Ashel Eldridge, Eli Lee, Anne and Christopher Ellinger, Phaedra Ellis-Lamkins, Elsa Rios, Emily Nepon, Ditra Edwards, Laurie Emrich, Lea Endres, Ray English, Randy Engstrom, Maya Enista and David Smith, Marisol Enyart, Kevin Erickson, Alyssa Erickson, Espo, Zoe Estrin and Griff Foxley, Chloe Eudaly, Christian

Ettinger, Jodie Evans, Ian Everhart, Matt Ewing, Zack Exley, Shepard Fairey, Celeste Faison, Dapo Fakunle, Kirstin Falk, Diane Feeney, Michael Fiore, Steve Fenberg, Gary Ferdman, Kim Fellner, Danielle Feris, Deepa Fernandes, Demain Fernandez, Bob Fertik, Tom Frank, Fikes family, Michael Fiore, Charlie Fink, Jose Flores, Laura Flanders, Donna Frisby, Mike Foerstel, Natalie Foster, Louis Fox, Jason Franklin, Diana Frappier, Judith Freeman, Jeff French, Sarajo Frieden, David Friedman, Ryan Friedrichs and Jocelyn Benson, Ivan Frishberg, Ellen Furnari, Anna Galland, Tracy Gary, Margarita Garcia, Grant Garrison, Karen Gasper, Robert Gass and Judith Ansara, Michelle, Jim and Lynnette Gaza, Chico Gibbons, Colin Greer, Melissa Giraud and Andrew Grant-Thomas, Ira Glass, Anne Glickman, Rha Goddess and Corey Kupfer, Chris Golden, Arlene Goldbard, Holly Roberson and John Goldstein, Elspeth Gilmore, Harmony Goldberg, Thomas Goldstein, Leslie Goldstein, Micah Gordon, Jim and Suzanne Gollin, Adelaide Gomer, Belma Gonzales, Scott Goodstein, Cyrus Gould, Sara Gould, Alex Grashow and Yasuko Tamaki-Grashow, Billy Grayson, Ian Greenfield, Grandma Betty Greenman, Sarah Greenwalt, Ben Griesinger, Patricia Griffin, Julia Grob and Khalil Almustafa, GQ, Sebastian Gross-Ossa, Sean Gardner, Hadley Grousebeck, Katie Gunther, Sarita Gupta, Sara Haile-Mariam, David Halperin, Suheir Hammad, Allen Hancock, Julie Handa, Andrew Hoppin, Ruth Ann Harnisch, Stan Hallett, Anne Hallett, Jill Harris, Tate and Shawna Hausman, Liz Havstad, Jeremy Hays, Alissa Hauser, Don Hazen, Nancy Hechinger, Mia Herndon, Courtney Hight, Jethro Heiko, Judith Helfand, Molly Hein and Dan Griffin, Tad Hargrave, Martha and Bill Heinemann-Pieper, Jessica Heinemann-Pieper and Param Srikant, TJ Helmstetter, Nikki Henderson, Vauna Shai Hernandez, Bracken Hendricks, Tracy Hewat, Jack Hidary, Dalton Higgins, Terry Rochelle Hollingshead, Stephen Hightower, Sander Hicks, Marielena Hincapie, Yolanda Hippensteele, Lee Hirsch and Cynthia Lowen, Stacy Ho, Ying-Sun Ho, Danny Hoch, Chinaka Hodge, Esme Hoffman, Ilyse Hogue, Christina Hollenback, Brooke Holt, Sarah Shanley-Hope, Stacey Hopkins, Florence Horberg, Ben and Elizabeth Horberg, Bill Horberg and Elsa Mora, Marguerite Horberg and Shelby Richardson, Miro, Natalie and Diego Horberg, Jay Horberg, Katie Horberg, Jeff Hull, Courtney Hull, Megan Hull, Kristin Hull, Blair Hull, Holmes Hummel, Amy Hundley, Michael Huttner, Ian Simmons, Tenisha Idowu, Joe Iglesias, Invincible Illana, Daria Illunga and Mark Reed, Edie Irons, Idelisse Malave, Ian Inaba, Sarah Ingersoll, Randy Jackson, Naomi Jackson, Maura, Maurita, Maurissa, Maurice and Maurci Jackson family, David Jacobs, James Pearlstein and Chitra Subramanian, Quentin James, Taj James, David Jay, James Jankowiak, James Bernard, Aimee and Cara Jennings,

CJ Jenkins, Ana Jimenez, John Hunting, Chad Jones, Dalton Jones, Ruthie, Chris, Matt and Jeff Jones, Kofi Jones, Van Jones, Whit Jones, Tyrue "Slang" Jones, Ron Kahn, Elaine Kamiley, Shalini Kantayya, Ragini Kapadia, Amy Kaplan, James Kass, Daniel Katz and Maggie Lear, Norman Lear, Doug Kelly, Katherine Keon, Linda Ketner, Brian Kettenring, Naina Khanna, Navina Khanna, Cietta Kiandoli, Michael Kieschnik, Jee Kim, Ian Kim, John Kim, Kimball Stroud, Keegan King and Lyn Wilson-King, Bear Kittay, Bakari Kitwana, Brendan Kelley, Adam Klaus, K-Lite, Jane Fleming-Kleeb, Amanda Klonsky, Joanna Klonsky, Michael and Susan Klonsky, Jidan Koons and Bryant Terry, Rachel Knight, Jesse Koecher, Pete Koechley and Krista Williams, Sally Kohn and Sarah Hansen, Melissa Kohner, Brian Komar, Sarah Kovner, Justin Krebs, Kalpana Krishnamurthy, Robert Krulwich, Maria Teresa Kumar, Kso, Vivian Labaton, Brian Laguardia, Marc and Lauren Laitin, Brad Lander and Meg Barnette, Gara LaMarche, Anna Lappé and John Marshall, Frances Moore Lappé, James Laurie, Anima LaVoy, Mark Landsman, Phil Lawson, Kiese Laymon, Malia Lazu, Makuti Lee, Peter and Jonathan Lewis, Anna Lefer-Kuhn, Matt Lerner, Ken Lewis, Samantha Liapes, Becky Liebman, Angela Lindvall, Bill Lipton and Yasmin Ramirez, Amy Little, Kimi Lee, Laura Livoti, Jim Lodas, Tony Lodico, Laura Loescher, Grace Llewellyn, Genaro Lopez-Rendon, Karen Lopez, Nica Lorber, Eric Lotke, Kris Lotlikar, Juliet Lu, Mario Lugay, Kevin Luklan, Mike Lux, Josh Lynch, Kalia Lyndgate, M1, Alyssa Macy, Jackie Mahendra, Josh Mailman and Monica Winsor, Juliette Majot, Mahfam Malek, Shiloh Maloney, Marianne Manilov, Adam Mansbach and Victoria Haggblom, Ashindi Maxton, Alisha Thomas Morgan, Mervyn Marcano, Natasha Marsh, Easter Maynard, Marianne Moore, Mary Beth Maxwell, Alec Maybarduk, Robery Mayer, Shamilia McBean, Dani McClain, AJ McClure, Rodger McFarlane, Alexis McGill and Rob Johnson, Neva McIlvane, Rob McKay, Rodney McKenzie, Ada McMahon, Marisa McNee, Elizabeth Mendez-Berry, Paula Mendoza, Bryan Mercer, Barbara Meyers, Mandara Meyers, Geri Mannion, Julian Mocine McQueen, Vera Miao, Sandra Mikush, Michelle Miller, Wyatt Mitchell, Daniel Mintz and Kesa Huey, Jenny Montoya Tansey, Hallie Montoya Tansey, Jayme Montgomery, Pete Miser, Nupur Modi, Cristina Moon, Molly Moon Neitzel, Hans Morsbach, Camron Moore, Rowan Moore Gerety, Greg Moore, Mik Moore, Reggie Moore, Eddy Morales, Esther Morales, Maria Moreno, Xochi Moreno, Emily Morris, Khari Mosley and Chelsa Wagner, Taij Moteelall, Kate Moulding, Peter Murray, Jorge Mursuli, Karl Muth, Julia Nagle, Tony Nagy, Richard Nash, Rozz Nash, Rishi Nath, Ngani Ndimble, Gaylord Neely, Samarra and Max Neely Cohen, Matt Nelson, Mk Nguyen, Sara Nichols, Sarah Nichols, Vanessa Nisperos,

Kwabena Nixon, Kwazi Nkrumah and Sabina Virgo, Shamako Noble, Theresa Noll, Hez Norton, Jessica Norwood, Dara and Laura Nussbaum-Vazquez, Pauli Ojea, Diana Onley-Campbell, Jenny Overman, Bergin O'Malley, Jenn Pae, Celeste Palladino, John Flajnik and *Lucia*, Simone Palladino, Arthur Palladino and Robyn Marcow, Grandpa Arthur Palladino, Jessica Palmieri, Mikhail Pappas, Eli Pariser, Avi Peterson, Billy Parish and Wahleah Johns, Iara Peng and Brent Copen, Annabel Park and the Park family, Lynda Park, Harris Parnell, Mandy Parrish, Eboo Patel, Sam Patton, Sunil Paul, Erica Payne, Andrew Pearson, Portia Pedro, Analia Penchaszadeh, Gabe Pendas, Jill Perosky, Gihan Perrera, Tom Periello, Avi Peterson, April Pederson and Chris Lundberg, Han Pham, Steve Phillips and Susan Sandler, Phonte, Jessica Pierce, Drummond and Liza Pike, Supriya Pillai, Karen Pittleman, Crystal Plati, Beth Pollack, Aijen Poo, Stephanie Porta, Africa Porter, Pam Porter, Sasha Post, Erin Potts, Kevin Powell, Marc Powell, Kevin Pranis, Jacquie Pratt, Rose Pritzker, Susan Pritzker, Bryan Proffitt, Gita Punwani, Megan Quattlebaum, Sofia Quintero, Ben Quinto, Julie Quiroz-Martinez, Manju Rajendran, Kavita Ramdas, Debroah and Andy Rappaport, Andrew Rasiej, Lavie Raven, Marvin Randolph, Jay Readey, Karen Rechtschaffen, Stephen Rechtschaffen, Rene Redwood, Heather Reddick, LaDonna Redmond, Cynthia Renfro, Reverend Sekou, Katie Redford, Kyung-Ji Rhee, Julia Rhee, Ian Rhodewalt, Breeze Richardson, Hans Riemer, Chris Rigopulos, Elsa Rios, Mark Ristaino, Gibran Rivera, Kristina Rizga, Rhymefest, Holly Roach, Magda Rodriguez, Ocean and Michelle Robbins, Heather Roberson, Doria Roberts, Lekedra Robertson, Favianna Rodriguez, Kassie Rohrbach, Robbie Rodriguez, Howard Rosenfeld and Sheryl Leach, Kristin Rothballer, Margie Roswell, Mary Rower, Justin Ruben, James Rucker, Marianna Ruiz, Lisa Russ, Jeff Rusnak, Mark Rudd, Cynthia Ryan, Jessamyn Sabbag, Jonah Sachs, Deborah Sagner, Brenda Salgado, Bari Samad, Shana Sassoon and Abram Himmelstein, Sam and Adam Seidel, Lee McDermott-Schaefer, Joanna Schaetzke, Regina Schaffer, Paul Schmitz, Holly Schadler, Jordan Schuster, Marsha Scott, Melissa Schweisguth, Rinku Sen, Amy Scott, David Segal, John Sellers, Yosi Sergeant, Lisa Seitz-Gruwell, Han Shan, Robert Sherman, Jamie Schweser and Angela Hasnedl, Stephanie Shafran, Lanya Shapiro, Lindsay Shea, Nazon "Kep" Simmons, DJ Sake One, Daniel Souweine, Rob Stein, Naomi Swinton, Ben Shute, Martin Hershey Sims, Chris Silva, Veva Silva and Stephen Feuerstein, Matt Singer, Michael Skolnik, Adam Smith and Karynn Fish, Frank Smith, Heather Smith, Jefferson Smith, Leah Schraga, Ladan Sobhani, Joel Solomon, Joel Solow, Thenmozhi and Theeba Soundrarajan, Jessie Spector, Deborah Schneider, Alvin Starks, Rusty Stahl, Alicia Steele, Sam Stegeman, John Steiner, Adam

Stenftenagel, Suzanne Stenson O'Brien, Jeannine Stepanian, Matthew Stephens, Kyle Stewart, Shannon Stewart, Kabira Stokes, Matt Stoller, Tracy Sturdivant, Kayana Szymczak, Lisa Sullivan, Rhea Suh, Jennifer Suh, Nish Suvarnakar, Elle Swan, Naomi Swinton, Marge Tabankin, Kofi Taha, Agita Talwalker, Meighan Tauck, Betsy Taylor, Brennan Taylor, David Taylor, Robin Templeton, Elizabeth Tetrault, Steve Theberge, Erica Thornton, Luckar Thach, Shaunna Thomas, Monique Tilford, Alejandra Tobar-Alatriz, Christina Tolcari, Carlos Toro, Jessy Tolkan, Rev. Romal Tune, Jodie Tonita, Gloria Totten, Gigi Traore, Anasa Troutman, Vien Troung, Jessica Tully, Lynne Twist, Jade Netanya Ullman, Matt, Susie and Lindsay Ungar, PJ Urquilla, Marian Urquilla, Marta Urquilla and Jomo Graham, Sam Utne and Utne family, Clyde Valentin, Tobin Van Ostern, Bill Vandenberg, Myra Villalobos, Rhea Vedro, Jenna Vendil, Phil Villers, Amy Verebay, Christina Veran, Alex Visher, Wendy Volkman, Amy Wagner, Jason Walsh, Warp, Becky Wasserman, Anthea Watson, Geoffrey Watts, Rafiq Washington, Mary Washington, Mattie Weiss, Lisa Wennerstrum, Erica Williams, Calvin Williams, Kip Williams, Thomasina Williams, Maggie Williams, Reid Williams, Saul Williams, Steve Williams, Barbara and Chris Wilson, Antha Williams and Sam Boykin, Mexie Wilson, Alicia and Mark Wittink, Bill Wetzel, Jenny Wilburn, Ben Wikler and Beth McCarthy, The Wimsatt family: Mary, Mike, Mike, Chris, Ted, Alyssa, Ashley, John, Kathy, John, Jeff and Kim Innes, Elijah and Kestrel Innes-Wimsatt, Tim Wise, Rebecca Winsor, Rabbi Alyssa Wise, Scott and Christy Wallace, Lisa Witter, Jonah Wittkamper, Rosalyn Wolfe, Amy Woloszyn, Desi Wome, Angela Woodson, Toki Wright, Jen Wylegala, Christiana Wyly, Paul Yandura, Rev. Yearwood, Bethany Yarrow, Peter Yarrow, Mario Yedidia, Jane Yett, Nancy Youman, Eric Zeil, Kristin Zimmerman, Emily Zimmer, Monet Zulpo-Dane, and a lot of other people who have touched my life . . . but I had to stop somewhere or this would turn into Facebook.

What a community—let's keep building it!